MIDDLE GROUND

The MIT Press
Cambridge, Massachusetts,
and London, England

MIDDLE GROUND

Angus MacDonald

THIS BOOK WAS SET IN FOTOTRONIC CRT BASKERVILLE,
AND PRINTED AND BOUND
BY THE COLONIAL PRESS INC.
IN THE UNITED STATES OF AMERICA.

ISBN 0 262 13073 4 (HARDCOVER)

LIBRARY OF CONGRESS CATALOG CARD NUMBER: 70–148845

For Monaise

Contents

The true profession of man
is to find his way to himself.

Hermann Hesse

Safe Deposit

I still have the little cast-iron bank my father gave me when I was five, the same bank his father had given him when he was my age. It is a model of an old-fashioned office safe, with a door that swings open when you twist and turn the combination dial until the two tumblers fall in place. But a safecracker wouldn't really have to know the combination, for underneath protrudes the head of a rod, and if you give this a half turn parallel to its slot—klack! the bank falls apart, spilling all its secret contents. As I soon discovered to my dismay after monkeying with the rod to see how the thing worked.

In tears I gather up the ruins and take them to my father who patiently fits the pieces together and, holding the massive safe in the palm of one hand, with the other jiggles the tie rod into its slot.

"Here son," he says in his measured way as he hands the bank back to me intact, "remember, I gave it to you because I thought you were ready to take care of it."

That was some thirty-five years ago, and now, as I toy with the dial to find the right combination, I wonder if I will find my boyhood safely deposited within.

This cube of "silver bullion." How many cigarette packages picked up from how many miles of gutters did it take to peel and compress so much foil?

This piece of coral, bleached just as white as when I brushed the algae off with an old toothbrush after draining my aquarium the day the family moved from Penrose Avenue. It's only about half the size of a hen's egg, but once it seemed to me a mountain of coral in some far-off lagoon where schools of highly colored fish swam in and out of its dark cavern. Yes, the hole is still there, where at least a shark or maybe an octopus could hide.

A "gold coin." It is engraved on one side with a curly-headed wide-eyed girl framed by a horseshoe and the words, "Radio Orphan Annie's Secret Society. Good Luck. Ovaltine 3 times a Day." And on the other, "Good Luck," repeated in a dozen languages.

A folded sheet of spiral notebook paper, on which is carefully printed in purple ink:

Penrose Stamp Co.
2220 Penrose Avenue
Baltimore, Maryland

I. There shall be no arguments!
II. Each salesman shall gets a 2¢ profit on each sheet of stamps he sells, he is allowed to buy stamps from the company if he wishes.
III. No stamps may be reduced unless the stamp company's manager is reduced it first.

Manager—Henry Garner
Ass. Manager—Junior MacDonald
Company organized November 19, 1935.

A pair of flyer's wings with a shield in the middle on which is embossed an aviator's head and the words, "Jimmie Allen; Richfield Hi-Octane, and Flying Cadet."

An old banknote the German lady gave me that says "Deutschösterreich" and "Eine Krone."

An announcement-card envelope bearing the written message, "Congratulations from Parent-Teacher Association."

Another folded sheet of paper with this cryptic message:

Crusaders Club

1. Dues 1¢ a week
2. Members

Rusty
Junior
Jeff
Hoby

Meating Thursday 8:30

Chief Rusty
Cobsina
Lemonade next Thursday

Ah "Cobsina"! Our secret word that meant so much to us because none of the grown-ups could possibly know it meant nothing at all.

And finally a many-folded envelope with this message written across the back flap: "Vigilando agundo, bene consuliendo, prospera omnia credunt. Do not tutch until 1960."

Do not tutch! The year 1960 has come and gone, but the charm is still potent. The genie of the past has escaped from time's lamp, and I am back again on the street of my boyhood. It's the end of the line for Penrose Avenue, pointing a finger to the rising hills of red clay where Indians must once have roamed and the cliffs and abandoned quarry beyond. This block of identical two-story houses was born the same year I was; we are both children of the same pre-Depression optimism. The houses are still new and young with hope, like the forty families that inhabit them, all about the same age and means. Houses without much borning, since everybody seems to have had their kids before coming here, and without much dying as yet. A small town in itself, with all the closeness and gossip but none of the tradition and quiet.

It is one of those rainy afternoons in autumn when there's nothing to do, and a bunch of us lie sprawled on the rug in the living room of Henry Garner's house, wondering how we could do more with our packets of foreign stamps than just collect them.

"Why not form a stamp company and sell them?" I suggest.

It's only right that Henry should be manager. He's older than I am. He's ten, and I won't be ten until January. But I can draw up the corporation papers.

"Where's that fucking pen?" I say, every inch the busy man of affairs.

Suddenly Mrs. Garner, who has been quietly dusting in the dining room, looms over me, no taller than my mother but twice as big.

"Junior MacDonald," she says sternly, "I'm going to tell your mother you used that word in my house."

"All I asked for," I protest, "was that. . . ."

"Don't you dare say that word again," she explodes.

Henry is trying to hide his grin. Nobody seems to care that my older cousin uses the word all the time, but my father is sure to give me a licking when he learns of my transgression.

"You make up a sales route," Henry says. He is busy pasting rows of stamps on sheets of paper to sell to our prospective customers. As I watch him, I can see myself, stamps in hand, leaving our house by the front steps and, turning right, walking past the row of wooden porches, all painted gray with white railings between them, all alike, the way the houses are. It's hard to tell, from the front of these houses, in which ones the kids live who'll buy my stamps.

In the back, it's different. The neighborhood comes alive in Penrose Alley. No mistaking who lives in those yards, ranged side by side and separated by low wire fences, some with garages but most with gardens. All the good kids live down the alley, like Henry, and Rusty, and Hoby.

The only reason I ever go up the alley is to play with Jeff when we aren't fighting or to walk to school or visit the German Lady. I used to be up the alley all the time, though, to visit Granny when she lived upstairs from the Strykers, and Mr. Stryker would show me his paintings and tropical fish tanks and the real parachute he stretched through all three rooms and packed for jumping out of airplanes just for the fun of it.

Across the alley there is only Bunky, who just

happens to be the best baseball player. Nobody across the street, either, except Spooky, Henry's cousin, and the Jones boys.

I can't think of one of them who will want to buy our stamps.

"Hey, Henry," I say, suddenly discouraged, "I don't think we're going to sell many stamps."

"Mr. Stryker gave it to me. A real piece of coral and Mr. Stryker gave it to me," I announce, padding around the kitchen in my Indian moccasins with beaded fronts. "Look, Mommy," I hold it in my outstretched hand for her to admire. "I'll put it in my pretzel jar with 'Mother Swordtail,' and when the babies are born, they'll have a little cavern to swim into."

My mother is sitting on the stool near the porcelain table tearing apart pieces of bread with little pecking grabs of her fingers, all with such seriousness and urgency I know I must not bother her. Bread for her potato dumplings, no doubt, which, she always says, are so light and fluffy and not like the rocks Aunt Martha makes. I always know when we are going to have "sour bratten and gatooful glass," even before the smell of vinegar and bay leaves like tonight, because there are ginger snaps around for the gravy, and I get into them and eat some. Mother pays me no mind so I skate my way across the newly polished floor to the pretzel jar and hear the reassuring "Stop that!"

My red swordtail's stomach is so round and stretched the scales hardly overlap anymore, and you can see shiny skin between them. Her "black spot" has grown so big there must be a hundred babies curled up in there. I remember my Mother Guppy when she had her babies right before my eyes, dropping the little round balls out of the place the black strings usually came from. They looked all eyes until they uncoiled like a spring and swam away, only to have mother guppy turn around and gulp them up. My angel fish, "Daddy Longwhiskers," ate some too; he's always hovering around looking for live food. I'm glad I put that stupid Mother Swordtail by herself in the pretzel jar with all the hair grass so they can get away. The minute she has them, I'm going to dip her out, and I'll feed the babies until they're so big nobody can eat them.

Rolling up the sleeves of my flannel pajamas and plaid bathrobe over my elbow, I slowly lower the coral to the white sand, taking care not to frighten Mother Swordtail who is peacefully lying in the grass in one corner. When I mound the sand to one side and to the rear of the coral and plant several pieces of eel grass behind, it looks like a piece of the ocean floor to me.

"Ann, you're not going to let that boy play like that with his arm in the water all night, are you? He'll catch his death of cold!"

In my preoccupation with my south sea adventure, I fail to see Granny come into the kitchen through the wide portal to the dining room just to the right of me. But the demanding tone coupled with my mother's name always means trouble for me, and the very thought of a cold and Musterole rub on my throat, which suffocates me with fumes like the ether mask I remember when I cut my ankle, frightens me so I jerk my arm from the jar, leaving it wobbling on its perch and maybe about to come crashing down.

"He's not going to have his arm in the water all night, and he is not going to catch cold," my mother says in a quiet and rather slow way, but I notice she squeezes her dumpling ball a little harder and pats it into shape even more determinedly.

"Well, if his father was home, he wouldn't have his arm in that water," Granny sniffs as she leaves the kitchen. You can always tell when her feelings are hurt.

Now she's going upstairs to her bedroom. She spends a lot of time there, particularly when her feelings are hurt. She keeps her pills and creams and salves in her room and that roll of cotton she uses to make the balls she thinks nobody knows she wears in her cheeks to keep them filled out. Sometimes I sneak in when she's not there to look at the picture of the lady on the bureau named Sally Rand who has no clothes on at all but you can't see hardly anything because she is holding a huge white feather at her neck which goes almost to the floor.

Granny always says my father "wouldn't let me do this, wouldn't let me do that," but it's not so. Anyhow, he works most of the time. Still, he did lick me with the hairbrush last summer when I got home late and Henry's mother told him I'd been playing on a freight car.

The memory makes me uneasy, and I whine peevishly, "When is Daddy coming home?"

"You know Saturday is your father's long day, Junie Boy," my mother says, as she gently drops her dumplings into the boiling water, one by one. "He has to see that all those people out in Roland Park get their big orders delivered on Saturday."

I go to the kitchen window and look out into the fading light. The first snow of the season is on the ground, and I can tell from the crystal glob that seems to ooze from the curved end of the downspout that the water is frozen in the pipe again, and my mother will be on the roof with buckets of hot water trying to thaw it when the snow starts to melt and runs down the shingles of the house, making leaks. I remember crouching before the end of the spout last summer in a sudden downpour, dry in my oilskin and sou'wester, my cupped hands delighting in the rainwater as it gushed from the spout, all warm and smelling like wet pavements in summer sun.

I see the end of my rock (and the number "3" sticking out from beneath the spout), which my father thinks is better than the brick for holding the spout in place. It's the rock Henry and I spent all that time on last summer chiseling the date "1933" into it with a railroad spike and Daddy's ball peen hammer.

Thoughts of summer make me feel better, and I go back to the jar to wrap a heavy blanket around it, first taking one more searching look for babies. None yet. How can she be so big and not explode, I wonder, as I make the jar snug inside the blanket, knowing that it will be warm when the coal fire dies down in the night, and in the darkness Mother Swordtail will not be able to see the babies to eat them.

Presently I hear the spikes that are used to prop open the metal garage door being dragged across the ice in the alley, first one, then the other. And then the steady "rum" as the car is backed into the garage, and the "rum . . . rum" as the engine is raced. Quiet, broken by the slam of one door and then the other, and the slap, slap, slap as my father pulls three times on the handle to make sure the latch has caught.

I know how long it will take him to walk through the yard, so I am there, ready to open the door when he kicks his overshoes against the sill to knock the snow off.

"Hi Daddy," and he comes through the door in a swirl of cold fresh air, his chin straining to keep above the large cardboard box filled with groceries he holds in his arms. He puts it down on the table next to the pantry, and as I stand on tiptoe to see what good things are there for me, he boxes my face between his huge black leather gloves and with a rub says, "Hi son." For a moment I am bathed in the cold air he still carries with him, but I feel more than a chill because I sense something is wrong. He didn't call me "Sonny Boy," as he usually does, or take off his gloves to give me a knuckle rub on the head until I cry out, and when he says, "Hello, Ann," to my mother and gives her a peck on the cheek, neither of them seems to be aware of it. I feel sorry for his sad face as he walks through the kitchen.

Soon we are all seated around the kitchen table. Dinners are scary times because somebody is usually unhappy and, sitting there having to look at one another, the tight feeling spreads around the table. And then, too, something always seems to happen. Like last Thanksgiving when the dining room table was set as pretty as can be, with Mommy's Irish linen tablecloth and her tall water goblets with rainbows in them, I reach for my glass and crash! over it goes, just missing the real cut-glass celery dish the nice lady in Roland Park gave Mommy. She breaks into tears and, after picking up the broken pieces and dabbing at the wet spot, disappears up the staircase that opens down into the dining room. I am sorry for what I have done to her and I look at my father, but he has nothing to say to me and he seems a little frightened too.

Or like when we had kidney stew and I slipped the stinky kidney onto the cross brace under the kitchen table and it fell on the floor bringing with it the whole moldy collection of meat I had previously stacked there.

Or in a different way like when I told of my day in school and how I drew the different parts of a flower—the stamen, pistil, and ovary—and my mother laughed and laughed about Junie Boy talking about ovaries and I didn't know what she was laughing about.

Or like the time I left the table the Sunday the Boyds were our guests to go to the bathroom at the head of the staircase—and peed for a full minute with the door open. When I came back to the table, everybody looked as if I was dead or something and later my mother said I had mortified everybody at the table.

The "sour bratten" is the best ever, but Granny is still sniffing and only pecks at her food. Daddy is glum, and nobody wants to talk. I start thinking about all of the things I am kept away from because

Granny worries about me. Why, if she loves me as much as she says, does her worrying always turn out so bad for me? Why doesn't she give some of her worry to Jeannine? I think, but quickly retreat from this idea. I am sort of glad Granny doesn't worry about my little sister.

"Mom, there's something I have to talk to you and Ann about," Dad says as Granny starts to leave the table early in a final demonstration of her hurt, then sits down again without saying a word, and I know whatever is going to happen tonight is not going to happen while I am there.

"Goodnight son." "Goodnight Junie Boy." "Goodnight Junior."

As I pass through the dining room, I straighten the fringe on the tablecloth my mother crocheted, and after turning out the light at the head of the stairs and seeing my sister is still asleep in our front bedroom, I creep back down the staircase and sit there in the dark leaning against the newel post.

"The way trade is falling off, Mr. Mueller says he may have to let me go."

"Oh, Mac!" says Mommy. "Jesus wept," says Granny, and I am really afraid now because she only says that when I hurt myself and come running and crying. A loose chip of paint I have been picking at on the post comes off in my fingers.

I've been to Mueller Bros. Fancy Delicatessen,

and I don't see how Mr. Mueller can let my father go. Who would go to the market at six every morning and buy the special melons and vegetables and meats that are the only things good enough for Mr. Mueller's customers? Who would smooth things over, like when that lady asked for stronger cheese, and Mr. Mueller said, "Lady, if the cheese on that counter were any stronger, it would get up and walk away." Why, Mr. Mueller would have to close down the store before he could let my father go.

People are always talking about the depression and hard times, but things can't be too bad. The German Lady's husband is still sailing his ship. Jeff's father leaves just as early in the morning with his paperhanger's board and painting ladder on top of his car. I saw Mr. Stryker leaving yesterday with a big painted poster. Yes, and Rusty's father and Henry's father are still being policemen, aren't they? Hoby's father's cab isn't doing too well, though. Hoby said so.

"He says people just aren't buying like they used to, Ann, and he has to cut back someplace. He's right about the customers. I had a fellow come in the other day and ask me for twenty cents' worth of Polish ham. If Mr. Mueller had been there he would have given him the ham and said, 'Here, smell it.' And our customers who are still buying aren't paying their bills. He says he's going to let

Sam the butcher go, and if I can take over his work and take a $5 cut to $35 a week, well, maybe he can keep me on."

"What did you tell him?" I hear Mommy ask apprehensively.

"What else could I tell him, Ann?"

"What about Sparky and Roswell?" my mother asks.

"They'll be the last to go, Ann. The whole business depends on delivery, even if it's a pound of butter."

Sparky and Roswell. I feel happier just to hear their names, thinking how Sparky lets me ride with him on the delivery truck. And Roswell, with his motorcycle and sidecar and black leather leggins. Roswell is always joking, and when he came to pick up my fat rabbit to give it a good home for its old age, he told my father, "Yes sir, if I could have a white son, I'd have one just like this one."

I am sad again though, remembering my new white rabbit, and how he got into the coal bin and when I washed him he died stiff as a board. I could never eat vanilla ice cream after that.

White. Black. The colored boys playing on the "cliffs" last fall and having fun sliding down the hill on those bent pieces of tin. And then, Pow! one of them hits a rock and nearly cuts his finger off. He runs off screaming, leaving his thick red blood behind him on the tin, and Louie—he tells me his name is Louie—just stands there crying. He's afraid to go home because he will get a licking for letting his brother get hurt. But the tears that wash away the red clay dust in little streaks under his big white eyes finally stop, and he even laughs when I show him how to go down the high slide sitting on a piece of waxed paper. We play all afternoon and I feel good, but that all changes when I get home because Mrs. Garner saw us playing together and tells my mother. The way Mommy laughs when she tells my father about it makes me feel ashamed for playing with colored children.

Mommy and Daddy and Granny are talking about all sorts of money for this and money for that and Christmas coming and suddenly Mommy asks, "Mac, can't we have an old-fashioned Christmas, you know, like it used to be before you went to Dr. Willmore. It will make up for some cutting back on the toys."

I almost clap with joy at the thought of Christmas like it used to be, but Granny says, "That's a terrible thing to ask, Ann. Don't you realize how sick he is? There's not an ounce of pity in this house for my son."

I know Mommy means Christmas with fruitcake and cookies and all the candies she made before Dr. Willmore put Daddy on that silly diet—no this, no that. Why do we have to give up everything, too? Nobody else's back hurts, except maybe

Granny's. Mommy says half our money goes for doctor bills and that metal-and-leather thing like a corset Daddy has to wear. He got his backache right after my sister was born, Mommy says. I wish it would go away so he could have fun again like the parties he and Mommy used to give in the cellar and I could help him make the home brew and use the bottle capper again.

"Okay Ann," I hear my father say, and I am so anxious I pull another peeling of paint off the newel post, "we can have sweets at Christmas if it will make you happy." The way Daddy says it I get the feeling he is full up with hurt.

All of a sudden Granny, who worries about my fish with me, is shouting, "There they are, look at them, those little red things swimming everywhere. There must be a hundred of them!" When I hear, "Wake Junior up," I can see myself getting stepped on in the rush to my bedroom so I scramble up the stairs as fast as I can.

It doesn't happen though, because my father says, "Surprise him in the morning." And I listen at the top of the stairs while they all "oh" and "ah" about how flat her stomach is and then catch Mother Swordtail in my net and take her back to her husband in the living room.

I crawl into bed next to my sister who is so little and think about my swordtails and Christmas like it used to be.

"Be good to your mother, be nice to Little Orphan Annie," my mother says. We are sitting in the living room and my hands are outstretched, like the surgeon in the movies waiting for his gloves, with a new hank of wool draped around them and the wool looping off as she winds it into a growing rust-colored ball.

"Are you going to be good to Little Annie Rooney when you grow up?"

It always makes me feel uncomfortable when she talks about herself as if she was somebody else, but all I can do is fidget and say, "Yes, Mommy."

She seems to want me to know she suffered some big disappointment when she was a little girl. I guess that's why she works so hard now to make things better, in spite of everything.

I know she is the best mother in the neighborhood, everybody says so, even the other mothers, like Rusty's, who shakes her head from side to side like a sad Saint Bernard and says, "Junior MacDonald"—she is the only one who calls me by two names—"your mother is always on the go, I've never seen anything like it. Knitting, cleaning, painting, cooking, even working at the store when your father's sick. She's a bundle of energy, but mind you, she'll wear herself out. I hope you're good to her."

"Tell me again how you got the gold wire, Mommy. Let me feel where it is."

I am always amazed that there could be a piece of gold wire in my mother's leg. When she pulls her skirt above her knee, I stare in disbelief all over again at the long scar in the sunken place just above her kneecap, and I poke the hole trying to feel the wire as she extends her leg to make the depression more apparent.

"If it hadn't been for my father getting his German up, your mother would have a stump for a leg."

I know the story by heart, but I like to hear it repeated because I want to know something about my real grandfather. I have two grandmothers but no real grandfather.

"Yes, Junie Boy, your grandfather was a man who knew his mind. 'I'll kill the man who cuts that little girl's leg off,' he told them in my hospital room. 'Find me a doctor, not a butcher!' And they did. He said he'd try his best, and he wired my leg inside with gold wire. Said it had never been done before."

"Where were you when it happened, I mean, when you broke your leg so badly."

"Oh, I remember the evening so well. Every year father took me to watch the fireworks at Patterson Park. I was seven and still on crutches from the leg I broke falling down the stairs as a baby. It never healed right and was sort of stiff at the knee and bent back, and getting smaller because I didn't use it. It was such a lovely evening. A rainstorm had swept through the city in the afternoon and now people were filling the park from all over, some lying on blankets, most sitting on folded newspapers on the wet grass. The sky was clear and the park a little misty. They were setting off the finale, and you know how exciting that is, Junie Boy. First the sky is filled with red stars, then blue and gold, and blue comes out of gold, and they all crisscross and cascade, and 'vomp,' 'vomp,' 'vomp' at the end. And I stepped back into a mud puddle and there I was, my leg stabbing at me and Daddy asking, 'Which leg is it Annie, which leg hurts?' and I am frightened to death when I have to tell him, 'My bad leg, Daddy.' "

The very mention of fireworks makes me wish the Fourth of July would hurry up and come. The most fun I have, ever, ever, is playing with fireworks. And almost as much fun as picking them out. The roadside stand, draped with bunting; my father knows the best one. The shelves with the neat open boxes, displaying their marvelous contents. The fifty-cent-apiece rockets are on the top row, with their fat red-, white-, and blue-striped bodies, pointed caps, and long sticks. Not little, like the five-cent ones I buy or the penny ones on the bottom shelf we shoot at each other out of pop bottles, they are so harmless. But oh, so fast, fffft!

I am allowed five-inch salutes and even cherry bombs since I have promised never to light one in my hand. Haven't I heard over and over from Granny's father, Great-grandfather Keenan, how he lost an eye picking up a five-incher he thought was out. Granny lives in terror of the Fourth and tries every year to frighten Daddy out of letting me have fireworks. "It will be your fault when he comes in here with his eye hanging out." My one-dollar allowance buys me some of everything I want, even a small pinwheel and Vesuvius fountain and maybe a few red spit devils looking like dried apricots.

"Were you out of school long, Mommy?"

"So long, I got a whole year behind and never did go back. I had to help my mother take care of my three younger brothers, too."

"How did you get to know so much then, I mean about furniture and sewing and adding up as fast as you do, things like that?"

"You can do anything if you put your mind to it, Junie Boy. I may not speak the King's English like some of those hotsy-totsies out in Roland Park, but I can run rings around them in everything else, even with my bad leg!"

She sure can do anything she puts her mind to. Like stretching Daddy's salary to buy me a real Indian tom-tom and wigwam when I wanted to be an Indian. And sending me to art school on Saturdays when I became interested in Mr. Stryker's pictures and decided to be an artist.

"When did your father die?" I ask.

"When I was seventeen."

"What killed him?"

"He was a cloth cutter all his life and had a lot of lint in his lungs. He drank a lot, too."

"How come you didn't marry Pop-Pop Jenkins? You always say when we visit him and Granny Jenkins and I play with his model planes in the cellar that I almost had him for a father and then wouldn't I have had fun."

"Oh, I never said it that way. I never said you almost had him for a father. I said he and I dated before I met your father."

"Then why didn't you marry him?"

"Because my mother took a liking to him, and the first thing I knew they were in love."

"Was he your age?"

"I was seventeen; I guess he was in his late twenties. I met your father the following year, and we decided to marry. What a fuss Granny Jenkins put up about that. Right in front of our house she told me never to darken her doorstep again for planning to marry out of the church, and I even had to stay a few days with your father in Granny Chamberlin's house because I had nowhere else to go. You were born almost nine months to the day after we were married. How I remember your father in the back bedroom on Washington Street marveling at how perfect all your toes were and worrying when he heard me say the doctor cut off your belly button so close he hardly had any left to tie off. You were a real love bug too. Almost your first words were 'Tooty Mommy, more tooty Mommy.' "

I know what she means by "tooty" and it embarrasses me, so I try to think of something else. Like death, for instance. I wonder if Daddy's father died of lint in his lungs, too. And Granny's second husband, Pop-Pop Chamberlin, died several years ago. When he and Granny lived up the street at the Strykers' before he went to the State Hospital, I used to see him almost every day. "One little, two little, three little Indians," he would sing as he bounced me on his knee. "Show me how you blow glass, Pop-Pop," I would say, and he would puff out his jaws and pretend to blow through a rod he had dipped in molten glass and was twirling it in his hands as he blew. I remember going to that funeral parlor to see him. Pop-Pop was the only dead person I'd ever seen.

My mother is about finished winding the last hank and none too soon, because my arms are tired. As I look at her, I think again how pretty she is, with her wavy dark hair, looking a little like Claudette Colbert in the movies.

I love my mother. Our house is full of plants and flowers she fusses with; even the cellar windows have white curtains. She's always doing things, learning things. She tells me herself how she is always making do, pinching pennies. She picks up remnants, she says. Even the yarn she's been rolling up for my sister's coat. The homemade things I see around the other kids' houses all look fake, but not hers; hers look better than the store kind.

And taste better, too. Like her Christmas cookies. Nobody makes thinner Christmas cookies than my mother. It seems very important to her to make thinner cookies than anybody else. I get to cream the sticks of butter with the wooden spoon in the big mixing bowl and then work in the sugar, little by little, and the sweet smelling vanilla extract that tastes bitter when I try to drink it, a pinch of salt, baking powder, sifted flour, and a little milk. We have all sorts of secrets between us, such as just how to grease the cookie pans and how to put the flour on the rolling pin to keep the cookies thin. Ducks, stars, Santa Clauses, Christmas trees, lifted out on the spatula, brown and warm and smelling indescribably wonderful!

She takes such good care of me when I am sick. Propped up in bed with a fluffy pillow and sheets smelling like the outside air, I read my *Big Little* books on Buck Rogers and Flash Gordon, or the first real book she bought me, *The Story of Mankind.* I love to look at its cover, with the picture of the mountain, and fish at the bottom becoming alligators, then dinosaurs and birds and cavemen, and finally people like us near the top. When I start getting really well, I am allowed to make a tent with an extra sheet over the four bedposts to make me feel snug inside.

As I watch my mother knitting, her fingers a blur of motion, I rub my right ankle against the leg of the chair. The tender, not painful, but unbearably strange feeling in my ankle jolts me back to that day in Penrose Alley when I was almost five. I am kneeling in my red wagon, which has lost a tire, pushing with my right foot and steering with one hand. One of the kids begins to push me so I take my foot off the ground, and it gets caught between the wagon and the metal rim of the wheel which grinds at my ankle like Mr. Mueller's meat slicer. I scream and scream but he keeps pushing until Mommy suddenly appears in a cloud of pain and terror, sweeps me up in her arms, and carries me to the kitchen where she bathes my dangling foot in a pot of water red with my blood. I am afraid when I see her stretch to the top shelf of the pantry for the box of grey mercury tablets she keeps there, and really scared when she drops one with a skull and crossbones on it in the water.

"Am I going to die, am I going to die, Mommy?" I sob as she rushes four blocks with me in her arms to the Bon Secours Hospital.

My sister Jeannine almost died there for real. When she was three she had a pain in her side, and the doctor first gave her an Ex-Lax, then was very upset when she was rushed to the hospital with a ruptured appendix. Everybody said she almost died.

She was so happy with the little green metal baby carriage I bought her with a clay baby inside tucked under the covers. The Sister there told everybody who came in what a naughty girl she was to open her ice pack during the night and drink the water out when she had been forbidden to drink anything at all. But I could see that everybody really thought it was clever, else why would they talk about it so much.

I love my sister, at least most of the time I do, when she isn't teasing me or telling on me. I tease her a lot, I guess, but I only tell on her when she is doing things I don't think she should do. Maybe I should stop those things that really make her angry, like holding her in the closet too long or handcuffing her hands behind her back to the bedpost even though she lets me talk her into it each time.

"Fire in the cockpit." I can feel as well as hear the crackling flames as I sit on the edge of the red plush chair, the base of the standing ashtray between my legs, steering my wounded plane to safety, until with one turn too many the top of the tray screws off in my hands.

Just as well though, for the adventures of Jimmie Allen are over for another night, and I tune the radio for "Buck Rogers and His Solar Scouts." This is my best program, and I sit on the floor next to the radio, picking at the rug just out of sight under the sofa. I know the bare spot and ball of pickings will be discovered some day, but I can't help it, the program makes me so excited.

These programs went far deeper than the fun and games of "Little Orphan Annie" or "Chief Wolf Paw." Long after they were over, there was something in me that resonated to the knowledge they offered. Like many boys my age, I received a whiff of the future from them; I was touched by the sky and beyond.

My father must have sensed the depth of my interest. We didn't do much together—no baseball like some of the other fathers. He seemed to work longer, and besides he didn't have much to say to the other men in the neighborhood. But one Sunday, as we were about to leave the dining room, he said, "Sonny boy, how would you like to go up in an airplane with me this afternoon?"

"Can we Daddy, can we, can we?" and like a flash I was all over him with such a barrage of questions, "Who, where, how?" that all he could answer was, "Hey, hold your horses!"

Granny was upset. "Mac, you aren't taking that boy up in one of those things, are you?"

"Mom, it's perfectly safe. Chamberlin has been

taking hundreds of people up all over the country."

"Chamberlin, Chamberlin who? That's my name," she says, surprised to hear her own name.

"Chamberlin, the famous aviator, who flew across the country without stopping."

The very mention of his name makes me quiver with impatience and heightens my fear that Granny will get her way.

"What makes you think that motor isn't going to stop when you get that boy up there?" she persists.

For some reason, Daddy is not at all influenced by Granny today. "It has three motors, Mom, it's called a Ford Trimotor, and it only needs one to stay up. Get your coat on, Son."

Granny can see no amount of sulking will help, and Mommy is smiling because she feels happy for me.

It's fun to be driving in the car with my father alone. "Pop-Pop Chamberlin wasn't your real father, was he Daddy?" I ask, as I tuck one leg up under the other, trying to become accustomed to sitting in the front seat. "No, he wasn't, Sonny Boy," he says somewhat wistfully.

"Tell me about your real Daddy."

"Well, I really didn't get to know him. He died when I was eleven."

"What killed him?"

"Pneumonia."

"Is that what I caught from you when I was born?"

"No, that was diphtheria."

"Did I almost die?"

"I wouldn't say almost, but you were very sick."

"Did he work at Mr. Mueller's?"

"No, Son, he was a cooper. He made barrels. I have his business card that says 'Angus MacDonald, Dealer in Barrels'—his shaving mug too, with his name on it in gold."

"Oh, that's the cup with the picture of the horses on it, pulling a wagon full of barrels."

"That's it."

"Did you want to be a cooper?"

"I didn't have much time to think of what I wanted to be. Your Granny and I lived alone, you know, and I always had to work part-time. Soon as I was out of vocational school, I went to work for Uncle Dan at his delicatessen. And when I married your mother a couple of years later, I met Mr. Mueller and he asked me to come to work for him."

"Is vocational school where the picture of you on the wall over the tool chest in the cellar was taken, the picture of you in the funny uniform with your arms folded when you were a champion?"

"I wasn't a champion myself, Sonny Boy. All of us in the picture were part of a team."

"Is vocational school where you got the magnets in the tool chest?"

"Yes."

"And the spark coil and the mercury and your hammer and all of that?"

"Sure was."

The very thought of the tool chest and the cellar, particularly on this occasion, sparks the same surge of joy I feel every time I go through the door off the kitchen and down the skimpy wooden stairs into the whitewashed basement. In the kitchen and dining room I eat meals or make cookies; in the living room I listen and fidget; upstairs I sleep and tinkle and look through my father's chiffonier at his father's watch with the gold chain and polished elk's tooth and little paper *Maggie and Jiggs* books I don't understand.

But the cellar is for doing. And sometimes thinking about my father. His things are there, and they make me want to know what he was like when he was a little boy. I see lots, and even without thinking I know some things. I know he is sad now. But when I lift the lid on the black trunk with big brass latches next to the coal bin and root around in its musty smells, I find sheets with black music notes all over them—music for the saxophone, it says—and it makes me laugh just to think of my father, whose face is very red anyway, puffing away on a brass thing and twiddling the keys with his fingers.

I know he went to school as I do because there are arithmetic papers, and there is one page, which he must have copied over and over like I do for handwriting class, with fat flowing letters, called "The American's Creed." His teacher didn't see he misspelled one word even with all the copying because there is a neat red "100" in the corner.

I can tell from the old pictures scattered in one of the trays that Daddy was a gay blade, as Mommy says. Still, even in his fancy suit and striped shirt standing next to his best friend Andy, he isn't smiling. The wide brown belt he is wearing in the picture—holding the handles of the plow at Mr. Brinkman's farm—lies coiled in the trunk, and I buckle it sometimes and drape it across my shoulder pretending I am carrying bullets like the soldiers.

I have the most fun with his magnets, or maybe the bottle of mercury. They are big U-shaped magnets, not like the little toy ones. When I press them toward one another, I can feel the sticky attraction just before they touch, and when I turn them, they bounce as if there was rubber between them. They pick up a whole string of nails from the nailbox and under a piece of paper make my iron filings march around like a smiling moustache. They stick to the furnace and hang upside down from the furnace pipe. They're keen.

I have to be careful with mercury, though.

Daddy says it is very valuable and poisonous if you swallow it. It's a whole medicine bottle full and the heaviest thing I have ever felt. It lies in a soft puddle on a piece of clean paper, and then I poke it and watch it run apart in globs and then snap back together again. I take the two big bell batteries down from their nesting place in the rafters and get flaky whitewash in my eyes doing it. When I wire up a Christmas tree socket between the batteries and dip the open ends of the wires in the mercury, the bulb glows, and when I seal them in a test tube with a cork, the light goes on and off as I tilt the tube back and forth and the mercury runs down to cover the ends of the wire. I think I have made an invention, and when I put the batteries back, I make another discovery, because I accidentally short out the wires and the doorbell rings and Granny goes to the door and is mystified. Soon, all over the neighborhood, when kids are in the cellar, there are mysterious callers until one day some funny-pants tells.

Sometimes I hook the batteries up to the spark coil from some old car, and when it gets vibrating, I play Frankenstein with his lightning machine. I can draw a flashing blue spark almost two inches long to the end of the big hammer. But I'm afraid, too, that someday the electricity will get to me through the wood.

Every time I go to the tool chest and flip the latch, I see the picture on the wall above it with the line of boys and my father standing next to his friend Scotty in the middle who is holding the soccer ball with "1920 City-Wide Champions" printed on it in white. I wish he would do some of that now, some of those things he used to do.

Or even some of the things he did before he got his backache and had to go to the doctor's all the time. Like parties and making home brew. That was fun, being with your father when he takes the cheesecloth off the top of the large brown and white crock and decides that the hops and yeast and gloppy things he puts in have worked long enough and you're waiting to fill the bottles like a production line after he sucks on the hose and gets it started—amid delicious smells like nothing you've smelled before. But first you have to wash the bottles on the attachment that shoots a swirling jet of water into the bottle and makes the pipes rattle when you take it off. Then when the bottles are filled, you put each one under the bottle capper and press the shiny caps onto the top with a pull-down on the handle.

It's even more fun because you know you are helping for the New Year's Eve party and when the night has finally come you are allowed to twist the red and green bunting and tack it to the rafters from the highest ladder and sprinkle dance wax on the linoleum until it's hard to stand up. There's a light socket without a bulb in it lying next to the wall and, peering inside, I decide to push the little tab down with my finger. Yow! From my fingertip to my shoulder I feel a throbbing jerking burning pain like nothing ever, and the next thing I hear is "Jesus wept," and I am put to bed still afraid and crying and knowing I have spoiled the party.

But at twelve o'clock my mother carries me downstairs, and I see my father reaching behind the shoe box on the top shelf in the hall closet for his .38 pistol which he thinks he keeps hidden from me. Soon everybody is pouring up out of the cellar door, and peering through the window I can see my father in the yard yelling "Happy New Year" and bang, bang, bang—firing his blanks up into the night. Everybody is talking and laughing about the one-man band he hired for five dollars in advance and how, when the man arrived with his harmonica and drums and cymbals all on a stick, he looked around and said, "Where's the piano?" Now they are all crowding into the kitchen and people are kissing one another and my father keeps saying to anybody who will listen, "How was I to know the one-man band needed a piano?" Then he laughs and they laugh and he goes off to buttonhole somebody else with his funny story.

I am roused out of my daydreaming by the banner over the fence gate at the old Baltimore airport: "Chamberlin's Airplane Rides—$1 per person." And there it sits, bigger than I could imagine, with its three propellers and movable ailerons and rudder and elevators.

I duck my head when my father goes up to Mr. Chamberlin and explains, "The boy is in love with airplanes," but my shyness leaves when the man walks me around his plane, allowing me to touch it here and there, and, unbelievably, takes me to the cockpit and allows me to sit in his seat and rotate the wheel on the control column, as I gleefully watch my action move the ailerons up and down.

We are strapped in our seats. With mounting excitement I hear a door slammed shut and latched, the whine and cough of first one engine, then another, and another. The whole plane is quivering now, as if it can't wait to get started, and then we are racing down the field. I have a scary feeling the takeoff is going to be like the roller coaster at Carlins Park, but to my surprise we are already floating in the air. Higher and higher we fly, the grass like the green-dyed sawdust "moss" we spread in our Christmas garden under the tree each year, with the little gravel paths leading up to the cardboard houses with cellophane panes. A mirror for a lake and around the whole thing the Lionel trains my father bought just before he met Mommy. I see them all—my head to the window, delighted at each new sight—the Pennsylvania tracks with the steam locomotive chugging smoke against its long load, the glassy shine of Loch Raven reservoir in the distance, the tower of the Baltimore Trust Building.

Too soon we are down and walking toward the gate, feeling light, looking back, talking together. All the way home I stick my hand out of the car window and rotate it in the blast of the wind, first flat, and then at an angle, imagining I am an airfoil, feeling the air break off the top of my hand as I reach the stall point, and then I see my hand plummeting to earth in a spin.

My airplane doesn't stall, the one I built out of two banana boxes nailed together, with my sister's baby carriage wheels in the front, a roller skate under the tail. My backrest is made of wood stringers covered with cloth and tapers back to the tail surfaces of stiff cardboard with rudder and elevator attached to wires I can move by jiggling a stick between my legs. My wings have real wooden ribs and can be detached to get the whole thing out of the cellar. I become so convinced I have built a real plane that when I touch the wires of Pop-Pop Jenkins' electric motor to the bell batteries between my legs and the propeller rotates and Rusty gives me a final push down Bentlow Street hill, I think I will surely fly, and do for a moment—when I hit a bump and bounce into the air—but then my airplane splits in two when the banana boxes are jolted apart.

When we bring the pieces home, Rusty tells Granny I tried to fly off the cliffs and no amount of explaining will convince her otherwise.

Too soon Daddy and I are home and the car is in the garage. But that evening is magic, too. The dried Christmas trees the kids have been collecting for a month are now in one grand pile, maybe a hundred of them, on the hill and the gang stands expectantly around as the oldest boy, Lon, tosses the burning paper. The fierce, crackling bright, pungent evergreens light the entire neighborhood, and when the roaring blast becomes skeletons collapsing in upon themselves, we rake some of the coals into a circle of rocks nearby and sit there roasting potatoes and talking, talking about my airplane ride, about many things.

The feeling of happiness, of everything being just the way it should be, is too much for me, and I leave the other boys around the fire and walk over to the cliffs. My corduroy jacket is heavy with the smell of burn, and as I stand there staring at the stars, I become suddenly, intensely aware that I am here and they are out there. My mind leaps from one star to another, farther and farther, all the while asking, "And what then, where can it all end?" If there is ecstasy in the question, there is also terror, the same feeling I had when I saw a dead puppy in the grass and watched the maggots eating at his putrid flesh. The mystery is too overwhelming for my groping mind, and I hasten back to the comradeship and security of the circle around the fire.

"Cobsina." The secret password is spoken by our Chief. "Cobsina," and we huddle around the upended orange crate, where the candle sheds a flickering light in the dark cellar. "Cobsina," and the members of the Crusaders Club are all the warmest of friends, bathed in the feeling of belonging, and everybody else is enemies to be talked about in hushed tones. "Cobsina!" Gone is any thought of last week's quarrel or yesterday's taunt.

The sound of pennies tossed onto the wooden top and the "glunk, glunk, glunk" of the ritual lemonade we are swallowing. The web of secrecy draws closer and warmer.

Hoby gets us laughing when he tells about his surprise trip to Washington last week. The freight train he was "hopping" got going so fast he didn't dare jump off again.

Then Jeff has to be funny-pants and keep asking me to tell them how the man shaved his moustache off. I say, "Shut up Jeff," but he won't, and he tells them, snickering in such a way I want to bash his head in.

"You remember how last summer that bum came walking through the weeds on the hill and gave Junior and me 10 cents for letting him show us his peter. When Junior's mother asked him where he got all the candy, he tells her, and she tells my mother and everybody in the neighborhood about 'that nasty man,' and when Junior sees him again, she calls the police and has him locked up."

Hoby looks a little uneasy even in the dim light, and I am sure he is remembering several years ago when my mother chased him out of our cellar and down the alley, flailing at his bare behind with a broom.

"Well, what you don't know is Junior's mother says somebody has to do something about people like that, and Junior ends up in court with the judge."

"In court!" says Rusty in awe.

"Yah, in court," says Jeff. "I know, because my mother wouldn't have anything to do with it, but she took me to court to hear everything."

"Now tell them about the moustache, Junior."

I am feeling better now and not nearly so angry at Jeff.

"I was in court all right, and a darned scary thing it was, with my mother and Jeff's mother and Granny and all the other people sitting there and the judge way up there alone. I have to swear to tell the truth, and the judge asks me to tell the court in my own words what happened. I tell how Jeff and I ran at first because he looked like a bad man coming out of the weeds. And then he says not to run because he has something for us.

"And do you know what that judge asks me to do? He says, 'Tell the court what the man asked you to do for the 10 cents.'

"I'm really scared now and say, 'He asked us to look at his, well, you know what.'

"The judge leans over and says, 'Young man don't be afraid. Tell the court the exact words the man used, it's important you know.'

" 'Don't be afraid,' he says. His mother and Granny aren't sitting out there! I look at Jeff here, and what does he do but squirm and look up at the ceiling. Finally the judge says, sort of kindly, 'Go ahead, son,' and I say, 'He asked us to look at his peter.'

"People laugh and I feel terrible and the judge bangs his hammer.

"But that isn't half of it. Now they bring in a line of men and ask me which was the man. Nobody looks just like him, but one looks very much like him so I say, 'I think it's that man, Judge.'

"And the judge, all serious, says, 'What do you mean you think, son? This man may go to jail. You have to know!'

" 'Well, he looks just like him except he had a moustache, and now he doesn't,' is the only thing I can answer, and the judge asks somebody if the man had had a moustache, and seems very angry when he hears he did and was allowed to shave it off.

" 'I can understand your hesitation, son,' he says, 'but you have to tell me, is he the man or isn't he?'

"I look at the man with his hair combed and everything, staring straight ahead, and what can I say but 'I can't say for sure.'

" 'Case dismissed,' says the judge, and soon we are all standing on Pratt Street next to the court, with the ladies all saying how terrible it was they let the man shave off his moustache, and Jeff here standing behind his mother's back trying to make me laugh, saying the letters 'p-e-t-e-r' with his lips so they can't hear him."

"Wow, what a thing to have to say with parents there," says Rusty.

I am not accustomed to this feeling of wholehearted approval and develop a growing awareness of wanting to share. Even Rusty, who usually becomes interested in everything I do, doesn't seem to consider me enough sometimes. Jeff and I have some interests in common—mainly looking for birds' nests and catching butterflies and bees—but we fight most of the time. And Hoby is like the rest of the gang, not interested in much except baseball.

I feel on the outside of most things. At the same time I want to play my games and the other kids' games as well. I want to be part of everything. "He's into this, that, and everything," my mother says.

I have such an itch to go the whole way now and tell them about my secret watermelon. Ever since I started growing things in my backyard when I was too young to be let out, I have wanted a watermelon vine. But our garage leaves a much smaller yard than most—all in concrete, except for a strip two feet wide just in back of the garage. It is here that I have my garden, in this strip and in two large wooden banana boxes from Mueller Bros., painted green and filled with dirt.

Here a packet of round brown seeds becomes a double row of fat red radishes and a shriveled-up kernel of corn a whole stalk with several ears and hundreds of perfectly formed kernels topped with corn silk. I dig the soil from around the seeds every day watching them progress. Parsley, string beans, lima beans, carrots, tomatoes, red peppers, onions, even potatoes—and a wisteria vine, trained up the garage, given to me by my wonderful Uncle John who drank a pitcher of beer and ate a square of Limburger cheese every night before he died. Pansies, zinnias, black-eyed susans, and everywhere petunias with their conical seed pods and hundreds of tiny black seeds.

But nowhere a fat, juicy watermelon. Until one day, a few weeks ago, while poking around "the dumps," past "the cliffs," near "the trees," where in the past I found tomato vines growing, I see among the scrawny green weeds the dark green fuzzy leaf of a watermelon vine and after following its many runners like a rat in a maze, come upon a watermelon nestled in the bushes. Yowie! Gently I pick it up, taking care not to break the stem. I smell it, I put it down, I put two fingers on it and thump them with a third as I have seen my father do in the early market, choosing Mr. Mueller's fancy watermelons.

Each day thereafter I visit the watermelon, approaching its protective cover with a racing heart. What if somebody else has found it!

I share my secret, but nobody seems to care except maybe Rusty. I feel a little put out and somewhat guilty that they don't like what I like. Maybe this isn't sharing at all, this telling them about something they don't have.

The next day I visit my watermelon and it is gone! I race up the cliff and across the hills to the street where the gang is playing baseball.

"Where's my watermelon?" I demand of Hoby.

He rolls his eyes and rubs his stomach.

"We all went to the dump," says Lon. "It's a free country."

"But where is it?" I persist.

He points to a rock near the weeds, and I can see it there, wantonly smashed.

I light into him in a flailing rage that throws his

head back and soon we are in the dust, punching and rolling. Then suddenly Granny's there yelling and chasing the kids and when I stand up all dusty and smeared I break into floods of tears—loving her for coming, and hating her, too.

There's always a going back after such happenings—and pretty hard, too, when they are all standing on the corner of Penrose Alley with brothers and friends and that's where you want most to be on a summer's night. No trouble; kids forget. You melt right back into your niche.

Presently Hoby, trying to be nice, says, "Boy, look at those shoes," and all eyes are on my brown wing-tip shoes I had put on especially for tonight, a little large perhaps, but handsome with their pebble finish and in stark contrast to the customary sneakers. "They're my fifteen-dollar shoes," I explain precisely (not adding that they were given to me by Mr. Mueller whose son had outgrown them even before getting around to wearing them).

"Ya, ya, ya, fifteen-dollar shoes, tell us more," and the group breaks up in laughter. But I don't care. I have the feeling I am better than they are.

"How long do you think it will take to heat up?" says Rusty, the brush of his crew cut sticking just above one of the two trash cans we are crouched behind at the end of my yard.

"Beats me, but it has probably melted by now."

The wooden racing hull looks sleek sitting there in the middle of the yard in its cradle, and I can just imagine it one day skimming across the model boat basin in Druid Hill Park at unheard-of speeds, belching bubbles of white smoke from its stern.

The alcohol tray under the boiler continues to flicker. Suddenly, there is an ominous gurgle. A shaft of white smoke jets from the copper tube sticking out of the rear of the hull and—ffft wham! Stuff clanks on the cans and garage and all over. Rusty beats it down the alley, and I head up. Never a noise like this before! A whole explosion! The squad car is sure to come. Better disappear.

I unlatch the German Lady's gate and walk carefully up the yard, avoiding the smelly piles of dog turds baking in the sun and making no quick movements that might be misinterpreted by Kurt as I edge past where he stands like a bully, snarling at me even though he sees me every day in the summer.

What meets my eyes as the screen door slams behind me is seldom any different: The German Lady sitting at the round kitchen table that is littered with newspapers, clippings, paste pot, and scissors. She glances up at me, and her bulging eyes, magnified by her thick glasses, seem the biggest things in the room. She is wearing a saggy blue and white house dress, and her round puffy face is set on her shoulders like my snowman.

"Take a load off your feet, Junior," she says, "and tell me what you've been up to today. But don't try to tell me you had nothing to do with that noise a minute ago. It's all over your face."

"I made a rocket boat out of the hull Mike carved for me and it blew up. Rusty and I ran, but I'm sure it's ruined."

"Don't worry about the old hull. You know Mike will carve you another one. But a rocket boat, that's different. What is it, anyhow?" she says, stubbornly dabbing the paste brush on the back of a clipping.

"Well, you see, I got the idea from my putt-putt boat I play with in my bathtub. I put an eye dropper of water up its tube, and when the tiny little candle has heated it to steam, it 'putts' out under the water in bubbles and makes the boat go forward. But that's for babies and bathtubs. Now I have my chemical laboratory and can make rocket powder. So I started thinking, why not put a boiler on my hull and solder a tube in it sticking out under the water. If I put some of my powder inside and heat it until it wants to burn, it will come whooshing out of the tube."

"What happened?"

"It whooshed all right, but it couldn't get out

the tube fast enough, and the boiler blew up. Like the can of beans I put on the fire at the Boy Scout camp without punching a hole in it first. Mike wondered whether the tubing was wide enough when he gave it to me, but it was all he had. And I didn't want to gunk up my good boiler on the inside, so I used a Shinola shoe polish can. Filled it half full with powder."

As I talk, I can see Mike's face when he returns from sea, and I tell him what happened: his black eyebrows arched high on his tanned forehead and the roll of his blue eyes, mouth tightly pursed, no words. None are needed. I know he's saying, "Why tell me? There are things you could have figured out in advance. Now you are a little wiser, aren't you? Let me know if I can help." And I learn more from the roll of his eyes than I ever learn from all the other yack-yacking, "You should have done this, you shouldn't have done that."

The German Lady's white-haired father comes padding into the kitchen, his crew cut just as bristly as Rusty's. I like it when he appears, even though he never smiles, because I get to hear some German.

"Will you have some angel food cake with Pop and me?"

"Yummy! First, can I look at Mike's things down the cellar?"

"Do you have to ask?"

I miss Mike now that he has become almost

twenty-one and gone to sea like his father. The cellar is just like mine, but dark and crowded like the rest of the house. One whole wall is piled high with hundreds of dusty old magazines—*National Geographic, Popular Mechanics, Field and Stream.* Over there is the real Navy hammock I lie in and hold onto for dear life while Mike pulls the ropes and tries to flip me out playing "Shipwreck." The canvas wrestling mat is rolled to one side, and next to it are the dumbells and the barbells. And there is his workshop, right where my laboratory is, next to the coal bin.

His wood vise is still holding the six-foot-long block of clear pine he has partly shaped into the new battleship which will house the miniature steam engine he is now making in the machine shop at sea. The sharp wood gouges are hanging neatly on the wall with all the other tools, the soldering iron is in its cradle, the metal vise half open. The shelves are stacked with parts boxes, some waiting replenishment from his last port of call, New York.

My laboratory is so dinky compared to Mike's: one shelf, containing three pharmacist's jars labeled potassium chlorate, sulphur, and charcoal; an old kitchen table with a few test tubes in a rack, an alcohol lamp, a mortar and pestle. And a pile of toilet paper cores, for making rocket bodies. I know the druggist thinks I use the potassium chlorate for gunpowder, and no amount of talk about rockets convinces him otherwise.

I suppose I miss Mike because he is like a big brother to me and Rusty. He's so quiet and strong and would take up for us if we ever really needed it. Not that he takes sides. He doesn't seem to get involved with the other fellows his age—seems to enjoy doing what he wants to do, like listening to those Gilbert and Sullivan records of his and making boats to give away. When he does get involved, he knocks every ball a home run or swan dives off the very top of the quarry, while the others are splashing around below. Not much fun in that for him too long, though.

"Come get your cake!"

The thought of the last time I had cake with the German Lady makes me smile: There we were, Hoby, Rusty, Jeff, and myself watching the jugglers at thc Hippodrome Saturday morning, before the big movie, and she picks that moment to pull the string off her cardboard box, takes the kitchen knife out of her purse, cuts up the fresh angel food cake, and passes a spongy piece to each of us. She's so nice to us. But we all want to crawl under the seats later when the little girl toe dancer is twirling around and the German Lady claps her heart out when nobody is clapping.

"When is Mr. Braun coming home?" I ask, taking my place at the table.

"In a few months now."

"I heard one of the mothers say once, 'Pity poor

Mrs. Braun—I'm glad I don't have a ship captain for a husband.' Don't you ever get lonely?"

"Pity poor Mrs. Braun, my ass," says the German Lady. "They're busy pitying themselves even at the thought of not having somebody else around to suck at, those yo-yos they have for husbands. Excuse me, Junior, but I know there are a lot of old battle-axes in this neighborhood who just can't stand it because I don't seem to bother with anybody. They just can't stand living and let live. If they want to pity anybody, let them pity Mr. Braun—he's the one who'll be out there soon again in winter storms. But they can't even do that because he loves the sea. They're just a bunch of rubbernecks, butting into everybody else's business."

I know what she means. I was with her when a neighbor tried to rubberneck in her window, and she stuck her head out from between the curtains, making bug eyes and thumbing her nose.

"No, I'm not as lonely as you might suppose. Each week, when I've gotten all of the advertising cut out of the newspapers and sent the packet off to him, I feel we've done a little something together."

"I heard another mother say, 'Pity poor Mike. She has always let that boy do just as he pleases. Why, I understand now he even dives off the side of his boat.' "

"There they are again, wanting me to get my sticky fingers all over somebody else like they do. I'll tell you something nobody around here knows, Junior. Mike had an older brother who was drowned. Fell through the ice, was a good swimmer, just like Mike, but he got trapped under the ice. Don't think I didn't have trouble keeping that from influencing me in bringing up Mike. But he's strong and on the move and into things. It's his nature. Tell me, who would I really be concerned about if I sat on him?

"Now you had better start home. You're going to be in enough trouble as it is. First go into the living room and get the Buddhas off the piano."

As I pass through the dining room, I admire the picture from South America made of dark butterfly wings and glance at the former resting place of the intricately carved and painted gourd she gave me last year.

Ah, the Buddhas, though. I run my fingers over their fat stomachs of polished redwood and admire their ugly jolly faces.

"Take them, they are yours, I want you to have them."

"Oh thank you, thank you, I'll keep them always," I say, as I back through the door, one in each hand, half in embarrassment at the unexpected gift, half in fear they would be taken back.

I pass by the Strykers' house on the left where Granny used to live. I see myself as a little boy, going up the alley to School 86, opening the gate every morning and standing expectantly under the upstairs bedroom window. It slides open and Granny's head appears. Slowly a brown paper bag descends toward my eager hands as she pays out the string hand over hand. I know by now it contains a penny and a piece of black walnut cake.

"Come visit me after school, Junior!"

The school orchestra has just finished playing "Smoke Gets in Your Eyes," and Miss Collett is on the stage again. It can't be long now.

I look down at the crease in my pants and fidget with the vest of my dark blue suit. For a moment I see myself as the parents will see me: standing next to Rusty in the Easter picture I carry in my wallet, the same blue suit, hair combed straight back but still slightly unruly in spite of Granny's globby green wave set, a look of the good boy on my face, so good it makes me feel uneasy.

I remember how Rusty and I ate the chocolates shortly after the picture was taken, the chocolates he warned me against buying for my first real girl friend, Ernestine. He always kids me about her, calls her Flash Gordon because of the blue cape she wears with the red lining. Rusty is around the corner, and I walk up the six white marble steps and ring her doorbell. She stares wide-eyed at the wrapped box in my extended hand. And then turns and bolts indoors.

"I told you so," says Rusty, all in stitches. I can't figure out what I've done wrong, what makes her not like me, and I decide I never liked Ernestine anyway.

I hadn't expected to be on the stage for graduation, hadn't even thought about it before Miss Collett called me into her office in the spring. You only came to her office when you were in real trouble.

"As principal of this school, I recommended you for a very special program. . . ."

I am staring at her face as I stand before her but, failing to read good or bad there, I am not relieved until I hear the word "special."

". . . And it is my happy privilege to be able to tell you that you are one of the thirty-five boys selected from the entire city. I hope you will take advantage of it. Of course, it will mean leaving Junior High at the end of this term and going right into the ninth grade at Baltimore City College, missing your graduation next year, and, I daresay, missing your classmates. But I think that is a small price to pay for joining the Academic Accelerated Course at City and, by skipping the ninth grade, receiving the equivalent of a year of college free."

"You have planned to go to City, haven't you?" Miss Collett says, sensing a complication beyond my natural hesitation.

"Well, I really haven't thought much about it, Miss Collett. I'm interested in rockets and chemistry, and a friend of mine who went to Poly says that's the place to go."

"It is if you want to be an engineer. But if you really want to be a chemist or scientist, I think a sound academic course is the thing for you. This rocket business, well, I wouldn't worry about that. It will take care of itself as you grow older."

I know what she means by that. I know how all grown-ups think about rockets, including even my Uncle John, but they haven't read in the library what Professor Goddard is doing with his rockets in Worcester, as I have.

"Have you thought about college? If you take this program, you really ought to be thinking about going on to college. The last year's credits are accepted at most colleges without question."

"I don't know much about college. Nobody I have ever known went to college, except a friend of my mother's, Mr. Warren. He went nights to the University of Maryland and says it's the thing to do. He went to City, too, come to think of it."

"Then you talk to your mother and father and let me know next week. I hope you'll accept. We'd be awfully proud to have another of our boys in the program."

Now I am nervously eyeing the potted palm on the high stand which is in a direct line between where I am standing in the wings and Miss Collett at the microphone on the stage. I notice there is one on the far side of the stage too, sort of framing the rows of kids sitting in their chairs for graduation.

"And now," I hear her say, "I will have join me a young man"—this is my cue to walk onto the stage and, with my preoccupation with the palm, actually brush it (I look over my shoulder and see it teeter, Yipes! but it settles down)—"a young man who, up to a few days ago had given up any thought of being on this stage at graduation, the winner of this year's Parent-Teacher Association Award for the highest grades in the school, Angus MacDonald, average 96⅘. Good luck at City."

I open the little envelope, see it contains a five-dollar bill folded around a card, weakly speak my thanks to all and walk back to the wings in a wide arc.

As soon as the school song has been played and people have started to leave, I race into the audience through the side door off the stage and find my mother, beaming, talking about her son with a group of people. Mr. Warren is beside her.

Mr. Warren had started coming to our house in his long hooded black Chrysler Imperial shortly after Christmas. At first he was just that short man with thick glasses and thinning straight-back hair, but now Mom says he is a very close friend and they go for rides all the time. She says she met him at Bernie's, where she used to stop in to see the owner's wife Pearl, who is also a friend of Mr. Warren.

I have him to thank for the bike I am about to sail home on—the biggest, best, reddest bike any boy ever had, with even an electric horn and lights. When I picked it out last spring at his friend's bike shop, Mom said how wonderful it was, because my father never gave me anything of value.

I feel very uneasy having Mr. Warren around, though, especially today. I don't know what to tell the kids why he's here.

2

Growing Up

I was fourteen and resolved to be "a great chemist for the good of mankind," according to the message to myself in my cast-iron bank, dated March 30, 1940—the message nobody was supposed to "tutch" until 1960.

How American that evangelical note, "for the good of mankind," when I had just made the amazing discovery that one could earn as much as $10,000 a year—an enormous sum, it seemed to me then—by working as a chemist for Du Pont.

"Better things for better living through chemistry," said the sign in the window of the exhibit room at the base of Steel Pier in Atlantic City, where Mr. Warren, my mother, sister, and I were sojourning.

And test tubes! My eyes devoured the exciting array of glassware in the same window.

I edge my way through the crowd of adults as

the demonstrator casts a nervous glance in my direction. "Ladies and gentlemen," he is saying, "notice as I tip this test tube slowly on its side, the contents,"—it looks like castor oil to me—"while viscous, are still liquid. With further processing they became—this!" and firmly he raps the table with the crystal-clear rod he holds in his left hand and now holds up for all to see.

I am astounded by this piece of magic and push my way to the front row of onlookers.

"Lucite, ladies and gentlemen, the plastic Lucite, yet another product of our research laboratories, staffed by some of the ablest chemists in the country, to which we have added more than our share from the graduating classes of 1939."

Policemen . . . grocerymen . . . painters . . . glassblowers . . . these I knew about. But a fellow could become a chemist, too—if he went to college.

". . . and to attract the top Ph.D.'s with broad experience, Du Pont pays as much as $10,000 per year and provides them with the finest. . . ."

How much was that a week? Let's see: 52 goes into 10,000 . . . 52 goes into 100 . . . once with some left over. No . . . start over: 5 goes into 10 twice . . . $20 a week, that's it. Almost $20 a week! No, there's another zero. Good God! $200 a week!

Stunned, I run back to the lobby of the hotel to join my mother, Mr. Warren, and my sister, who is still a bit green around the gills from the basket of

Concord grapes we ate in the back seat during the drive to Atlantic City.

"Boom! Boom!" says Mr. Warren, taking the cigar out of his mouth and slapping me on the back. Over the years I was to learn that these words were his single expression for a galaxy of emotions ranging from joy and approval to disappointment and despair. "Boom! Boom!"

The trip would be fun, Mom had said, and besides, we could get to know Mr. Warren better. He and I were sharing a room down the hall from my mother and sister. Ever since my mother had called me into the back bedroom at Penrose Avenue at the beginning of summer, I had shared the front bedroom with my father. But sleeping in the same bedroom with Mr. Warren is a different matter. It's . . . spooky.

"Sit here on my bed, Junie Boy," she had said. "You love your mother, don't you?"

All I can do is nod my head. I feel too choked up to say anything.

"Well, she loves you too, and she wants to see you have some of the things in life that she never had. Junie, what would you say if I told you your father and I can't live together any longer, and I want you and your sister to come live with me."

"And leave Daddy and Granny?"

"Yes. But you won't be far away. Now, now, don't cry like that. You're making me cry too."

"But why can't you? Why can't you live together with Daddy?"

"Your father doesn't love me."

"He does, too. He does, Mommy. He does."

"No, he doesn't Junie Boy. All he does now is read those Christian Science books of his morning, noon, and night. God is love, he tells me."

"But what about my laboratory and wisteria vine and . . . oh . . ." The tears are running down my face. ". . . Daddy's trains and the Christmas garden."

"We'll take the trains and garden and transplant the wisteria vine just like when you brought it home from Uncle John's."

"Will we have a yard?"

"A yard, why, you'll have a whole yard, all full of dirt, and we can have a real garden. And what a laboratory! You'll have a whole cellar for your laboratory. I've talked to Mr. Warren about it, and he said he'll have a special table and shelves built for you and—hold your breath!—a gas jet for a real bunsen burner."

"Really?" The rain has suddenly stopped. The sun is coming out again. "And maybe running water too?"

"Sure."

"How far will we live?"

"On Hollins Street, next to Mr. Warren's house. You can visit Granny every day after school."

"City, Mom, City. I can't go to City in the fall if I live down there. I know because my friends at Boy Scouts have to go to that stinky Southern High."

"I don't know where the line is. You may be right. We'll be one block south of Baltimore Street. That won't be a problem, though. Mr. Warren is in politics, you know."

Warren was his middle name. He was one of those men who prefer a first initial. From all I have heard he was brilliant, hard working, effective, but I never saw this side of him. When I met him, he was already on the way down. He had been a member of the Maryland House of Delegates as his left-over stationery and its official heading attested. When my mother first met him, he was Assistant U.S. District Attorney in Baltimore and still in his early forties. His office was on the first floor of the three-story building where he lived with his mother, and I liked visiting him there because I could browse through his *Encyclopaedia Britannica* and the medical books of his uncle who had been a surgeon. His framed law degree on the wall from the University of Maryland Night School impressed me no end.

Mr. Warren had married his first wife while still in law school, my mother said. There had been a second wife, too. He was very active in politics and his followers—to whom, apparently, he was a source of patronage—said he would be governor some day. Later they said he could have been governor.

"Warren here could have been governor if he wanted to, couldn't you, Warren," they would say, drinking his liquor at Dubner's Bar.

"Boom! Boom!" he would answer, sipping his Schenley's and water. "Maybe we'll show them anyhow, one of these days."

The turning point seemed to have been his loss of an election for district judge. Somehow Franklin D. Roosevelt must have figured in the defeat, for at the very mention of the name he would snort, "That —— cripple!"

Still, I was very impressed when I sat at the top of the stairs leading to his basement, which served as the Democratic Club of the Sixth Ward, and listened to the rallies for the mayor and U.S. representatives and senator. And pretty proud, too, when he called me down to meet Senator Tydings one night and introduced me as his son.

My relations with Mr. Warren were surprisingly good at first. He gave me my Boy Scout sheath knife and made me give him a penny so the knife wouldn't sever our friendship. Before our Friday night troop meetings he would take me to Bellow's Delicatessen, a client of his, where each time I had kosher corned beef on a bagel, Pepsi Cola, and Butterscotch Tasty Cakes. The first Christmas, before we moved to Hollins Street, he even bought me the most elaborate chemistry set and three-power microscope the May Company had to offer.

But soon the special efforts dwindled away, and our relationship became one of growing disappointment on my part. Before our first Thanksgiving dinner together he was slobbering asleep on the couch —he seemed to spend half his life asleep on the couch—and would only come to the table after a scene with my mother. When I was old enough to drive, he would promise me his car for the evening and then renege a few minutes before I was to leave. I never knew what he would say if I brought a friend home. "What is he, some sort of a fairy?" he remarked, somewhat in his cups, when I introduced him to an English boy whose accent offended his American ears.

Had Mr. Warren not been his own worst enemy, if his clients had not had to search for him when he was supposed to be representing them in court, were he not clearly a disappointment to everyone with whom he came in contact, I might have suffered the guilt of competing with him for my mother's love. Had his fall been more subtle, I might have taken it on my shoulders. As it was, he gave me every advantage.

He is dead now. He died the night my mother returned from her visit with me, my wife, and our new baby daughter on Long Island, after we had left

Oak Ridge some seventeen years ago. "Ann," he said, "I don't feel well," and he lay down on the couch, and in a few minutes he was dead. I went to his funeral and suffered that overpowering feeling of how different things might have been—if only. . . .

In the last few years of his life his practice had virtually dried up—a few divorce cases here and there was about all he had left. He drank constantly, and I suppose that's what got him in the end, although who can say. Others have the same conflicts that must have been eating away at him and still manage to hold the outside together. Even so, Mr. Warren was not the only man I have known who seemed to will his own failure. The reasons lie deep, and undoubtedly reasons there are, but none for judgment.

I never liked Hollins Street. Not the apartment itself, with people living on the first floor below and the third floor above, and walking up and down my stairs and going into my cellar. Nor that dark dirty cellar, with an old desk for my laboratory work bench, cluttered with the trash of many years, which none of my sporadic attempts at house cleaning ever seemed to change. Nor the backyard, a shabby affair even with the thriving wisteria vine threatening to engulf the garage.

The row of houses with white marble steps were

merely doorways through which people drifted or in which people sat on hot summer evenings—nameless, faceless people. Women in pants, up from the South, to work in the war plants. Some single, some with husbands. A whole block of hillbillies.

The move would have been a more painful experience had it not brought me close to the Boy Scout troop I had joined two years before. Now I lived within a few blocks of the boys who were the most fun in the troop. And a rough lot they were.

The doorbell rings of an evening, and I can tell from the raucous voices on the steps below that the gang has arrived.

"How's about our listening to your records and then shooting some rats with your BB gun," says Ted, the skinny Pole, as they push their way into the downstairs hall even before I reach the door. In the dim light, I also see Stan, the Lithuanian, with the pushed-up nose, and Howie, the Irish boy, with the big eyes and sunken cheeks.

"The Polka Dot Polka" and "The Rose of San Antone!" None of my Beethoven tonight.

"Hey guys, put that bottle away! You'll get me in trouble with my mother if she comes home."

"What the fuck do I care about your old lady?" says Howie, passing around the pint bottle of blackberry wine for one more swig.

"Hey MacDonald, what the fuck are you doing studying all the time?" says Ted, twirling over to my desk in a polka step. "Look gang, Cicero, and French," he exclaims picking up my books. "Par lays voos fon casey."

"I'm going to be a chemist and make $200 a week."

"Do ya hear that, gang! $200 a week! Sounds to me like he's been jerking off too much lately. Let's get the fuck outa here."

"Hey gang, first do you want to see some of my dirty pictures down in the cellar?" The need to belong is strong in me.

They stampede past me down the stairs but stop abruptly at the cellar door.

"Not me. I'm not going down that cellar. I know that knucklehead means it," says Stan, pointing to the sign on the door 'BEWARE TNT BELOW.' "I saw him with his eyebrows all burned off when something exploded in his face once before."

"Oh, forget it Stan, I just put it there to keep the kid on the first floor out."

That isn't quite the truth. That's why I put the sign there, but there is TNT in the cellar—from the nose of the 75-millimeter shell Mr. Warren finally let me bring over from the Democratic Club. Its fuse is out, and it's mostly hollow, but one day I poked inside with a curtain rod and chipped off some of the TNT that was still stuck to the bottom. It burns like mad, but I can't get it to explode.

"Where's the pictures?"

"Hold your horses." (I want to give them a chance to admire my glassware, still hooked up on the desk from the experiment I was making after school, especially the new glass retort I saved up for for six months. There it is, its glass bottom nestled in the tripod, looking like a comma on its side.)

"This place stinks. Where's the pictures?"

I go to the shell which stands upright next to the desk and with all my strength lift the hollow steel nose off the brass cartridge case—empty except for the rolled-up sheath of pages torn from the medical book next door called *A Handbook of Obstetrics.*

"Jesus," says Stan, looking at the outstretched wide-open legs, "I've never seen pussy like this." And for once they are all quiet as the pages are handed back and forth.

"Hey guys, do you want to see how I discovered a new way for making iodine out of potassium iodide?"

I am startled as Ted grabs my retort from its perch, holds it between his legs with both hands and shouts, "Look gang, I've got a big one."

On the way down to the Hollins Street market to shoot rats, we pass Union Square and Stan says, "Let's go in and tease the queers."

"No, let 'em alone," says Ted. "We'll get in trouble marching around too much with this BB gun."

The marketplace is empty at night, and its wooden stalls are completely bare of the daytime piles of food and goods. Only the smells of fresh sauerkraut, smoked fish, and cheese remain. We quietly take our places side by side atop a stall and wait for the overfattened shapes to come slinking out of the shadows.

"There's one, there's a big one! What the fuck are you doing, missing him like that?"

I was playing the pinball machine at the gang's hangout in the Oriole Restaurant when the familiar strains of "You are my sunshine, my only sunshine . . ." on the radio was interrupted by the first dramatic announcement of the events at Pearl Harbor. Instantly, it seemed, the old noise and activity came to a halt and silence took over as we gathered around the radio, exchanging glances of incomprehension and alarm.

Hurrying home alone—the restaurant had suddenly emptied as people followed their animal instincts and made for their burrows—I continued to experience the same bewildered feeling of dislocation. Then all afternoon and well into the evening a seemingly endless train of olive green trucks and tanks, looking monstrously out of scale in the small, peaceful frame of Hollins Street, rumbled by. The ashtrays danced on the coffee table in our second-floor living room as I looked down on the chugging, backfiring tanks that shook the street beneath their steel treads. Later I learned that "war plants" on the east and west coast were considered subject to imminent Japanese attack; the convoy was on its way from Fort Meade to the Glen L. Martin Company's airplane plant on the other side of town. Overwhelmed with excitement, I scribbled the words "War with Japan. December 8, 1941" on a scrap of paper and deposited it in my cast-iron bank.

With the outbreak of war, jobs became plentiful. Work as a part-time soda jerk was all I could find during the summer of 1941, and then only because the owner of the drugstore was a client of Mr. Warren's. But after Pearl Harbor the demand for workers was such that I had my pick of several jobs.

As soon as school was out in the summer of 1942 I went to work for the American Hammered Piston Ring Company—my first real job, seven days a week, twelve midnight to eight in the morning, as a hammering machine operator. With time and a half for Saturday and double time for Sunday, I managed to make a little over forty dollars a week at the basic hourly rate of sixty cents. Under the incentive program I added a few more cents, but very few, for although I reached the point of having three machines going at the same time and cut my fingertips to shreds sticking the razor-edged piston rings in the machines, the standards were set by a miser and could seldom be excelled.

Rusty, whom I continued to see on my periodic visits to Penrose Avenue, became a riveter at the Martin plant. Older than I, he had already graduated from high school and was awaiting the draft. By the time summer came, he was making enough money to buy a horse which he kept at a riding academy in the suburbs. That's what I liked about Rusty; he was always doing interesting things, like buying the horse, and, before that, skis. Who else in our neighborhood would ever think of owning a horse, or skis? They were for the rich people who lived in Green Spring Valley.

A good bit of my earnings went to support Rusty's horse. In return I was allowed equal riding time. By the end of the summer, I had learned a little about the finer points of horsemanship—a little, but not very much.

It was a wonderful summer. True, the war was on. But nobody was getting hurt, at least nobody I knew, not yet. I was seeing less and less of the gang on Hollins Street whom I had never really liked, much as I tried to think I did. I enjoyed the freedom of a few bucks in my pocket that I could spend as I wished. But freedom comes high, and toward the end of August, exhausted by working all night and playing all day, I thought I would take a few weeks' vacation before the beginning of school. That was when I met Sally.

Our first moments together were typical of young people who are introduced by older people and resent it (the matchmaker was one of Mr. Warren's tenants who knew Sally's family).

I had just arrived at the family's summer cottage on the Magothy River outside Baltimore and had headed toward the beach with her mother to find her.

"Hi," said Sally, waist-deep in water next to the wooden dock on which her mother and I were now standing.

Then, as if suddenly aware of my presence, she slid beneath the water, and emerging slowly to face us, she swept her long brown hair back from her sun-tanned forehead and gave a hike to the bra straps of her tight-fitting orange-yellow bathing suit.

"Well, aren't you going to invite Mac in for a swim?" asked her mother, breaking the silence that followed. "That's what he came for."

"Baloney!" Sally was thinking. You could see it in the way she shifted her eyes. She knew I was there to meet her. And so did her younger brother and cousin who were squinting up at me, their heads cocked at an angle, arms folded on their chests. Kids have an uncanny knack of figuring age down to a few months, and the two boys had already paired me off with Sally.

"Let's play submarine," said her brother, ignoring his mother's words, and with that they were off, diving and surfacing like porpoises in an underwater game of "gotcha!"

"Those kids will never learn their manners," said her mother as she showed me to the bathhouse.

Momentarily hurt by the kids' snub, I was soon too busy getting into my bathing suit to dwell on it. Once I was in the water though, the feeling returned. Except for a half-hearted lunge in my direction, the cousin, who was temporarily "it," spent all his time pursuing Sally and her brother.

I was relieved when I noticed that Sally had an eye cocked in my direction whenever she came up for air, usually directly behind and tantalizingly close to her perplexed pursuer. Taking a deep breath which swelled her ample bosom, she would again slip out of sight and continue to outsmart the boys. What engrossed me was not the game but Sally's lithe body as it moved swiftly and effortlessly through the water.

Now her brother, whose ability to swim under water was more fishlike than human, just missed her as she plunged to one side. Without surfacing, he headed for the next body in sight. "Gotcha!" he shouted as his head popped out of the water, but after he cleared his eyes and saw that it was my wrist he had grabbed, he dropped it as though it were a sea nettle.

For a discreet interval I devoted my efforts to the boys, but soon I was in hot pursuit of the blur of orange-yellow beneath the surface. My frustration grew as she eluded me with a nonchalance designed to spur me on. Finally, after one last all-or-nothing lunge I found myself clutching a wet slippery thrashing leg. The squiggly feeling that had been developing in my stomach suddenly dropped lower.

"Gotcha!"

Aside from my strong physical attraction to Sally, what appealed to me about her were the same qualities I value in a woman today. Different words and images then and now, no doubt, but the same qualities. She was game for anything—a good sport, ready to pitch in, fun to be with, a happy girl. Young as I was, I saw in her clear, intent eyes a look of knowing her own mind—strength, endurance, quiet independence, the capacity of seeing things through. And with all that, she was a loner, just like me. In short, I was enthralled.

At lunch after our swim she sat as far from me as possible, a fact of some consequence, since meals were served in the "mess hall" (white frame like the nearby main cottage and the lonely outhouse off in the trees) whose interior was dominated by a thirty-foot-long, picnic-style table with benches for seats. Were it not for the delicious food and easy informality of the place—wet bathing suits, sandy feet allowed—I would have felt put out again. As it was, I dug into the mound of brick-red hard-shell crabs, steamed in vinegar and beer like Granny's, I noted, and with nutcracker in hand began to extract the tasty meat. Kids and grown-ups were eating and talking on all sides—there were about twenty in all, counting Sally's family and the families of her mother's sister and two brothers who shared the cottage—and I immediately felt part of them.

It was not until several months later, after I had taken her to several "City" football games, that I sensed any movement on Sally's part toward me. And then it happened, all at once: we were crazy about one another and were together every possible moment for the next year.

Although I didn't give it a thought then, it surprises me now how anxious I was to date other girls after I left for the Navy in the fall of 1943. Yet, when I was home on leave, it was always Sally. For me, love was all-taking, and so it would continue to be for some years to come.

Toward the end of the war Sally got wind of the fact that I had a girl in Boston. The day after I was mustered out, she arrived at my house in a truck driven by a blond boy dressed in work clothes whom she introduced as her fiancé.

"We've come for your pictures of Sally," he said.

I protested that they were my pictures, taken with my camera, and that it would ruin my photograph album to remove them.

"Give them to her," he demanded.

He was twice as big as I was and seemed to mean business, so I produced the album and stood by as he proceeded to remove every picture in which his sweetheart appeared.

That was the last time I ever saw Sally. And so, as the poet says, a world ends, not with a bang but a whimper.

I have never forgotten Sally. She is a part of me to this day.

3

Professor Templeman

The fall of 1942 was the beginning of my last year at City. Crowning a tree-studded hill, its gray stone arches and Gothic tower exuding high purpose and inspiration, City had come to be identified with what I instinctively felt to be the style, the substance of my life. I had become increasingly aware of education as my "sure thing," an attitude from which I have never fully recovered. Let there be a falling out with the gang, let Mr. Warren play with me like a cat with a mouse over the use of his car . . . my mother unhappy with her life . . . people quarreling, fighting, always fighting . . . my father reading his Christian Science books . . . my sister not behaving as I think she should—in the end, nothing seemed to matter but my education. It became for me an intensely personal, living thing, something beyond the conflict and disappointment of ordinary existence. Naturally a growing boy does not think in such terms, but the feeling, the conviction, was already there.

"Remember," my mother would say, "your education is something nobody can ever take from you."

I have forgotten the names and faces of most of my teachers, but three remain with me. There was Mr. Fisk, who taught me what little I know of German. A little, sickly faced man, who was reported to collect jade pieces, he wore a green eyeshade, a Hitler moustache, and quieted each ulcer-produced belch with a glass of hot water poured from an ever-present thermos bottle. Any overt or suspected malfeasance always produced one of two set pieces, delivered with flashing eyes and forefinger outstretched toward heaven: "The wages of sin is death," or "You'll be *sporlos versenkt!* Sunk, without a trace!" And occasionally a third, delivered in solemn tones with the same forefinger pointed to the picture of Napoleon on the back wall: "For what is a man profited, if he shall gain the whole world, and. . . ."

Then there was Miss Paris, in Music, who spent four years trying to change our full-voiced pronunciation of the key word in the school song from "Ciddy" to "Sitee."

And Professor James P. Templeman.

"*Arma virumque cano.* I sing of arms and of a man. *Troiae qui primus ab oris.* Who first set forth from the shores of Troy." I felt a twinge of excitement as the words rolled from his lips, perfectly enunciated, his tongue flicking to the roof of his mouth on the second syllable of *virumque.* I had expected quality —the mere fact of having Professor Templeman, Head of the Department of Ancient Languages, suggested exclusivity, for he taught only third- and fourth-year Latin—I had expected quality, but not excitement.

Ah! Listen! *"Infandum regina. . . ."* The very first day of the term he reads to us from Virgil's *Aeneid.* No review of declensions, *amo, amas, amat,* no *is, ea, id* bit. Right in, head first! My God, it suddenly occurred to me, he likes it, too!

And now, we were beginning our last year, our surrogate first year of college. Often, at lunchtime that fall, a small group of us would sit around in a tight circle on the grass, working on our translations of Horace. Latin was forever with us, classes every day in the week and twice on Monday.

On this particular day, there were four of us sitting cross-legged in the sun. Abe, always the boy to beat. Year in and year out he had the highest grades in the class and was possessed of the only truly photographic memory I have ever known. Abe was completely sedentary, pig-faced, flabby—he flunked physical education, being unable to swim, even after four years in the pool, and was incapable of a single setup, which he always approached with a look of grim determination; he had no apparent interest outside of his schoolwork. Terry, second in grades, son of the principal of Forest Park High, was sallow from spending every spare moment practicing the piano and the organ. He was the only boy in the class who knew precisely what he was interested in.

That Terry was giving a recital the next week of Bach's Fugue in G (which he had practiced on the organ for a year), or was studying under Dr. Courboin at the Peabody Conservatory, or was taking a lesson from Virgil Fox or E. Power Biggs made a difference to me. I remembered it. Words, such as contrapuntal, came in one ear not out the other. Part of this I attribute to my affinity for the esoteric, like magnet for iron, with its comforting suggestion to myself (and to others) that there is more to the inner core than one might suppose. To put it more simply, I was horning in on Terry's uniqueness. But also, I had independently developed my own love of classical music and when by myself loved to play my favorite records over and over, although I must admit I may originally have heard some or all of this music drifting down the stairs in the German Lady's cellar. (Whoever knows what in truth is strictly his own?) But most of all I envied Terry his love of music, which he was pursuing with effort and accomplishment, while I knew I would have to gather education for some time to come wherever I found it, like a child depositing bits of silver foil in a cast-iron bank, convinced of its ultimate value. Only it was not so much his love of music I envied Terry, as his dedication, for though I nourished a secret passion for rockets and read everything I could on the subject, I had not his single-mindedness.

The fourth member of our group was Izzie, a rather short, heavy boy, a bit flip and somewhere in the middle of the class in grades. His father and mother ran a grocery store, a seemingly unrelated fact which I recall with singular vividness (for good reason, as we shall see).

Sprawled on a hillock nearby, in the shade of the large oak trees around us, still in full leaf except for the new growth scattered on the ground by the sharp-toothed squirrels in search of plump acorns, were Bill and Penn, matching pennies.

"Even . . . Even . . . Even again! . . . And again! . . . Hey, and again! . . . Hot damn, five in a row!"

Bill and Penn were the big boys in the class, especially Penn, who would make two of the rest of us, and as such were on the football team (second string, our class not being distinguished for its athletes). When they had not prepared their translations, which was not unusual, they would hover around waiting for us to finish and invariably talk one of us into lending them his book—"Come on, MacD, you're a regular guy." "Okay, but this is the last time."—long enough to memorize enough of the penciled-in translation to avoid the dread zero in Professor Templeman's notebook.

We all liked Bill—he was a natural leader—and each year chose him our class president. Most of us wore suits, which made us look like little old men, and I could not help but admire Bill's rich, brown sports jackets, foulard ties, button-down collars, gray flannels, and cordovans. In fact, I admired (envied) a lot about Bill. He had quality, however different it might be from Professor Templeman's or Terry's.

Social quality. He was draped with the words cotillion, tea dance, deb as naturally as with his sports jacket, words that evoked for me smells flowing from a bottle labeled "sweet essence of substance." I arrived at our first dance in a rented tuxedo, with Ernestine, driving Rusty's $25 Model T; he, in his own black tie, with his father's Buick, and his steady girl, Anne. Ernestine had to be home at midnight; Bill's party was going on to a drive-in on York Road.

Since our class was a special one made up of students from all over the city, none of us saw anything of the others after school. Only twice was I invited to another boy's house. Once, by Bill, for a meeting of class officers (I was vice-president). His house in the Homeland section of Baltimore, his gracious mother, the painting of her in oil over the dining room sideboard—all spelled substance to me. My other invitation was to Terry's house, near City, and there I sensed a different substance: academic.

I had with me the new hand-tooled leather briefcase my mother had bought during a visit to Mexico with the Spanish Lady upstairs. I had rested it against the piano bench in the living room, and as Terry was introducing me to his mother, a look of horror spread over her face and her hand went to her mouth. I turned in the direction of her gaze and saw their dog, with lifted leg, using the Aztec calendar on my bag as the bull's-eye.

"My God," I groaned within, embarrassed, not for myself but by the thought that I was embarrassing Terry's mother by causing her dog to pee on my new briefcase.

"I'm so sorry," she said, wiping it with a dust cloth, "he must have been attracted to the strange smell."

"It doesn't matter at all," I said, very much the gentleman. "It's made of cowhide."

"Odd. Come on baby. Odd. And odd again! Hot spit!"

"Parcius iunctas quatiunt fenestras," reads Terry from *The Odes of Horace,* beating out the meter with his right index finger,

iactibus crebris iuvenes protervi,
nec tibi somnos adimunt, amatque

ianua limen,
quae prius multum facilis movebat
cardines; audis minus et minus iam
"me tuo longas pereunte noctes,
Lydia, dormis?"

"Good heavens!" He looks up in amazement, a shock of hair falling over his forehead. "Is he saying what I think he's saying?" His finger stabs at the lines, a physical aid to his scanning eyes as he mentally unscrambles subjects and predicates.

The young bloods come round less often now,
Pelting your shutters and making a row
And robbing your beauty sleep. Now the door
Clings lovingly close to the jamb—though, before,
It used to move on its. . . .

"Say, what's the word *'cardines'* ?"

Abe, as solemn and squat as Buddha, flips through his dictionary and runs his stubby finger down the page. "Hinge."

It used to move on its hinge pretty fast.
Those were the days—and they're almost past—
When lovers stood out all night long crying,
"Lydia, wake up! Save me! I'm dying!"

"Why, it's an ode to an aging whore," says

Terry, delighting in his acute perception of things wicked.

"Ode to a whore!" Bill exclaims, and he and Penn scramble over to our circle like two linemen as the ball is snapped back.

I start to snicker as the picture painted by the poet begins to sink in: "Leave it to old Horace to say she did a roaring business, by speaking of her well-used hinges." We all roll with laughter as we picture dark shapes in the night, moving through Lydia's door, a squeak perhaps, now and then. All of us, that is, but Abe. Even he, though, manages a smile and a sly "Heh, Heh, Heh."

"What makes you say she was a whore?" says Izzie. "Why not just popular with the boys?" He is given to questions you want to swat like a fly buzzing around your face.

"Abe, why don't you finish it?" Terry says.

Soon your time's coming to be turned down
And to feel the scorn of the men about town—
A cheap hag haunting alley places
On moonless nights when the wind from Thrace is
Rising and raging, and so is the fire
In your raddled loins, the brute desire
That drives the mothers of horses mad.
You'll be lonely then and complain how sad
That the gay young boys enjoy the sheen
Of ivy best or the darker green

Of myrtle: leaves that are sere and yellow
They throw to the east wind, winter's fellow.

The sureness of his translation convinces me that he has worked on it at home. I'll bet he knew all along that *cardines* means hinge. And his phrasing—a bit too elegant. Sounds like a trot. I wonder if Abe uses a trot.

Bill purses his lips in that impish mannerism that makes the sides of his mouth curl upward like Jerry Colonna's moustache. "Hey fellows, what do you say we make a pact that if one of us is called on we start by announcing 'An Ode to an Aging Whore'?"

"Can't we say prostitute?" Izzie says.

"No, Old Temp would like whore better. He's a regular guy, you know, his being in the war in France and all of that."

"He might be sore at our poking fun at a woman who is more to be pitied," Terry suggests.

"Aw, come off it," scoffs Penn, who has been taking everything in quietly until now. "If he likes women, why isn't he married?"

"Because he thinks it would be unfair for him to marry a woman, that's why," I say, hot in Professor Templeton's defense.

"What's unfair about it?"

"His being gassed in France, that's what's unfair, and not wanting to tie a woman down to a sick man."

"How do you know?"

"That's right," Terry intercedes. "My older brother had Professor Templeman, and he told me the same thing. He wasn't drafted either; he volunteered, and was gassed so bad he almost died."

I am glad Terry spoke up. I don't remember how I know. Maybe it's something everybody says or maybe somebody told me—I don't know.

"Imagine Old Temp volunteering," Bill says, "a Latin and Greek and Sanskrit scholar volunteering—that proves he's a regular guy." The word Greek evokes for me the delight on Professor Templeman's face as he recites his oft-repeated favorite line from Homer, " . . . rosy fingered dawn," face tilted upward, looking at something, somewhere, and I feel irritated at Bill's implied derisiveness. At the same time the wake of the word "Sanskrit" washes over me, and I feel a twinge of excitement at the thought of learning Sanskrit some day.

Terry looks at his watch. "If we don't get going, we'll be *sporlos versenkt!*"

As we double-time it up the long flight of broad stone stairs leading to the top of the hill, Izzie, on my right, says, "Say, didn't you tell us your father is a lawyer?" I slow down so the rest can continue on ahead of us.

"What do you mean?"

"Well, my father says that the salesman from Sunshine Cookies who has been selling his store for years got talking to him about his son at City the other day, and my father, making conversation, says 'That's interesting, my son's there too. He's in that academic accelerated course.' 'Really,' says the salesman, 'my son is too. What year is yours?' When my father tells him I graduate in June, he says, 'Well, I'll be, after all these years I find out your son is in my son's class at City.' And his name is the same as yours. How is that?"

"He's my real father. My other father is a lawyer," is all I can say, my voice trailing off into the sinking pit of my stomach. I feel sick, dizzy, no good. Izzie is pleased with himself for having uncovered my deception.

From the time of my arrival at City, I had told my classmates my father was a lawyer, feeling socially more at ease with such a parent when the fathers of my classmates included a minister, a high school principal, a doctor, and even the vice-president of a company. But that was not the whole of it. I was profoundly ashamed that my mother continued to live next door to Mr. Warren in an apartment owned by him, in spite of the fact that he had reneged on his promise to marry her. Somehow, picturing him as my father, though on the deepest level I hated his guts, made things seem a little better, a little more acceptable to people on the other side of town who I hoped would never know the difference.

Nor was this all. "Warren cares more about you than your own father," my mother would say. "Your father doesn't care anything about you children."

On occasion she would even say I looked like Mr. Warren, usually when a lot of other people were around, maybe at Dubner's Bar. "Look at Junior's nose. Why if that isn't Warren's nose I'll eat my hat. Warren, turn your face this way. See, Junior even has his chin," she would continue as I squirmed in my seat, wanting to get up and run out the door. "If I didn't know better, I would swear he was Warren's own son."

But a boy has only one real father, and I know now I must have loved mine. Even allowing for a boy's sentimental feelings toward his family, which were particularly strong in me—every boy should have a mother and father and sister and Granny and live in the same cozy house forever—it was with genuine emotion that I made a wish on every falling star, well into my teens, that somehow my father and mother would get back together again.

Not that my feelings toward my father were unmixed. I suppose the most obvious thing that angered me was his way of saying "nope" to so many things I asked of him—no explanation, just "nope," and nothing in the world could budge him.

He sometimes said "nope" to Mom and Granny, but it usually had to do with something that could be blamed on his sore back, like not allowing any cookies or candies in the house because the doctor said they were bad. Or, later, his going on a diet of an apple a day until he became so weak he couldn't get out of bed, and my mother had to take over his job at Mueller Brothers for several months.

But when I wanted to hear him say "nope" to them and prove himself the head of the house, he didn't. Like the Christmas morning I was given the bow and arrow set I had wanted for so long.

"That looks like a strong bow, Sonny Boy," I heard my father say as I unwrapped the last of the holly paper. "I'd better show you how to shoot it. Let's go down to the cellar."

For weeks I had slipped into my mother's clothes closet at odd times and, parting the hanging dresses, admired the six arrows stapled to the cardboard backing next to a stout-looking bow. Once, in my excitement (I had despaired of ever being allowed to have real arrows) I drew blood when I pressed my finger against one of the sharp metal points.

But looking and touching isn't having, and now, after an eternity of waiting, I was thrilled to be in possession of my treasure. After all the trouble with Granny about real arrows, my father seemed to be on my side and genuinely joining in on my excitement.

We put a large cardboard box filled with newspapers atop a stool in front of the coal bin, and as my father aimed an arrow at it from about 20 feet away, I could see the bow was stiff, for he had trouble drawing the notched arrow all the way to his cheek.

And then Zing!——Crash!

The arrow had gone over the box, through the window, and out into the street beyond.

"Are you going to tell Mom and Granny?" I asked, worried what would happen then. I wanted him to laugh the whole thing off, or at least say everything was all right.

"I guess I have to Son," he said. I could see he was scared, and I think at that moment I felt sorry for him and resentful, which is no way for a boy to feel about his father.

"I knew he'd put somebody's eye out with that thing," was Granny's reaction to the news.

"He didn't put anybody's eye out," my father said, almost in a whisper. "And besides, I did it."

My mother was angry about the broken window, but all my father did was get quieter and quieter the rest of the day.

He always seemed to hold things in. Except

once when he grabbed the kitchen table and threw it over on its side without saying a word, and I knew it took more than the scrape I had with my sister to make him so mad.

I never remember him openly angry again. He just kept things bottled up more and more tightly in himself.

Like the times Mr. Warren drove up in front of the house and took my mother off in his car. I knew something was wrong and wanted desperately for my father to get up from his books and do something, but he didn't make a move. He just sat there with the muscle in his cheek twitching and never said a word. When Thoreau said that most men lead lives of quiet desperation, I think that even as a boy I knew what he meant.

My mother's answer to everything was that my father was selfish, that he thought only of himself. Although secretly I felt he had let us down, and blamed him for it in my heart, I could never picture him as selfish. He always seemed too sad and grim, and I thought selfish people must at least look self-satisfied.

She missed no opportunity to remind me that she had left my father "for you children, to give you kids a break in the world I never had." I never really believed this, and I found it hard to lift my eyes to her when she said it. Somewhere along the line I must have said to myself, with the conviction born of despair, "I'm never going to let this happen to me." That was when I began looking around for heroes.

"MacDonald."

Professor Templeman says my name quietly but firmly, with a slight tilt upward of his head, but his eyes are still fixed on the grade book open before him on his battered wooden lectern. It is as if he mentally throws the dice each time and anticipates, by his random pattern, catching any student who hitches his preparation to an easily discernible pattern. We all learned early that it's like matching pennies—you can be called on five times in a row.

I walk to the head of the class and stand next to him, I in my salt-and-pepper suit, custom tailored for the Spanish Lady's husband in Mexico City some years ago, he in his dark blue worsted double-breasted (he could have been president of anything by the way he dressed).

"Please give us your translation of Horace's twenty-fifth ode."

I sense the pity of the rest of the class who take my nervousness for lack of preparation, the type of sympathy boys show when but for the Grace of God. . . .

"Ode to the Aging Whore Lydia," I begin, with the same mixture of smiles and uneasy seriousness that accompany the lead-off joke of a novice after-dinner speaker.

"Now that you have passed judgment on the contents of the ode, please proceed," is Professor Templeman's unmixed reaction. His beaklike nose looks a little more hawkish than owlish today. I have a sinking feeling, not unlike the one coming up the steps with Izzie.

"I'll see you in my office later," he says at the end of the class.

Professor Templeman's office—private, since he is head of a department—is on the top floor at the extreme end of one of the two wings on either side of the main tower of City. As I walk to the chair in front of his desk, I notice once again the dramatic view of a good portion of North Baltimore. For just a second my right eyelid stops twitching. I am more ashamed than frightened. I feel that what's on his mind must be something more than a petty peeve of his own.

My eyes sweep the familiar desk: the bronze box which I know houses the silver coin from the Age of Pericles, with the head of Athena on one side and her personal symbol, the owl, on the other, its ragged edges enduring evidence of the inflationary snippings of politicians past (did Socrates ever hold this very coin in his hand?); the corroded piece of Roman hardware he uses for a paperweight (Lydia's hinge?); the worn, leatherbound volume of the Upanishads (I know there is Sanskrit in there).

"What in the hell got into you today, Mac?" he says, pounding out the stub of his cigarette held firmly in all five fingertips. "I don't mean your use of the word 'whore,' although Abe looked as though he were shot dead. I mean the whole idea of it. You were reaching for something, and the effect was about as dry and unpleasing as a pithy grapefruit. Was it somebody else's idea?"

"A group of us thought it might be funny," I answer, pressing my index finger to my eyelid that's twitching again.

"Wanted to be a regular guy, eh?" He turns his head and his shoulders heave as he puts his hand to his mouth to cup the sudden cough. "You'd be better off as a cheerleader leading the regular locomotive—more in context, at least. Did it ever occur to you that you are a regular guy?"

"No. I'm not, not really."

"Now there's an interesting word: 'really.' Do you think you are 'really' quite intelligent?"

"Not really."

"And yet everything you do makes you *appear* really very intelligent. Not *really* intelligent. Not *really* a regular guy. O me misera! Do I detect a note of self-pity? You are intelligent, all right, and someday, if you are lucky, your intelligence will become part of you. You will see it for what it is, no more, no less—and you won't have to be denying it in performances such as today's."

"Denying it . . . ?"

"O mea culpa. I set myself apart and wonder why I am lonely."

"I still don't understand."

"I don't believe I do either, not *really*. But enough of that. I didn't call you in here just to confuse you. Tell me"—that wracking cough again—"Oh, damn it! Tell me about that V-5 pin in your lapel. I've been meaning to ask you about it ever since I read in the school paper you were the first from Baltimore to join up. How did it all come about?"

"Well, right after school began there was an assembly called in the auditorium and a naval officer showed us this here moving picture. . . ."

"Showed us *a* moving picture."

"Showed us a moving picture about how you can join the Naval Air Corps now without having graduated from college. What a picture! It showed pilots in these helmets in the flight line in Pensacola, and diving and doing barrel rolls and learning about navigation in classes. I decided right then I wanted to be a pilot and filled the application blanks out after assembly."

"Without asking your parents?"

"My mother had to sign—I live with my

mother and sister—because I'm still sixteen, but she always lets me decide for myself."

"What about college?"

"I figured I'd be drafted sometime after next summer anyway, and my education would be all ruined. My best friend Rusty was drafted into the Army even though he was working at Glen Martin's. And Lon and Bunky from my old neighborhood have already been killed."

"I'd suggest that was a very patriotic act on your part if I hadn't done a very similar thing years ago. But why complicate things. At that moment you simply wanted to be a pilot. By the seat of their pants. Boys do things by the seat of their pants and who knows how they'll turn out."

His words drifted off into memory, and for a moment I could see that his eyes were looking inward and not really at me. He seemed to be listening, however, to my lengthy description of the events leading up to the swearing-in at Washington: like how I had eaten raw carrots in preparation because I had worn glasses since I was eight and was afraid without them my eyes would fail the examination (no problem, 20-20 eyesight, slight astigmatism, but still no explanation of the headaches, the tension around my eyes and nose, why the squinting and blinking were relieved by the glasses); how after every imaginable physical test in the morning (revealing the scar on my right ankle and one over my left eyebrow) the afternoon was filled with written tests; how the train back from Washington stopped at the station behind the playground at Penrose Avenue, and I ran across the tracks (past the tree with the robin's nest, through the waist-high grass thick with underbrush from which I had once made arrows, down the red clay bank and up the alley) to the old house where I told my father and his new wife, Miss Edna, the news. ("That's good to hear, son," were his quiet words, in contrast to my mother's reaction of excitement and disbelief as I finally reached Hollins Street, out of breath, and burst into the kitchen.)

"I was in the infantry, damn fool thing to do," Professor Templeman says, the usual crispness and sharp awareness returning to his features. "Did you buck for any special duty in the Air Corps?"

"Yes, yes!" (I am so pleased he asked.) "Funny thing, after I was sworn in they asked if I would take one more test to qualify for bombers, fighters, or transports. Boy, was I surprised because I had only thought of being a fighter pilot, zooming up, and then, pushing my stick to the side, peeling off and slipping down on the tail of some Jap Zero—that sort of thing—no slow bombers or transports. But I knew just what to do. When I answered the questions, I knew I ought to be fierce about it. Like the question, 'Were your parents quarrelsome?' I checked off the box marked 'very.' And 'What kind of sex life do you think you will have?' I marked off 'excellent' with a big strong X." (I am so delighted with his hearty laughter I almost tell him my difficulty trying to figure out how a fighter pilot should answer the question, "Did you ever have intercourse with an animal?" I supposed a farm boy would look pretty fierce doing that, but on second thought I decided he would just look depraved, so I marked "no" with a big X.)

"Don't tell me your plot worked?"

"Fighters it was!"

"Kuh! Kuh! Kuh!"—the capillaries in his face redden with the violence of his cough. "Damn it, Mac, I'm sorry," he says, pounding out the cigarette he had lighted moments before. "Worst things in the world for me. But back to you, what do you want to do after you've shot up all the Japs, after this crazy war is over. Have you ever thought of being a teacher?"

"No. Why?"

"I guess I think you'd make a good one. Not one of those fellows just living out a contract with life. I mean a real teacher. You have a zest, enthusiasm, you want to see life passed on. I think what we all become down the road means something to you."

"Really what I want to do is be a chemist and work on rockets. Mr. Goldberg, my adviser you know, showed me this here catalog. . . ."

"Showed me *a* catalog."

"Showed me a catalog of a school called M.I.T. with a picture of an artificial lightning machine on its cover and all sorts of courses inside that would help rockets, oh, like stress analysis, quantum theory, vector analysis. He says it's the best, but I took one look at the tuition, wow! Not for me."

"Rockets! Really? If I've reached that stage of my life where I'm projecting my own wishes on my students, I've certainly gotten my comeuppance today. Vector analysis, quantum theory." Professor Templeman reacts to the words physically as though they turn around and spit at him as he utters them.

"Rockets are the only way to get to the moon and Mars."

"Ah, so that's it. I wasn't so wrong after all."

"What do you mean?"

"Oh, nothing. Tell me, now that we both know you don't anticipate carving out a life as a scholar, has all of this Latin touched you? Has it had any meaning for you, beyond the grades? Honestly?"

"Oh yes, Professor Templeman. And it's funny, too, because I don't like French or English very much, and German just a little. But Horace says so many things, without really preaching or anything, that I want to use in my own life."

"For instance."

"Well, what he says in his *Nil Admirari* epistle to Numicius: "Marvel at nothing, admire nothing, covet nothing, never be impressed.""

"Interesting you should choose that one. Do you think you're inclined to hold on to things a little too tightly? You know he isn't advising a swing to a life of noncommitment either. A poet is trying to get at the truth by stringing words together—a sequential process by its very nature—and time does violence to truth. Every so often, though, the lines he strings form a triangle and lo, behold, the truth hangs suspended. But then what you yourself bring to it makes all the difference."

"I know it. I know what you mean, and I feel someday it will mean even more to me."

"I think some day it will. 'Hold close with open arms,' the poet says. The only close embrace is the embrace of death. I have certainly found that when I settle on anything too intensely, I am on the way to killing it. Movement stops, death takes over. And speaking of movement, get the hell out of here before we run this into the ground."

A few weeks later, the Navy announced a new program, the V-12: high school graduates would be sent to certain colleges at Navy expense and, upon completing the prescribed courses (not necessarily leading to a degree), would be commissioned as ensigns. Free college! Bill and several others passed the stiff exams and were accepted. My heart sank.

"That's what I get for going off half-cocked," I said to myself, trying to shrug off my disappointment.

One afternoon in the spring of 1943, I arrived home from school and found my mother as usual in the kitchen. She was washing some fresh string beans, and, as soon as I appeared, she hurriedly dried her hands on her apron and gave me a letter she had stuffed in her pocketbook (so I wouldn't read it without her if she was still in the market).

"Go ahead, read it," she said with girlish glee, already aware of its contents.

I had one knee on the chrome-and-red-leather chair opposite the refrigerator—my usual stance when talking to her in the kitchen—and as I opened the envelope (blue seal of the Navy Department, official business, Cadet A. MacDonald), I was aware of her eyes on me.

"God, Oh God, God!" I shouted in my excitement, quite overwhelmed by the message. All V-5 cadets were being reassigned to the V-5-a Program and would complete two semesters of college at Navy expense before being assigned to preflight training. Particular consideration would be given to the cadet's own choice of college from the enclosed list. I was going to college after all!

We were looking at the list when Mr. Warren came in, still wearing his rumpled overcoat, and puffing from the climb up the stairs.

"M.I.T.'s not on it," I said ruefully.

"Why don't you try for the best? Try for Harvard, you can't go wrong with Harvard," he said.

It was just a name to me, which I vaguely associated with football and rowing, but he spoke with such authority I requested Harvard and received another letter ordering me to report in Cambridge on November 1.

Thus time and chance have their way with us all, and for one Baltimore kid for whom the possibility of attending so prestigious a university was beyond even his dreams, Harvard suddenly became a reality.

My reception by the Navy, when I arrived at Harvard that first morning in November, was something less than enthusiastic. As I entered Eliot House where I had been instructed to report, I was brought up short by a menacing bark.

"Where the hell have you been, seaman? You were to be here by 9:00 A.M.!"

"The Navy gave me my ticket and reservation on the train, and I came directly here," I said. "I assumed. . . ."

"Seaman, you can't assume a goddamn thing! And address me as 'Sir.' I'm putting you down for five demerits. Now fill out these papers."

Had I not been too dismayed to listen carefully, I might have learned a great deal about the military right then and there. The military are right even when they're wrong, and standing before me to prove it was their representative, ham-faced, bleary-eyed Chief Bosun's Mate Hazen.

About a week after my arrival I had a letter from Professor Templeman. Among other things he mentioned quite casually that he was ill, and the doctor had ordered him to go to California or Arizona as soon as possible. I promised myself I would visit him on my first leave, and on Christmas Eve I went with Sally to his apartment on the second floor of an old red brick house on Cathedral Street.

We had brought one of my mother's fruitcakes, wrapped with cheesecloth and soaked with rum, and when we rang the bell we were shown to his bedroom by a nurse. He was sitting in bed, propped up by pillows, in a navy blue robe with red piping. He looked so frail, so very frail, I was shocked. The darkness under his eyes accentuated their roundness and made him look more owllike than ever. His face was still red with the cough we had heard coming up the stairs.

"Come in, come in the two of you," he said, leaning on one arm, and extending the other over the edge of the bed toward us. "You can put your coats over there. You'll be the most comfortable in those chairs. Sally, I'm so pleased he brought you. I've been hearing a good deal about you, you know. So kind of you to give up some of your leave, and on

Christmas Eve, too. What, a present for me! No, that's too much. May I open it now?"

I glanced around the room. On his dresser were two photographs, one a fading, oval cutout of a man and woman in old-fashioned clothes, the woman seated, the man standing by her with his hand on her shoulder; the other, a picture of a girl standing next to a boy with his legs wound with puttees and wearing a Boy Scoutish hat. (For a moment the picture became the Victrola on Penrose Avenue grinding out the nasal "Over there, over there . . . and we won't be back till it's over over there.") Books everywhere. A stack on his night table. Familiar leather of the Upanishads.

This is a teacher's house, I thought, and I've never been in a teacher's house before. Serious business, this being where a man lives whom you admire and who has a degree of power and influence over you. Particularly when you have never seen him outside a classroom or his office, never run into him in the ten-cent stores, or seen him driving a car, or even met him on the street. I felt very much the schoolboy again.

"Ah, a homemade fruitcake," Professor Templeman said, stripping away the last of the holly gift wrapping and folding back the cheesecloth. "And with a civilized dowsing of rum," he added, "rosy fingered dawn" spreading across his face as he sniffed the fragrance, then held the cake on high like an ancient offering. "Let's have some with a glass of port. You're both old enough. Say, a party, what do you know. Something for me, a party for me!"

I was especially pleased that he liked the fruitcake. I had hoped my mother would come with us, but she had declined, as she had on a number of occasions in the past when I suggested it would be good for her to meet a fine man like Professor Templeman. "Who, me, go out with a Latin professor?" she would say, even though it had become obvious to both of us—and everybody else—that Mr. Warren was no longer the marrying kind.

"Seems to me last time we had a long talk you were impressed with *nil admirari.* I don't see much of it in your face when you look at Sally."

Sally glanced at me suspiciously. "Don't worry, Sally, that's a compliment," he said.

"How's Harvard, how's the old joint?"

"Well it's hard, because our courses are the same ones the civilians have, even though they have a Navy number on them to make it seem like we aren't really going to Harvard. And then all the rest of it, like running along the Charles River in our sweat suits before it's even light out, and jumping off the high diving board and pretending we're swimming under burning oil, and chicken sh—I mean stupid inspections where Chief Hazen runs his white glove over the tops of doors. But I have some time left for poking around. The first Saturday I went looking for the cyclotron—that's an atom smasher."

Professor Templeman smiled. "I at least know the language of science."

"I saw a cyclotron listed in the civilian catalog, but when I found the building, it was locked. I could see through a window, though, that the room was empty, except for wires and trash all over the floor. I asked everybody I saw what happened to the atom smasher, and nobody knew or seemed to care. Finally, one professor got very annoyed and said, 'If I were you young man, I'd forget about it, forget it right now, understand, forget it.' The way he said it, I knew I'd better. They give you demerits for everything around that place. What do you think, do you think it broke, and they sent it out to get fixed?"

"God knows what the scientists are up to. They're one of the few things the ancient world didn't have to contend with. What about those rockets you were talking about? Anything going on at Harvard?"

"No, but just before I came home, I visited Professor Marks, because the handbook he published has nozzle equations in it, and I asked him about rockets. He said a rocket society has just been started down the river at M.I.T. I'm going to try to join when I get back."

"You know, Mac, I'm not at all curious about

the machinery of things, but I am intrigued by the question why a boy, whose seriousness I honor, would set his cap for the moon and Mars."

"Not just me, lots of people."

"I've noticed that, now that I'm alive to the subject. You would be surprised at how much I've thought about it. One day last spring I was sitting in the park in front of the Peabody, trying to remain absolutely motionless, watching a skittish pair of cardinals out of the side of my eye. And, behold, a milkweed seed, dangling from its white puffy sunburst, floated past my eyes, so close and unexpected that I jerked my head and away flew the birds. No milkweed pods for miles around and there it was, trying to insinuate its life into that little plot of park. I thought then of all the countless mechanisms nature has provided her seeds to ensure their distribution: the hooks, the burrs, fuzz, wings, flotation bags, even the tasty flesh the appleseed surrounds itself with in quest of a minor ride around the barnyard in a pig's stomach. And I asked myself, is nature, working through the intellect of man, chipping away now at the singular problem of spreading her seed throughout the universe. Never thought of yourself as a pea in a pod jetting through space, have you?"

"No, not really." The image of a peapod clashed with my feelings of the power and importance of rockets. "Something to think about, though."

"Kuh! Kuh! Kuh! Damn this cough to hell. Excuse me Sally. And excuse me for neglecting you. What do you think of these dreams of Mac's?"

As they chatted, I thought of many things I wanted to ask Professor Templeman, but shortly he was saying, "I've been utterly selfish keeping you this long. I had no idea of the time. Thank you for coming, thank you."

I never saw him again, nor did I hear from him. He must have become very ill. Now and again I thought of making the extra effort of tracing him, but I never did. One day in Oak Ridge some years later I received a clipping from my Grandmother: "Templeman—On April 13, 1948, James P. son of the late Dr. James Albin and Ella Bryan Templeman. Funeral from Mitchell Home, 1900 Eaton Place. Due notice will be given."

4

Harvard

"You wore a tulip, a big yellow tulip. . . ."

The crowd around the piano moments before had melted away. Most of the fellows had left, but a few still lingered to chat with girls who had struck their fancy. The two of us were alone, she playing, both of us singing, her long dark hair dancing on her slight shoulders as her fingers enthusiastically struck the keys. Suddenly we both seemed to sense a new awareness of each other.

"My name is Marsha," she said, turning around on the bench and looking at me with even prettier eyes than I had imagined from my sidewise glances during the final minutes of our singing.

"Mine's Mac. Golly, I didn't expect to meet a girl at Radcliffe who knows the old-fashioned songs. Something besides 'Row Row Row Your Boat' and

'Frère Jacques.' I know we're supposed to go now so would you consider it presumptuous"—incredible, but I think those are the words I actually used—"would you consider it presumptuous if I asked you to the movies next Saturday night, I mean after knowing you so short a time."

"I'd love it."

"I'll look for you on the campus before then, but anyhow I'll be here at eight next Saturday," I said as she showed me to the door.

I walked to my "quarters" at Eliot House with my head in the clouds, aware for the first time in that long (though in some ways intensely short) first week at Harvard, that the Navy and college could mean more than hard work and missing Sally.

Earlier that week there had been a notice on the bulletin board in the main entryway to Eliot House: "The girls of Bertram Hall, Radcliffe, invite You to a JOLLY-UP Sunday, November 6, 4–7 P.M. Punch Served."

"Not me. I've heard about those Radcliffe girls," one of the fellows said. "They're all too smart. Jolly-up my eye." "Aw come on," said another. "What else is there to do on Sunday. We can't have Boston leave yet."

Since I was not enrolled as a civilian, it did not strike me as comical that every pretense that Eliot House was a red brick and gold-domed ship moored along the Charles River was rigorously enforced. I entered the "main gangway," checked the "scuttlebutt" on the bulletin board, spoke to the seaman (in hat and canvas leggings) who was on the "2000 to 2400 watch" in the "guardhouse" on the right, signed the "log," glanced in the direction of the captain's "cabin," opened the "hatch" to K entry, climbed the "ladder" to the fourth "deck," opened the "hatch" to my "quarters," K-42, which was divided by "bulkheads" into a "head" (with a tile shower—what a joy instead of the bathtub I had always known), two "staterooms," each with upper and lower Navy-issue "bunks," and a large common room. The latter name was one of the few holdovers from civilian days, perhaps because it had a cozy fireplace (which we were forbidden to use).

Nature seemed to cooperate with this charade. Shortly after we arrived, she sent a hurricane through New England, and we watched the fury of the storm from the "portholes" of our rooms, which overlooked Memorial Drive and the Charles River. The sapling sycamores lining the Drive were literally bent parallel to the ground.

Much of the week had been devoted to stenciling and learning the proper stowage of our "gear" (every piece of our Apprentice-Seaman-Third-Class uniform had a definite place in our "lockers"), developing the skills necessary to clean and dust our quarters meticulously, including the bedsprings and window frames. The "skipper" never went so far as to complain about dirty fireplace flues; the first time he opened the dampers, he sent more than one contraband load of liquor or radios crashing down into the fireplaces.

We learned to rub the gold lettering on our dress hats with dirt and salt and sleep with them under our mattresses to make them look old and "salty." We learned, too, that crossing to the other side of the street (a discreet interval ahead of time, of course) to avoid a humbling salute to an officer was a valid strategy on Massachusetts Avenue but might bring demerits on narrow Dunster Street, and we were warned that water fights with the Indian-brand fire extinguishers on each "deck" could result in a court-martial for endangering the "ship" and the lives of her "crew." Soon enough we began to chafe under all of the regulations, and such is the human capacity for ingratitude that even free college came to be criticized after the first twenty-four hours.

When I entered my "stateroom," my delight at having met Marsha at the jolly-up must have shown on my face. Hank, my roommate, turned around from his large desk facing the window, looked up from under his green eyeshade and said in his slow Iowa (Eagle Grove) twang, "Been whoring around already, eh?"

Hank had lots of seniority, which meant the small desk and upper bunk for me. He was older by a year or so, but more important, he was of the elite within our ranks, one of the few who had been a civilian at Harvard and had applied for V-12. Moreover, he was there on a scholarship—one of the handful of regional scholarships Harvard issued, under which all expenses were paid. He was also an athlete, as I discovered several days after we first met, and he asked "Do you have any sports?" "Yes," I replied with great enthusiasm, "wrestling, I was on the team at City" (I didn't add third string, only one match—which I lost). "What about you?" "I wrestle a little, too," he said. "Will you show me some of your holds sometime?"

I never quite forgave him the performance that followed in the athletic house. Had I not been carried away with my chance to show him a thing or two, I would have considered that, wholly apart from skill, he was in the 160-pound class and I in the 135-pound. I would have noticed more closely, too, his short stubby neck, broad shoulders, and stomach muscles which when flexed, although he was not in the least fat, made him look pregnant. We approached one another in the standing position. Twice within seconds, I found myself pinned on the mat after several lightning-fast moves on his part. When the surprise of his technique wore off, I was able to offer a little resistance. This was a mistake on my part; he literally wiped the mat with me, producing burns on my shoulders the size of half dollars. I found out later he had been Iowa State Champion. Since he was a gentle, quiet fellow all the time I knew him, I will give him the benefit of the doubt and suppose that he saw an opportunity to apply a dash of cold water to one who was given to shooting off his mouth.

When I went into the bathroom before "lights out," I found Sid (who shared the second bedroom with Pete) with one foot up on the washbasin, carefully drying between each of his toes. "You've got to take awfully good care of your feet, MacDonald," he mumbled. Sid was always worrying about athlete's foot, a concern he must have been taught in Boot Camp, for he was one of the small group of men who had come to the V-12 program from the fleet.

Groups within groups—Walt the civilian student, Sid proud of his fleet background, plain old Pete who came to V-12 from high school, and my group, the "fly boys," outnumbered by the V-12s five to one.

I opened the door to the mailbox marked K-42, and even as I reached for the single letter, I was aware of the delightful, fairy-tale fragrance. For me! I studied the white-splotched paper of the envelope and ran my fingers over the raised red seal of Radcliffe on the flap. Unfolding the letter, I noted the broad-point, very legible handwriting, the kind society matrons seem always to achieve.

. . . and my mother said it was very thoughtless of me, since I've been with you so much these past several weeks, not to invite you home for Thanksgiving. Will you have enough leave? We would all love to have you. Marsha

P.S. Your round trip train fare to Bridgeport will be $8.50.

We were met at the Bridgeport station the evening before Thanksgiving by her father who said we would have to hurry because Uncle Bert had decided to give a party for us that evening.

"Hello Ma'am," I said to her mother as she greeted me in the hallway.

"We're so pleased to have Marsha's friend from Harvard with us. This is young Bob. Bob, show him to his room, will you?"

I gathered during the drive to Uncle Bert's that his house was near the amusement park and that he owned it. We were met at the door by Uncle Bert himself, and it was clear from the white cast that extended up under his ears he had done something serious to his neck. "Good to meet Marsha's friend from. . . ." I stared at the black rubbery bow tie pinned to the cast where his Adam's apple would have been and was startled to have it wink at me, with a green light on one side and a red one on the other. Uncle Bert was a real cutup.

"So pleased to meet Marsha's friend. . . ." The whole family was there.

Before and during dinner, whenever Uncle Bert caught my eye, he would smile and wink his lights at me. Then, after dinner he put his arm around my shoulder and asked me to come into his club cellar with the men. Dominating the place was a stand-up bar, every bit as professional looking as the one in the corner saloon, complete with bartender.

"What would you like to drink?" I had never been asked this question before by an adult when it was clear he didn't mean a coke.

"Blackberry wine is my favorite." I was pleased with myself that I could name a favorite with so little hesitation.

"Blackberry wine!" exclaimed the bartender.

"You know, Jim, that special blackberry in the squat bottle over there we've been saving," said Uncle Bert, flashing his lights.

"How do you like that?" he asked as I sipped the wine.

"The best ever."

What a good brand, I thought; it tastes so different. After I had several drinks—I felt safe because I knew blackberry wine had a low percentage of alcohol—Marsha's mother called to me from the head of the stairs, asking if I would join Marsha who was about to play the piano.

The room was large and well furnished, and I threaded my way carefully among the ladies of the family who were smiling approvingly at Marsha, seated before the baby grand, waiting for me to join her on the bench. In almost military fashion I turned on my heel as I reached the bench and, taking care not to sit too close to Marsha, lowered myself with dignity—onto the floor! I had missed the end of the bench!

A gasp from the ladies. A horrified look from Marsha. In a flash I was on my feet and sitting on the bench as if nothing had happened. I had never heard her play serious music—Chopin! Beautiful! I felt positively euphoric—and somewhat dizzy. After she finished and people started filing out of the room, her mother approached me. "Do you feel all right?" she asked kindly. "What was Uncle Bert giving you downstairs?"

"Blackberry wine."

"Why, he doesn't have any blackberry wine. Bert! Bert!"

"You poor boy," she said, as she returned from the cellar. "He thought it would be amusing to serve you blackberry brandy."

During the train ride back to Boston, Marsha talked about her ambitions to be a biochemist and do graduate work, perhaps get her Ph.D., and I talked about me. After a while she became drowsy and put her head on my shoulder and fell asleep.

I took her to the Regimental Ball in December but saw very little of her thereafter. We didn't seem to click. Perhaps in those first critical weeks away from home we were just reassuring one another that somebody cared.

"We were sailing along on moonlight bay. You could hear the darkies singing. . . ."

The words repeated themselves in my head endlessly (a sort of cerebral mood music) as I sat at Hank's desk looking out over the Charles, only slightly aware of the racing sculls gliding down the river—"stroke . . . stroke"—and the couples stretched out on the grass, enjoying the May sun and the warm breeze just strong enough to ripple the water, this same breeze blowing through the open window and slightly ruffling the piece of paper before me. I had put off the assignment as long as possible, but now that I had chosen "Moonlight on the Magothy" as my theme and was coming in closer and closer contact with the mood of the evening last summer, I was almost enjoying writing my paper for English 2: "An Unforgettable Experience."

It was Sunday, though, and I resented the procrastination that had gotten me in this fix, sitting here alone, I of all people, while everybody else was out enjoying himself, even Walt who never went any place because he wanted to be faithful to his girl,

Fran. I warmed to the thought of my reputation for working hard all week, from chow time to lights out at 2200. All week? Well, most of the week, except sometimes right after chow, when Frank, Dick, and Jack Lemmon (the actor, whose name we pronounced Le Mon) gathered at the piano in the adjacent common room and sang their endless ditties. "I met a girl in Atlantic last year, whose hobby was swimming around the long pier. . . ."

I would like to have been more a part of this bunch—they were the "in" group, all three of them from New York, dating the sophisticated girls and accepted by Harvard's more traditional side. Quick, in-the-know, right there with it. Sophisticated, but not socially snobbish, like Stanley and Hobart, who were roommates in K-41 and were overheard on occasion commiserating about being forced to live among "such people." Stanley's father was a General in the Marine Corps, and Hobart returned from weekends in New York looking white as a sheet, emaciated, and hardly able to stand during Monday morning muster (those parties at the Stork Club, you know). In spite of his social prissiness, he always received demerits for the dandruff that blanketed the collar of his blue jumper.

I seemed to fall in more naturally with former members of the fleet, particularly a short, dark-haired, heavy-eyebrowed boy with a perpetually frightened look from Columbus, Ohio, named Phillip Harris.

My acceptance by the fleet men started with a note placed under a glass of milk served to me by Corrine, the buxom waitress who looked like a bureau with the top drawer open, as I moved my tray to the end of the chow line in the dining hall at Eliot House. She stood between the French twins (Canadian French, that is), stunning girls with rich black hair, from Bangor, Maine, and the Filipino, who attacked the deep can of ice cream with such nervous vigor that, summer or winter, beads of sweat dripped from his forehead into the container as he reached in for the next scoop.

I unfolded the note in my lap. "The twins are giving a party at their apartment at 9:00 on Saturday and said I can invite you. Will you meet me there?"

My throat was suddenly dry, the dryness of sly excitement a youth feels when he realizes he is in the presence of a sexually aggressive female. She was waiting for my answer as I looked up from the crowded table where I was seated and furtively nodded my head as our eyes met across the hall.

"Corrine asked you to the twins' party, didn't she? Hurray for you," said Topper from across the table, rolling his eyes.

"She's got the hots for you," Bo said, with a touch of envy in his voice.

"How do you know?" I was surprised and embarrassed.

"We're going too," Topper said.

Almost from the first day, they both had pressed admiring comments on the twins when no one at the officers' table was looking. In fact it was rumored they were dating the girls, although this was forbidden. The two of them, both from the fleet, sported service ribbons which must have been the envy of our "Skipper," a former high school principal. Topper, with his wavy black hair and tailor-made blues, was the perfect ladies' man, able to strike up a conversation with a girl any place, any time, without a shred of self-consciousness. Bo, the pharmacist's son from Tulsa, Oklahoma, with his country face, homespun ways, and folksy songs: "Who's that girl with the red dress on, some folks call Ida, stole my heart away from me, down in Louisiana. . . . Little bee suck the flower, big bee get the honey, black man pick the cotton, white man get the money."

To my dismay (or was it delight?) word spread around the table, and old smiling Frank, feigning the use of a stand-up telephone receiver, shouted "Long Distance, Long Distance" into his cupped right hand in mock manipulation of Corrine's breasts.

"I'm a tit man myself," said Topper.

"I'm a leg man," replied Bo.

"Gol-ly," was all Hank could say when I returned to the room. "Gol-ly, MacDonald."

When the three of us arrived (I with my V-5 pin in the space reserved for service ribbons), the apartment, off Massachusetts Avenue between Harvard and Central Square, was already half full. The twins had stacked the deck in their favor with civilians and Navy from Harvard, some townies, and a few extra girls. Corrine already had quite a bit to drink and kept hanging around me from the moment I arrived. I wished she would disappear; I had suddenly decided her eyes and nose were too small for her face.

"So drink chug-a-lug, chug-a-lug. . . ." Bo and Topper were next to the kitchen sink with a bottle of Four Roses. "Here, show how the fly boys do it," said Topper, handing me a tumbler half full.

"So drink. . . ."

"Ugh! How can Mr. Warren like this stuff," I thought. "I'm going to throw up if I finish it."

"Come on, we've all had one," said Topper.

I closed my eyes and finished it off.

As the lens of my inner microscope began to blur, I felt an exhilarating release from myself. My every move seemed to have a certain flair, a distinct cut. I wanted to do a little jig—no, more of a subtle shuffle, like Maurice Chevalier: "On ze boo, on ze boo, on ze booly, boolyvard." Everybody seemed so compatible—except Corrine; her face still looked piggish. In my expansive mood, I brushed her aside and directed my charms to a slim, dark-haired girl in a red dress, who had caught my eye.

"Tecum vivere amem, tecum obeam libens," I found myself saying (I always thought Latin had a lot of clout with the ladies).

"Ooo! You speak Latin," she purred.

"With you I would like to live, with you I would gladly die," I purred back, rather pleased with my ability to get right to the point with a girl, just like Topper.

But suddenly, a warm, shaking storm swept over me with no warning, and now my lens to the outside world was blurring. "Excuse me," I muttered, and like a wounded animal managed to escape from the smoky, packed room. A door, a bedroom, two daybeds; I threw myself onto one, holding on tightly as its lurching, spinning frame tried to dislodge me.

"Ma-ac, Ma-ac." Several hours must have passed. I looked across the room in the direction of the voice and made out the dim outline of Corrine on the other bed, plaintively calling out my name, over and over. She was too loaded to be aggressive, and by this time my initial dizziness and nausea had turned to stomach cramps which kept me bent over like a Mandarin during the walk back to Harvard.

"Pretty slick," said Topper, "slipping off to the bedroom like that."

". . . as we sang love's old sweet song on moonlight bay."

I finished the theme as the couples began drifting away, hand in hand, in the purposeless gait of contentment, the newspapers they had been sitting on left behind on the grass, curved to the bodies that had pressed down on them, looking now like white caps on a sea of green, in angry contrast to the calm water of the Charles.

"What ho!" I thought, as I read my essay aloud—in moments of enthusiasm I often speak to myself in someone else's idiom—"This isn't bad, no, not half bad at all." Now the music of "Pomp and Circumstance," ". . . dear land of ho-ope and glorey," filled my head as I recognized the nobility of my creation. Yes sir, I had captured the feeling of that evening sail with Sally, last summer, just the two of us, in her uncle's little sailboat. ". . . and my ears filled with the delightful cacophony of the water lapping at the hull and the chirping crickets, I gazed up at the moonlit sky and realized for the first time that the stars were mere pinpricks in the night, eyelid of the world." I had finally painted the smell of a rose. "Gosh, it's good to be able to express your deepest thoughts."

"Mawkish sentimentality . . . clichés. . . ." I stared in red-faced disbelief as the instructor continued his criticism of my theme before the class in

Sever Hall several days later. Such was my humiliation that my mind will still not allow him the dignity of a name or a face.

". . . pompousness. . . ."

I sat in terror as I heard him attribute the theme to me and then begin to read it, his voice full of sarcasm, his rhythm and modulation emphasizing my sentimentality. Terror of the kind one spends so much of one's life avoiding—the sudden unmasking. My lips were puckering as I stared at the heavily carved plank in front of me that served as a desk and settled upon a small hole bored through its hefty two inches by generations of enterprising wielders of pencils and pocketknives. Would I be called upon to say something and have my eye or face twitch, or at the very minimum would I give myself away as I spoke by a slight unnatural rigidity of my lips (as I do even now).

But you keep still, you aren't called upon, the storm passes. Already you are beginning to see yourself as simply more sensitive than others to life and nature and a starry night with Sally. And the instructor—he couldn't really have been a Harvard professor—is pleased with himself, too. What better thing could he do for the boy at this point in his life than kick all of that kind of crap right out of him?

Certainly education cannot be held accountable for the ineptitude, perhaps cruelty, of one of its servants. Yet even had the system ground on normally, I could only have received a poor grade and at most a conference after class—". . . too sentimental, try to get closer to the truth, do away with the clichés. . . ." And have gone on my way, untouched.

Education had unearthed something directly relevant to my life and was unable to handle it. A little matter, you may say. Mountain out of a molehill. Happens every day. But there was a message here for me far more important than all of the facts and figures that were being pumped into me.

The message was that sentimentality is a false emotion, a state of feeling all juiced up precisely because you dare not feel truthfully, dare not be aware.

Why had I not written about that evening on the Magothy the way it was? Why had I lied? That was the question unobserved and unanswered.

The sailboat was a small one, fourteen feet or so, built with loving care, no doubt, but with one significant flaw: a devilish leak at the forward end of the centerboard trunk where it meets the bottom, just under the deck, which no amount of caulking cotton and seam compound seemed to stop.

Sally's uncle had picked me up at my house after work for the drive to the shore—a beautiful late afternoon, with no anvil-topped thunderheads threatening in the distance, in spite of the heat. I was eagerly anticipating the evening sail, for the smells and sights of my job that summer before going to Harvard were beginning to get me down—a job at the local draftboard as a laboratory technician specializing in urinalysis.

Sally's uncle must have been surprised when he saw me come down the steps toward the car dressed in my riding boots (borrowed from a friend the summer before and never returned), breeches, yellow sport shirt, and tan ascot figured with scenes of men riding to the hounds. I was dimly aware that one wore a certain costume for sailing, but lacking a clear picture of what it was, I did the next best thing and wore the only sports outfit I had.

And so it was that Sally and I set sail that evening, I with one eye on the bailing can and, except for a fleeting awareness now and then of the accordion being played on the other bank, the freshness of Sally's cotton dress, and the phosphorescent trails of the fish darting away from our bow, numb to everything except a growing concern with the problem I would face should the leak get ahead of us or should we capsize in a sudden gust. How would I ever get my boots off? It was only with considerable soaping of my feet that I was able to get them on in the first place.

I was hardly the relaxed poet of my theme.

"Know thyself," I am told. And to help, education lavishes upon me the humanities. I learn all of the possibilities of the human condition from wicked stepmothers to Scrooge, Babbitt, Hamlet, Orestes, Oedipus, and the great white whale. I learn a lot about man, but very little about myself. Hamlet has his grand problem, but what of those shoddy little quirks and defenses it's not very reassuring to see in oneself.

I ask of education now as unknowingly I did then: show me to myself. Help me to see myself, to experience myself. Give me a framework on which to build myself. Above all, I want to know a little more how it is to be you and have you know a little more how it is to be me, for our shames may then become a little less governing.

"What the hell do you suppose that means?" asks Bo, as a group of us returning from class read the notice which has just been tacked on the Eliot House bulletin board. Word spreads fast. Others come running. "Due to a lowered requirement for pilots, all V-5-a personnel will remain at their present stations for another semester."

"It means the Japs haven't shot up as many of our men as the gold braid expected," says Topper, with his usual salty insight. "It looks like soon it'll be all over. Before Christmas we'll be fighting the Germans in France and. . . ."

"In a pig's eye! Who says so?" interrupts Bo.

"My brother overseas says we're committed to invade France before Christmas, probably sometime this summer."

"I'll kiss your ass if we do," replies Bo.

It was June 1, 1944.

As I climbed the stairs to my room, I had mixed feelings. On the one hand I had hitchhiked to the Quonset Rhode Island Naval Air Station at every opportunity during the spring and had sat in the cockpits whenever given the chance, fingering the pistol grip on the joy stick, imagining the whine of the inertial starters. But more and more I felt I was finishing a story in which I was no longer interested.

I had joined the M.I.T. Rocket Research Society and looked forward to each monthly meeting (a fifteen-minute streetcar ride down Massachusetts Avenue from Harvard Square) with the eagerness once reserved for play. My roommate, Hank, was the only one in whom I confided the reason for my disappearances. I had been ribbed about rockets enough in Baltimore. "Gol-ly, MacDonald," he would say, dawdling around my desk in those rare moments he had nothing to do, "why do you want to go to the moon?" Somehow, to Hank, I never seemed to add up, and he was forever trying to pry my secret from me in subtle ways. I was into too many things to suit him.

He once admitted he had written to his father, a high school teacher in Eagle Grove, about me, and read me the pertinent part of the letter in reply, a warm and perceptive paragraph, cautioning Hank against poking fun at another's budding ambition, at new ideas. "My father thinks you're to be admired," he said. After this I talked to Hank more freely about our meetings.

About how liquid oxygen in an open-mouthed vacuum bottle looks clear like water, but thick and syrupy, although it isn't, because you see the slight steel-blue tint and know it is incredibly cold. Jim Lask, the president of our Society, immersed a fresh bacon, lettuce, and tomato sandwich in the liquid oxygen with tongs and then, holding it in his gloved hand, hurled it over our heads to the wall beyond where it shattered and fell to the floor in pieces, like the most delicate Christmas tree ornament. A short length of rubber hose, its heat absorbed in the frenzy of bubbles as it was immersed, likewise shattered as it was rapped soundly on the large conference table around which we sat in amazed silence. Some of the liquid was poured on the table top and was transformed into white haze before our eyes. And then, in a moment of what appeared to us to be sheer folly, Jim pulled up his sleeve and plunged his hand into the flask up to his wrist, withdrawing it immediately as we gasped.

"For that split second," he explained, "the heat of my hand vaporizes a thin layer of oxygen and impedes the flow of heat out of my hand, like a dead air space—but just for that moment."

Part of our meetings were devoted to our test program, particularly plans for the summer test firing of a ten-pound-thrust rocket motor which Jim was machining out of steel and aluminum after hours in the Radiation Laboratory where he worked (on radar, I found out after the war). He brought the motor, about the size of a hot dog roll, to each meeting and showed us his progress. At one of these meetings he sat staring at the motor on the table before him, his tongue extended and clenched between his teeth, the way he always did when his attention was caught. We all tensed to the problem: how to remove the end of the tiny steel drill bit that snapped off in one of the ingenious rings of injection ports which sprayed liquid oxygen against an opposing stream of kerosene in the rocket's innards.

The half-dozen "M.I.T. Papers on Rocketry," a project started the previous year, were now being completed, and their proud authors presented them at our meetings. In one of them was this passage on space navigation:

This qualitative discussion would not be complete

without some statement as to the probability of such a sequence of events as outlined above actually occurring. If the problem of reaching the moon were left to individuals and groups motivated by the desire for the immense fund of scientific information available to man when he has explored the solar system, there is some question as to when sufficient money for such a venture could be raised, and sufficient personnel and equipment assembled. That it would finally be done is not greatly in doubt, although an estimate of fifty years time for reaching the moon would probably not be conservative. However, there is every indication that the fears of the men leading the independent warring nations of our present society will naturally shorten this time.

By the time I return to my quarters, I can no longer contain my enthusiasm. "Wowee, I'm going to see a rocket firing this summer!"

"Gol-ly, MacDonald, now what's eating you?" says Hank.

The men of Company D are standing around in small groups in the Eliot House court awaiting morning muster. Laughter and shouts of glee are mixed with back slapping comradery, in contrast to the usual preening before inspection. It is June 6, 1944, and news of the invasion of France has just spread through our ranks.

It's D-Day! Hurray!

"Wait-a-minute, wait-a-minute," says Topper as he winds his way among the men, looking for Bo.

"Ah, here you are, here's my ass-kissing friend." He drapes a long friendly arm around the neck of Bo, whose eyes suddenly show recognition of his plight.

"Company D is hereby invited to an ass-kissing ceremony tonight in honor of D-Day," Topper shouts into his hands, cupped in megaphone style. "And bring your friends at 2100." Everybody is laughing, even Bo, even ham-faced Chief Hazen.

Shortly before the ceremony is due to begin, Frank rushes into my room.

"Hey, they say you have a fancy Christmas shaving set."

"What's it all about?"

"Stop screwing around MacDonald, if you got it, give it to me. We're preparing his royal highness for the ceremony and want to do it up real brown. Get it."

I do. "But it's my good Old English Lavender set!"

"Give it to me."

"Okay, but use your own brush."

Topper is standing in the center of his room, naked, a silly grin on his face, his rear end spotlighted by one of the Navy-issue floor lamps, its shade cocked at an angle. The room is packed and the overflow of men fills the suite and extends out into the hall. Bo is given his choice of cheeks and glumly chooses the right one as the object of his affection. Frank, using more of my soap than I would like, lathers it up amid giggles from Topper, then produces a razor.

"No sir, absolutely not," declares Topper. "You'll give me a beard, and I'll have to shave my ass the rest of my life."

With great flourish Frank wipes off the lather and pats on the cooling lotion. "Hey, that stings." And then sprinkles on talc from the chrome-plated can.

Flipping down a shot glass of whiskey somebody has produced, Bo takes the cheek between the thumb and index finger of each hand and plants a kiss right in the middle to the accompaniment of Bronx cheers, whistles, and shouts of "Long live D-Day, long live Topper and his ass-kissing friend."

The end of the war didn't seem very far off that night.

3

M.I.T.

As the pulsating scream grew even more intense, I flattened myself against the dirt baked dry by the August sun and inched even closer to the two-foot-high barricade of old railroad ties behind which the ten of us were hiding for protection.

"I'm going to crack the lox valve a little further," Jim Lask shouted.

He twisted the control rod in his right hand, and the scream became a shriek. In the mirrors of my homemade periscope the long flame trailing behind the rocket motor, gripped in the jaws of our test stand apparatus, was all but sucked back into the nozzle. Now in its place there was an intense spike of luminescent gas.

The big black needle of the F for thrust dial, on the side of the wooden packing crate that served as our test stand, swung to the notch marked 10 and then jiggled there. P for pressure remained steady at 250, and T for time stood still—because the stripped-down alarm clock on the other side of the wood face never did work.

As I listened to the all-but-unbearable noise of the rocket held captive some twenty feet away, I thought, "the wailing of the banshees," suddenly recalling from somewhere in my childhood the description of a terrifying scream in the night that had sent shivers down my spine.

I looked over at Lask as he peered intently through the small wire-reinforced safety glass slit in the shield atop the barricade at his control position. Two control rods passed through holes in the sides of the shield, but it was so small that when his hands were on them, his elbows, in fact most of his arms, were fully exposed.

In that two-foot cube of the box he was looking at was a tank full of gasoline, and several inches from it a somewhat larger tank of liquid oxygen, both pressurized to over 500 pounds per square inch by a cylinder of nitrogen gas under several thousands of pounds per square inch lying next to the stand. As the now-boiling liquid oxygen built up its own pressure, the ball-and-spring valve on the top of the tank opened to release a white jet of vapor, whose hiss could not be heard above the din.

Everything, except the nitrogen cylinder, had

been machined and welded by our group in the M.I.T. laboratories.

Emboldened by Lask's exposure of his arms, I raised my index finger above the barricade to depress the shutter on my Kodak sitting on top of the logs. I was just about to bring the camera down for rewinding, when the exhaust became a shower of sparks, like a Vesuvius fountain on the Fourth of July.

"Lox off, fuel off," shouted Lask.

Except for the painter's blowtorch aimed up at the exhaust—the most reliable way of starting ignition—and the red-hot metal dripping down into the drip pan under the rocket, all burning ceased.

In the sudden silence the only sound was the hiss of the escaping oxygen as its valve popped off, and then the shouts of students playing baseball in nearby Briggs Field. I wondered how they could have resisted investigating the extraordinary noise of our test. Rolling over on my side I could see the Massachusetts Avenue entrance of M.I.T. and the dome beyond. I liked to look at the dome; it always told me, deeply, where I was.

"Okay, depressurizing the system," said Lask.

"Woosh!" The oxygen and gasoline tanks were vented.

After examining the burnt-through cooling jacket and all-but-destroyed nozzle, we gathered around Lask and listened to his plans for the next rocket: "The injection head can be reused. Why not a metal body next time lined with ceramic inserts in the combustion chamber and nozzle?"

As we were about to begin the drudgery of lugging the equipment back to our headquarters in the basement, Bill Rogers, a civilian chemistry major with thick eyeglasses and an almost entirely bald head, remarked that there was a large amount of liquid oxygen left in the Dewar flask. "Let's pour gasoline in it and see if it freezes hard as a rock," he suggested.

It occurred to me then that one of the chief attractions about rockets for a man like Bill was the potential violence associated with them. He was fascinated by explosives. He would show up at practically every meeting with a new type of bomb, usually a length of iron pipe with pipe nipples sealing off the end and a fuse to his latest mixture inside. Even though the rest of us were uneasy with these devices around, we all joined in the fun after the meeting and waited anxiously to hear the level of the explosion, usually by the edge of the Charles River in front of Walker Memorial.

So one of us wanted to see what would happen when we mixed gasoline and liquid oxygen, and another thought it was a great idea. He scooped out a shallow hole in the dirt and lined it with paper. Gleefully Bill poured in the gasoline and then the steaming liquid oxygen on top. Most of it vaporized instantly as it hit the warm liquid and surrounding earth. Finally everything was cooled down enough for us to observe the result. Instead of a frozen block, all we saw was gasoline floating around in waxy shapes like mothball flakes.

"Let's see if we can explode it," proposed Bill, and he and Fred Hardy lugged two of the railroad ties over to cover the hole, one on top of the other. "To contain the energy," Bill explained.

The rest of us moved apprehensively back to the barricade, as Fred ripped up an oil rag, laid the strips end to end up to the hole under the logs, and doused the strips with the remaining gasoline. Now he struck a match and tossed it at the end of the makeshift fuse, intending to run behind the barricade with the rest of us.

Instantly the flame leaped the ten feet into the hole and then—wham! Through my periscope I glimpsed Fred smacked to the ground in a cloud of dust, and looking up I saw the two logs tumbling end over end in the direction of a low-flying Piper Cub airplane. But it was noon, and in a moment we could not see the logs for the sun. Panicked, we made a run for it, our hands covering our heads, like so many newborn chicks in the shadow of a diving hawk. Flopping on the ground, hands still over my head, I heard—thud! One was down. Thud! Thank God so was the other.

Nobody was hurt. Except Fred, who was walking around in a daze. Had he not managed to turn an instant before the blast, the dirt and gravel embedded in his back would have hit him full in the face. As we later learned at the hospital, his only serious injury was two broken eardrums.

I was still savoring the memory of this first rocket field test at M.I.T. when a few weeks later, well into our third term at Harvard, a notice was posted on the bulletin board that all V-5s would meet individually with a Naval Board of Review. "Now what's up?" I wondered.

The moment I entered the conference room next to the captain's "cabin," I felt I was going to be playing somebody else's game for the next half hour. "They look so confident," I thought, as I peeked from under lowered eyes at the dozen or so officers seated around the long table, pads, pencils, and ashtrays neatly in place.

Only one of the many questions made any impression on me, and it was asked as I sensed the session was about to end.

"If you become a fighter pilot and shoot down a Jap plane, but the pilot bails out safely, what will you do?" asked an officer who had been silently eyeing me. "Will you shoot him down?"

"No Sir, that wouldn't be fair," I blurted out, and in that instant, shaken up by the spontaneity of my reply, out of nowhere came the memory of a "war card" I had found in a package of bubble gum in the thirties. In garish color it showed a Chinese in a parachute being machine gunned by a Japanese fighter plane, with two bullets just exiting from his body followed by exaggerated spurts of red for blood. We used to play a game with these cards, sailing them up against a wall from the curb, and the closest to the wall would win the other cards. A "leaner" was the best of all; you could collect a full set of the horror scenes if you had a "leaner."

"Unfair!" laughed one of the officers. "Have you heard of the Japs' atrocities, such as cutting the ears off our wounded?"

"Yes Sir."

"But suppose he had just shot down one of your buddies in flames, and you realized that he would be back tomorrow and shooting at you again?" asked another.

"Well, I just don't know," I said. "I mean sitting here like this. Maybe if I were over there and angry and frightened I would shoot him. Gosh, I just can't tell."

"What do you want to do after the war?" was the last question.

"I want to work on rockets so we can go to the moon some day."

In October, a notice was posted on the bulletin board: "The following V-5 personnel will be promoted to the rank of Seaman Second Class and assigned to Tarmac Duty at Floyd Bennett Airbase." Preflight obviously still wasn't ready for us. We were dismayed because we knew that Tarmac was a euphemism for washing airplanes. Anxiously I ran my finger down the list. MacDonald, A. N., wasn't there. I went straight to the Chief's office.

"I think you're going to be given a chance to transfer to V-12," he said.

For once, I liked Chief Hazen.

Perhaps it is only during a war, with all of its discontinuities and the creative possibilities arising from the confusion, that a young fellow can be faced, overnight, with a list of several dozen things to "be." "I'll have a licorice whip and some of those Ju-jubees and a couple of jaw breakers and. . . ." "No, you can only have one."

"Is there any one specialty that would most likely send me to M.I.T.?" I asked the Exec., as I ran my finger down the list of V-12 options.

"Well, as a matter of fact, the only schools equipped to handle the aeronautical engineering specialty are Cal Tech and M.I.T. I understand they're sending all the structures subspecialties to M.I.T."

I checked the box on the mimeographed sheet, signed my name, and within several weeks was reassigned to the Graduate House, M.I.T.

At first I had a feeling of shy joy, standing in

the Great Court of the Massachusetts Institute of Technology looking up at the dome, trying not to be obvious about it while reassuring myself it was not just a special trip down the river from Harvard that had brought me here. But then, as I was crossing the courtyard of the Graduate House, our new "ship" along the Charles, somebody behind me cried "Seaman!" and it was Harvard and the Navy all over again.

I turned to face the towering frame of our skipper, a former dramatics professor.

"Pick up that piece of paper," he said, in surprisingly quiet mellifluous tones, as he pointed a dramatic finger at the grass, and I got a sense of what it must be like for an aspiring Shakespearean actor finally to find an audience. I had been warned about our skipper and his ways, particularly his antics with the night watch guarding our "ship."

"Aha, seaman! Where's your whistle?" he was reported to have demanded of one young man self-consciously patrolling the corner of Massachusetts Avenue and Memorial Drive, whom he had first stalked, then grabbed by the shoulders.

"We aren't issued whistles, sir."

"Then how do you expect to summon help if the enemy attacks your ship?"

My fondest dreams were realized when I was

elected secretary of the Rocket Society and knew that one day I would be its president. The world was now aware of rockets, and I spent part of each day filling the orders that came pouring in: "I have been requested by His Majesty's Stationery Office in London to secure for them one copy of M.I.T. Papers of Rocketry. . . ."

Now it was winter, and another test was scheduled—a rocket using a "new high-energy propellent" proposed by Bill Rogers—and the Pentagon had sent two spit-and-polish colonels as observers. Boom! The rocket exploded in a shower of metal and flame the second the valves were opened, and everyone was glad the test took place in the pit on the Navy's obstacle course. One of the colonels was so frightened he stepped back off the wooden plank into the melting snow and mud at the bottom of the pit. "Let's get the hell outta here," he said to his companion.

But no such diversions could stem the torrent of problems that were the fallout of each day's classes. Those innocent-looking mimeographed sheets of problems you took back to your room and cut into slivers, pasting each question in the right upper corner of its own piece of paper. A neat, clean piece of paper. You read and reread the statement of the problem: "Given a beam of length 1 = 20 ft., freely supported at its ends and. . . ." You have learned to make a little diagram. Always the diagram now;

your life is filled with diagrams. You draw a beam—there is no artistry at work here, a beam is always a long narrow rectangle. Under each end you draw a small triangle, a knife-edge, showing it is "freely supported." You represent the load, a single weight in the middle, by an arrow pressing down on the beam, it's head a cusp made with one quick motion of the pencil and sometimes filled in black because it looks so neat. You letter in all the given facts, 1 = , w = . And finally you have that satisfying feeling of having the problem defined, of having "isolated" it, so that solving it becomes rather routine. And so you finish the task and draw a box around the answer, gratifyingly aware of your growing ability to solve the problems of the wood and steel of the world.

At some point the process comes alive, a shower of sparks, mild steel held against an abrasive wheel; if this is so, what about that? But wait, wait, do the here and now first. You know you must wait for the next class, the next course. You can take a peek, though. What if the beam is held at the ends, buried in cement? What if the weight is not still, but moving like a man jumping up and down. And before you know it, you are there, figuring out these problems—one spring, two springs of different stiffness, rotating shafts, flywheels, beams with irregular loadings. You even forget about the "oscillating bobo whose frequency is proportional to the heat of the meat and varies inversely with the mass of the ass."

You become so preoccupied with your little slivers of paper and pastepot that you begin to resent the nightly stampede into your room that happens to have the best view of the oscillating bobo in the Bexley Hall Apartments across the way. "Hey, lookit, she's nude even fixing his dinner," somebody yells, as the mob three deep at the windows jostles for position. "Yeah, yeah, they're newlyweds for sure." "Look, look, he's coming in the door, right on the button as usual," and all eyes shift to the bedroom next to the kitchen. You want to look, but you have to finish those problems even while envying the men stuck with the fire watch on the roof with their homemade telescope.

Everywhere there are forces. They become second nature to you, these little arrows, with the head indicating direction and the number next to it the strength of the force measured in pounds. They press down, up, pull apart, compress, resist, thrust, lift, drag, and rotate. In practically everything you do, there is a force lurking about to be ferreted out, if not for itself, then for its effect. Some are very sneaky. Mr. Coriolis, you learn, found a particularly elusive one and had it named after him. It becomes second nature to you to size up a situation in terms of its forces.

Gradually, you learn the significance of becoming an engineer. Newton has presented you with your starting point: a beautifully universal set of laws governing forces and motion. It is for you to apply them to the here and now before you. There is no cult of personality, quite the contrary; you use Blasius' equations and Clausius' inequality without so much as a tipping of the hat in their direction or even the passing thought of whether there was ever flesh and blood behind these tools possessed of men's names. There are always the applications, the torrent of applications.

And running through all the days of theory like an interlacing weft are the hours in the laboratory which allow you to form and feel and test the materials that are bedeviled by your forces. Sometimes it's amusing, like Testing Materials Lab with wiry, ever-serious Professor Stewart, as he prepares the sample batch of concrete with as much flourish and hurried activity as a French chef preparing a Grand Marnier soufflé. "Ah, see," he says, with the note of satisfaction cherished by those who live by the book, "the concrete is just right, not too thick, not too thin." To come to this conclusion, he has performed the "slump test." Before our very eyes, he has filled a sheet-metal cone with concrete, a truncated cone of particular and historic dimensions—12 inches high, 8 inches in diameter at the top, 4 at the bottom—and has turned it upside down on the table, withdrawing it smartly as a child does his sand bucket at the beach. The pyramid of concrete neither stands perfectly rigid, nor dissolves upon itself, but rather slumps a little, like a woman's breast removed from its restraints. And thus the foundation of all great buildings: very technical, Mamma mia!

You talk old Giuseppe in the metallurgy lab into helping you cast a bar of aluminum for a rocket motor out of the precious scrap you have collected. The metal is cooling in its mold, and you wander over to where Giuseppe is applying all of his considerable might to a huge stillson wrench, trying to loosen a large plug screwed into the end of what appears to be the recoil mechanism on the barrel of a cannon lying on the floor. "Hey Giuseppe, what are you up to?" "I'ma doa this for the war." "How so?" "It's a damma good thing we hava smarta men like the Professor. Ah, here she's a come." "But what does this have to do with the war?" "She's a captured German howitzer, and when Giuseppe cutta her up, the Professor analyze da metal and tell where she com'a from." "Say, that's keen." "He even knowa the town," says Giuseppe. . . .

Swoosh! The plug held by the last few threads pops off like a button and unleashes a huge spring, its coils as thick as a black snake. "Jesus Christ!" exclaims Giuseppe, as we both cringe, watching the unguided missile careen around the room, chipping cement, sparking steel, crushing wood, until its deadly energy is exhausted and it lies useless on the floor. "That's a teacha me good!" Giuseppe says.

At other times, surrounded by machines whose

functions are not unlike those that graced the Inquisition's dungeons when men methodically set about determining the limits of man, you take the measure of your materials, and never again will the battle with your forces, given life by your equations, be solely a thing of the head. "Load is 1,000 pounds," says your associate, reading from the dial on the tensil-testing machine that registers the force with which its jaws are trying to pull the steel test specimen apart. "Elongation is 4 ten thousandths of an inch," he notes, reading from another dial which measures the amount of stretch in the test section under the load. You shoot a glance at the specimen, about the size of a cigar, before plotting the information on your graph paper—over 4 on the elongation scale and up 1 on the load scale—and you make a point, which represents the relation between load and stretch at the moment. "Load 4,000 pounds, elongation 2 thousandths . . . 7,500, three thousandths." Suddenly the points, which have formed a straight line slanting to the right, deviate from this proportional relationship as the yield point of the steel is reached, and now the elongation increases at a more rapid rate. "Load 8,400, 5 hundredths, 14,200, 2 tenths, 14,700, 4 tenths. . . ." and "Womp!" the specimen breaks, necking down more like taffy than steel in the final seconds. You are so busy determining from this profile the numbers you want to know that you would consider absurd any suggestion that one day all the detail will melt into the background to be replaced by a simple feeling of understanding as you watch an airplane wing flexing on the way to Cleveland, or walk past the giant I beams within Grand Central Terminal, quietly bearing their share of the PanAm Building above.

Now the pace quickens as your basic engineering education is left behind, and you become like the canoeist when he feels the bite of the flowing water more than his own strokes and knows the excitement of the rapids lies ahead. The broad sweep of education begins to converge on a single object: powered flight, at first with the generality of "Aeronautics" and then with the blatancy of "Construction Details, Aircraft" and "Airplane Design Practice." Education is finally more than a distinction, it is a tool, a tool you can use to pry the lid off the world.

You find yourself contriving forces rather than merely coping with them, forces of air flowing over wings at speeds greater than the wildest hurricane the world has known, speeds that would force the proudest oak to its knees. But your wings are friends with the air and seem almost to smile on a foggy day when you can actually see something of the complex pattern by which they coax their lift out of the air—the vortices shed at the wing tips, like the turned-up ends of a moustache, as the high-pressure air under the wings finds a path to the low pressure on top of the wing and wants to go up and around at the same time as it is blown back in corkscrew fashion.

Forces of air, hot with the foul breath of burning gasoline, against pistons in radial engines which translate the linear motion of the pistons to the rotation of the propeller shaft—this and more as you learn the thermodynamicists' art of coaxing useful work out of heat flow.

Increasingly it is your ball game as you design beams and structures to handle the forces you have created. A far cry from the "given a beam of 1 = . . . , given forces of . . ." exercises of months past. You rather like this feeling of control that comes from knowing the consequences of everything you do in this system of yours, the system of an airplane in its environment. Everything is consequential, and you find enjoyment in playing with the variables, holding everything in a long string of possible variables still and moving the last, perhaps letting it wiggle a little, watching the ripples flow through the system, trading off consequences, optimizing, until you have the best combination.

Finally, stamped in a way that you don't realize at the time, you are an engineer.

And there I am, in June of 1946, standing beside my father on the small plot of grass in front of 2220 Penrose Avenue, Baltimore, with Granny taking our picture together, first in the white ensign's uniform borrowed from a friend (the Navy had mustered me out at the end of the term with a commission in the Naval Reserve) and then with borrowed cap and gown over the whites—my own private graduation ceremony after receiving in the mail, a few days earlier, my bachelor's degree.

The year before, as the war in Europe was ending, there had been a flurry of talk among V-12ers of being mustered out. But the prospect of becoming a civilian faded when the focus shifted to the war in the Pacific. It seemed likely that the completion of our training would coincide with the final drive on Japan, and we would be in the thick of the storm when it broke.

But in August 1945——"We've got em, we've got em!" one of my shipmates shouted as he burst from the doorway of the drugstore across the street from the main entrance of M.I.T. and ran full tilt into me on the sidewalk. "It's all over but the mopping up."

He threw his arms around me as if I were some long-lost friend and beat the back of my head with the newspaper clutched in his hand, all the while dancing up and down.

"Got what?" I asked, overwhelmed by his sudden familiarity, for while I recognized his face, he lived on another deck in the Graduate House and I didn't know his name.

"The Japs, haven't you heard, the Japs! Look!" and he unrolled the newspaper before my incredulous eyes.

ATOM BOMB DROPPED ON JAPAN

"Hey, wait a minute," I pleaded, but he tore the paper from my grasp and continued down Massachusetts Avenue, skipping and waving the paper in the air. "We're going home, we're going home!"

"How the devil does it work?" I kept asking myself as I scanned the headlines over my morning coffee at the drugstore counter. "How did they do it?" But it would be days before words like "plutonium" and "tamper" and "critical mass" came together sufficiently for me to conceptualize the actual device. Right now, I had to be satisfied with terms like Oak Ridge and Hanford and fission and thousands of tons of TNT.

Some years later Norbert Wiener's secretary told me Wiener had locked himself in his room most of the day after receiving news of Hiroshima. I was not that perceptive. Aside from my initial curiosity about the bomb, I shared the elation of my slap-happy shipmate. We had been told that Japan would never surrender and increasingly, in recent months, casualty figures for the final assault on Japan had been bandied about in the press and in the chow line. "A million Americans dead or wounded" was the common estimate, and several times that many Japanese—a reflection, no doubt, of the ferocity with which the Japanese had defended such outposts as Iwo Jima. Not that I had ever actually experienced fear at the prospect of being part of the last door-to-door shoot-out; it was too far away, and I was too busy with the next day's lesson. Nor did my lack of any sense of guilt because of the bomb stem from the desire for revenge and unconditional surrender that was stoked to red heat in us all. The only thing that mattered was to bring the war to an end, by whatever means. What a man like Norbert Wiener must have felt, the terrible suffering of the people of Hiroshima, was beyond my farthest reach.

What would happen if Japan did surrender? I wondered, putting the newspaper aside. Would the Navy muster us out? And if so, when would we be leaving? Such is the way an epoch-making world event can be cut down to individual size.

I needn't have worried, though. Soon after V-J Day, when servicemen around the world were adding up their "points" in eager anticipation of their day of discharge, the Navy decided our class would be allowed to complete the next two terms, and then each of us would be released to inactive duty.

There was never any question of what I would do upon graduation. I would work on rockets. But where? Then my helicopter professor told me his former roommate, Bensen, was setting up a rocket group at the Glenn L. Martin Company in Baltimore and arranged for my interview with him shortly after the end of the year—destiny, I thought, my hometown Baltimore!

Bensen's desk, in the middle of a hangarlike room filled with engineers and draftsmen as far as the eye could see, had on it a newly made sign, black with gold letters: "Pilotless Aircraft Section." Rockets and missiles were so new that some corporate mind was protecting itself from shock by this euphemism. The "Section" consisted of one—Bensen himself, a dark-haired boyish-looking man, handsome as a movie actor. It was to grow and produce the Matador, our first "pilotless aircraft," and the Viking, our first rocket approaching the V-2 in size. Bensen's "Section" in fact, became the major business of the company after the financial disaster of the early fifties when its commercial airplane business was written off. He was rewarded ultimately with the presidency of the company, and it was under his leadership that the Vanguard and Titan rockets were produced.

As sometimes happens, when one is listening with absolute attention yet is able to see other things with a clarity otherwise denied him, all during the interview I kept watching a balding draftsman a few tables away who seemed to have an attention span of five seconds. First the cigarette, then the peanuts, which he shook out of the packet into his palm and flipped into his mouth as if slapping himself in the face, then the walk to the water cooler. Now a stately gaze around the room, then back for another stare at the board before him, another round of cigarette, peanuts, and walk to the water cooler. The thought that this could happen to a man must have made a deep impression on me, for I remember it more clearly even now than much of what was said during the interview.

I left, though, convinced that Bensen's goal was the moon, although he realized it might take a lot of broken field running on military projects to achieve it. On my return to M.I.T., I talked with Max, a young professor in mechanical engineering. He was giving a brand-new graduate course entitled "Flow of Compressible Fluids," and I had eagerly signed up for it as an extra credit because of its applicability to rocket nozzle design.

"Have you ever considered staying on for your master's degree?" he asked.

"Not really. I couldn't afford it. I have to go to work."

"You could apply for an appointment as research assistant. Ross in the Gas Turbine Laboratory is looking for somebody with your interests."

I listened intently to what he was saying. For one thing, I had come to sense in Max the same integrity that had attracted me to Professor Templeman. And his enthusiasm for the new field of supersonic aerodynamics was contagious.

I still have the "Notification of Appointment" from M.I.T. I received early in May 1946 (does everyone save such things?): "I take pleasure in informing you that at the last meeting of the Executive Committee of the Corporation, you were appointed Research Assistant in Mechanical Engineering for one year beginning July 1, 1946, at a salary of $150.00 per month. . . . Please write me your acceptance of this appointment."

Several weeks later I received a letter from Bensen assuring me I had made the right move:

> . . . I must admit that I am somewhat disappointed that you will not be able to join us in our rocket work at Martin's this summer. I want to congratulate you, however, on your appointment as a research assistant and feel that the graduate work in Thermodynamics and Supersonic Flow of Fluids will be extremely valuable when you do enter the industry. I shall appreciate your keeping in touch with me and assure you that if we are still in the business here at Baltimore there will be a position available.

I carefully tucked the precious letter away with my G.I. insurance policy, convinced of its negotiability, a rain check, so to speak.

But I was not "destined" to work at Martin's. After being mustered out of the Navy, I spent the next year at the Gas Turbine Laboratory designing and testing a miniature wind tunnel that was the heart of my work for my sponsor, the Navy's Project Meteor. This research was the basis for my master's thesis: "An Investigation of Supersonic Diffusers for Wind Tunnels."

Peering through the flat glass sides of my tunnel with an instrument that made changes in air density visible in much the way waves can be seen rising from a hot road, I felt the excitement of digging deeply into the within of things. There, naked before my eyes, the air was reduced from a speed of two and a half times the speed of sound to subsonic speeds within the inches of my test section through a series of shock waves that appeared as dark lines. I was recording pressures, taking pictures at 3,000 frames per second, and then all over again with different inlet angles, all to determine how best to slow (diffuse) air down from high speeds.

Toward the end of the year, when I was beginning to contemplate a Ph.D. in physics, I was visited by a recruiter for the Air Force's NEPA Project, Nuclear Energy for the Propulsion of Aircraft.

"Hello there, Mac Duff," he said as I walked into the interviewing room.

It was Roger whom I had known in the Rocket Society and greatly admired. He had done his undergraduate engineering elsewhere, was a P-51 instructor during the war, and was going for his master's when I first met him. Always well dressed and well spoken, he had a wider range of interests than any of my friends.

"It's a chance of a lifetime," he said, after explaining the reason for his visit. "Our main effort is still the airplane, but we've been given the go-ahead on a nuclear rocket feasibility study, and you'd be the first employee."

"What's the principle of a nuclear rocket?"

"I can't discuss it until you have a Q clearance. Look, you'd be in on the ground floor. If you need more convincing, we'll pay your way down to Oak Ridge for a visit."

"What would the salary be?"

"We're paying bachelors $175 a month. With your master's we can make it $200. Oh, we might stretch it to $225."

A week before I left on my visit to Oak Ridge, a group of us were standing in the new addition of the Gas Turbine Lab, staring at an instrument panel in shocked disbelief.

The new compressor in the basement was drawing full power, but the airflow in the just-completed supersonic wind tunnel refused to go super.

"At M.I.T.! Could this happen at M.I.T.?"

"My God, do you think we assumed too high a diffuser efficiency?" exclaimed Professor Ross, violating his own "theory on answers" for which he was famous among students: "If the answer is simple, it is probably right, but otherwise it is probably wrong."

The word diffuser jolted me. My pride at having had my thesis consulted in the design, turned to fear.

"Maybe it's the compressor," I said defensively.

"No, it couldn't be," said a member of our group. "We have the test curves that were taken before it left the factory, and they're okay."

"Well, whatever it is, we'd better find it in a hurry," Professor Ross said, the normal pink color of his face deepening a little. "The dedication of the lab is only two days off."

The ensuing action resembled the proverbial Chinese fire drill; everything was checked and rechecked. Finally the problem was isolated: the compressor wasn't producing design pressure, and the factory representative was summoned. When the inlet casing was unbolted and removed, there it was, wrapped around the inlet impeller—a rag, obviously a welder's grease rag, left carelessly somewhere in the hundreds of feet of pressure piping. But no ordinary rag, this! It was part of a girl's beach coat, popular at the time, and among the several sayings printed into its fabric the most prominent was "Who'd a Thunk It?"

6

The Yellow and the Black

"Ain't got no pass here for any MacDonald," drawled the pudgy guard to my driver. "You better git on up to Jackson Square and fetch him one back here, that is iffin you want him to git in."

As I waited at the gate for the driver to return with the pass that should have been awaiting our arrival, I marveled that the entire town of Oak Ridge was surrounded by a chain-link fence topped with barbed wire, and the feeling of mystery—and importance—that had been growing in me during the drive from Knoxville Airport began to quicken. I noticed the guardhouse had its own long antenna and read the sign over the gate: "MILITARY AREA. Weapons—Liquors—Telescopes—Radio Transmitters—PROHIBITED. All vehicles and passengers subject to search." During the interview at M.I.T. Roger had spoken of the huge factories back in the hills and how the townspeople—peak population, 75,000—must have wondered at the thousands of tons of equipment and material coming in with nothing visible going out. But he had not said the whole town was surrounded by a fence.

"What did the people think was going on here?" I asked the guard, "I mean with all the activity, and nobody knowing what was being made. Weren't they curious?"

"Now I'll tell ya," he said in a confidential tone, "there was two stories hereabouts. One of 'em had it all those buildings was makin' Roosevelt buttons fer his fourth term. And the other of 'em had it they was makin' horses' hay-eds."

I was so awed with my surroundings that I bit, to his immense pleasure: "Horses' heads, what for?"

"What fer, I'll tell you what fer, young man. Fer shipment to Washington, fer final assembly with all the horses' asses!"

Now I couldn't shut him up. He knew he had a pigeon and trotted out the stories one by one: "Any man who asks me what I'm makin' when I'm workin' at the plant during the war, I tell him 'bout $1.35 an hour. And. . . ."

My problem with the driver, once he had returned with the pass and we were on our way to the center of town, was just the opposite: he said virtually nothing. When I asked him the most innocent questions, he acted as though the purpose of the place, which had been known to the world for the past year and a half, was still a hush-hush secret. He did admit, though, that he had known the area as a child and that as recently as 1942 it had been "mountain country." Jackson Square, he said, just below the Guest House toward which we were heading, had been a hillside dotted with cedar and pine, "You know, the kinda land that just sorta holds the world together."

After checking in at the hotel, we drove along the Oak Ridge Turnpike to the plant area. The clay along the roadside, red as if the earth were bleeding, was still uncovered by weeds. The old dirt roads off to the side were blocked with chains and signs, Keep Out—Official Use Only, some disappearing into the dense pines on the hillside, others leading to empty log cabins, each numbered as if stored for later use.

We had just passed the sign, Leaving Anderson County—Entering Roane County, when I saw a convoy approaching us: a truck with a square, gray, windowless body behind the cab, preceded and followed by a black sedan, each vehicle sporting the ubiquitous whip antenna. As they passed us, moving at less than half our speed, I noticed that the man next to the driver in each sedan was armed with a shotgun.

"What's that?" I exclaimed. The driver reacted like a parent whose child, upon first passing a mausoleum, asks, "Who lives in there, Daddy?" After his initial shock, he replied laconically, "A shipment," but then appeared dismayed that he had been so specific.

"Were you here during the war?" I inquired, thinking I now had an entering wedge.

"Yep."

"What did you think they were making?"

"About the best I could figger out was that they was making sympathetic rubber."

Soon we came to a fork in the highway, and as we bore to the right, I studied the sign X-10 pointing down the somewhat more narrow road that appeared to lead into another valley.

And then, suddenly, the hillside on the right fell away into flat land, and there it was, with all the surprise of Shangri-La, K-25, a mile or so in the distance, the gaseous diffusion plant where the fissionable uranium-235 is separated from uranium-238. The statistics in the Smyth Report, "100 acres under roof, 1,000 miles of piping . . . ," hadn't prepared me for what I saw: the vast expanse of buildings, three or more stories high, windowless except for a tiny row at the top, hundred of ventilators studding the roofs. "Why, it must be the largest plant in the world," I marveled, remembering what the Report had told me was happening inside: corrosive gaseous uranium hexafluoride being pumped through miles of pipe by upward of 5,000 centrifugal compressors meeting countless "barriers" along the way. The "barriers" were solid except for billions of minipinpricks less than a millionth of an inch in diameter, so small, in fact, that the minute difference in weight between the U-235 and the U-238 molecule slightly favored the U-235 getting through so that after enough "cascades," as the individual units were called, the gas was greatly "enriched" in U-235. The whole thing was one gigantic sieve!

"In there, right over there someplace, is U-235," I thought, hardly able to contain my excitement.

While K-25 was still off to the right, a huge smokestack appeared over the hill in the direction we were driving, and soon I could see the outlines of a power plant and an impossibly large mound of coal.

"The S-50 area you're going to is over there next to the power plant," the driver said.

As we approached, I observed that the entire area was enclosed by the same type of barbed-wire-topped fence with elevated guard towers at strategic points as was K-25. Fences within fences!

"Hello there, MacDuff, welcome to Shantytown," shouted Roger as he joined me at the gate while the guard carefully examined my pass.

Roger had not changed since our Rocket Society days. In the role of recruiter, he was proceeding with the same blend of style and substance I had observed in him earlier. "I've arranged for you to meet our chief engineer," he said as we walked toward a long, narrow barracks-type building, "and a few of our section heads. We can't tell you much about the project—just enough to whet your appetite, I hope. Then I'll try to give you a taste of Oak Ridge living. You came out on the Oak Ridge Turnpike, didn't you?"

"Yes."

"Then you've already seen K-25. We'll swing over to Bethel Valley Road so you can see the pile at X-10, the plutonium pilot plant, you know, and double back to Bear Creek Road for a look at Y-12."

"What is Y-12 again? I've forgotten what the Smyth Report said."

"You've been doing your homework, I see. Y-12 is the electromagnetic separation plant. We should have time for a drive along Outer Drive just about sunset. Quite a view, with the Cumberland Mountains in the distance. And then on to the Stud Farm for dinner."

"Stud Farm?"

"Yes, that's where I live; there are six of us bachelors, all from the project, in a D House. We rented the house from Roane-Anderson just before the postwar population slump ended and they reimposed their rules against bachelors having family houses."

"Who's Roane Anderson?" I thought, as we entered the building. I got a strong whiff of wood, like an attic under a hot summer sun.

"These 'temporary' buildings were part of the administration and laboratory complex for the S-50 thermal diffusion plant. The plant itself was in the large hangarlike building we now use for our experimental test rigs. The equipment inside was dismantled after the war. But here I am, talking to an expert. If you've just read the Smyth Report, you undoubtedly remember more than I do."

His flattery pleased me. "Yes, I remember he said the process needed lots of steam, and that's why they put it next to the power plant. Smyth said something about heating long columns of liquid uranium hexafluoride and having the lighter U-235 tend to diffuse up. Or was it down? I don't remember. At any rate, he said it was never intended as a production plant in its own right."

Roger introduced me to HB, Assistant to the Chief Engineer, who was just coming out of his office. HB's background was nontechnical, and his role was that of executive officer. I learned later that he had had a distinguished war record; the "baby" carrier he commanded toward the end had come under intense kamikaze attack.

As we talked I saw none of the restless, spiritual side of HB which was to have such an effect on me. Rather, I was aware of a certain condescension and loftiness in his manner, magnified, perhaps, by his height, his military bearing, and the sharpness of his features. "Hope you'll be coming aboard," he said, as he hurried down the narrow corridor, a sheaf of papers in his hand.

We followed him at a slower pace, Roger sticking his head into a doorway here and there. "Say Dick, do you have a minute? I'd like you to meet. . . ." Signs made of neatly lettered slats of wood protruding into the hall gave shape to the project as we walked the length of the corridor: Aircraft Design, Analysis, Materials, Power Plant Design, Controls, Experimental Engineering.

"Where is the atomic work?" I asked, as we came to a large drafting room at the far end of the building and I realized I had been through the engineering department.

"Each section has its own unique problems relating to the nuclear power plant," Dave explained. "Specifically, studies of the reactor itself are in Analysis, and there is a separate Experimental Physics Department in another building."

"All of this has to do with the airplane, doesn't it? What about the rocket?"

"We haven't really started the rocket work. That's what you would be doing, in Analysis, working for me. Let's go meet Don Kendrick, my boss; he's the one I want you to spend some time with."

Kendrick's office was sparsely furnished, like all the others, and as we entered, he was hunched over his desk, staring intently at a wooden and cardboard device he held steady on the desk with his left hand while with the right he slowly pulled a string that was part of its mechanism. It looked exactly like a model of a guillotine with one side faced with cardboard in which a slot had been cut near the base. He must have known we were peering over his shoulder, but he was intent on finishing. He let go the end of the string, and the "blade" fell briefly exposing a series of numbers pasted to its side as it flashed past the slot.

"Aha!" he exclaimed, as he jotted a seemingly random set of numbers on a pad and compared them with those on the blade as he pulled the string a little so they would appear again in the slot. "I've finally reached eight."

"How do you like my homemade tachistoscope?" he asked, turning to us.

"Well, it's very nice," I said, somewhat bewildered. "What's it for?"

"Don, this is Angus MacDonald down from M.I.T.," interrupted Roger.

"Oh yes, you're thinking of joining us. Well, if you do, you'll find one of our biggest problems is reading all the background information we need to make some headway in this project. Most of it is written in bureaucratic gobbledygook."

As he spoke, the only way I could relate him to anything atomic was that he had a certain gaunt look about him and a prominent Adam's apple, like pictures I had seen of Robert Oppenheimer, although Kendrick's hair was anything but close-cropped, bushy as a matter of fact. He was one of those people whose head appears to be cocked at an angle even when it isn't.

"Half an hour a day!" he said enthusiastically. "Think of it, only half an hour a day, and you can learn to read twice as fast. Think what that could mean to a project such as this," as though it was entirely natural for us to be discussing such a subject our first moments together.

As I listened with rapt attention while he described the speed reading experiments at Maxwell Air Force Base, I learned what his little device was all about. The tachistoscope, it seemed, was a device for flashing a random series of numbers on a screen for brief intervals, say a second down to hundredths, even thousandths, of a second. You start with a few digits and a relatively long time interval, and over the weeks expand the number of digits you can recall after flashes of shorter and shorter duration. Kendrick was elated at just having achieved an eight-digit recall during a flash he calculated to be less than a tenth of a second.

"The eye," he explained, "doesn't read as it moves across the page, but rather 'sees' only when it is still, during a 'fixation.' By practice, the span of a single fixation can be increased so that the number of fixations per line is decreased. Experiments even show most people can increase their span to a newspaper-column width so that they can read right down the page."

"But don't you remember less when you read faster?" Roger shifted his weight from one foot to the other, annoyed I hadn't let the subject drop.

"That's where the reading rate controller comes in," Kendrick said. "It's a machine you can put a book into and have a metal cover move slowly down the page—you adjust the rate with a knob—so that you have to read so many words a minute, say 500, to keep ahead of the edge. Your comprehension actually increases as you read faster. Most people stumble along at 200 words a minute or so, verbalizing everything as they go. The controller forces you out of this habit."

Talk of speed reading eclipsed the remainder of our discussion. I found the idea of tinkering with yourself, improving your own machine, exciting. More horsepower, not through greater size but increased efficiency. At no time had formal education suggested this approach. "Concentrate, concentrate," I had been told. "Read more and you will read better."

As we talked I noticed several rather odd furnishings in the office. "Why does Mr. Kendrick have a red wastebasket with 'Burn' written on the side, sitting next to the green one?" I asked Roger as we left.

"We all have them. The red one is for wastepaper of a secret nature and is emptied every night into a special incinerator."

"But why the big eyeball on top of his filing cabinet?"

Roger laughed. "That's Don's rebellious streak showing itself. Did you notice that all the cabinets have a combination lock and a card lettered 'Open' stuck in the handle? One day Security sent a memo to all section heads asking them to 'keep an eye on their safes' whenever they are open. So Don had one made of clay in the model shop."

I had seen only a fraction of Kendrick's quixotic nature. Over the next four years I found him full of surprises. He hated bureaucracy and gave the impression of preferring Thoreau's life at Walden, although he was an admirer of Clarence Streit and an active member of the local Atlantic Alliance group who advocated a first step toward world government. This hatred of government red tape was undoubtedly why he was the only one on the project to buy a farmhouse in the hills outside of Oak Ridge. There he grew worms in barrels filled with a special mixture of dirt and garbage, and then released them on his property. The very thought of these creatures working for him around the clock, performing their wonderful duties of aerating and fertilizing the soil, made him ecstatic. The world's food problems would yield to the increased cultivation of the lowly worm, he said. Bread, too, was a passion with him, and he made his own flour from kernels of wheat patiently ground between two suitable stones.

Always interested in self-development, he was convinced there is more to the human psyche than we have even begun to understand. He kept a daily graph of his daily ups and downs, trying to determine his personal cycle. Subjective as the graph was, he felt it helped him avoid making important decisions on the wrong days. Midway through my stay at Oak Ridge, when I went from engineering into administrative work, he was an ardent supporter of my trip to Maxwell Air Force Base to be schooled in speed-reading techniques so that I could start a course in the Engineering Department. He was well known on the project for his frequent memos on the techniques of straightforward writing in which he lashed out at the scientist-engineer's predilection for such phrases as "It is believed by the writer" instead of "I think." When later I began a public speaking course for the department at lunchtime, he was one of the most active participants.

The chief engineer's office was only a few steps away, and as we entered, he looked up from his desk, head thrust slightly forward, eyes half smiling behind round steel-rimmed glasses. His whole manner of friendly expectation seemed to me exaggerated. As I got to know him better, I felt he was either covering up for a basic shyness or else resented deeply having to deal with people.

Like Kendrick, the chief engineer was in his thirties, maybe thirty-five. I gathered from Roger that he had come to Oak Ridge from Pratt and Whitney where he, Kendrick, and a number of the other project personnel had worked on the development of the "free piston engine," a tantalizingly attractive concept that never succeeded commercially.

From the beginning of our meeting, it was clear that the chief engineer would be painting the broad outlines of the project, and I was elated, for the central question, "What is a nuclear airplane?" had been swamped, as is so often true of questions we pursue, by distractions along the way.

I still had the lingering notion that nuclear propulsion had somehow to do with the hollow sound emitted by the shiny, bell-shaped protrusions that lifted Flash Gordon's rocket without visible effort from the surface of the moon. Now, as the chief engineer spoke, I saw it in terms of a heat transfer problem of heroic proportions. No one had cried "Eureka" upon discovery of an entirely new means of propulsion. No new secret had been pried from the atom, no antigravity machine invented (had it been, the very existence of the project would have been a secret). In a sense a step was being taken backward. Except for the use of falling water (which nature's cycle of evaporation and rain makes possible) to spin electric generators, all the world's significant power has come from the burning of fossil fuels in air—a chemical chain reaction started by ignition, which produces heat energy through the molecular rearrangements that take place during formation of the products of combustion. In the beginning the heat of combustion was transferred to a "working fluid"—water—in a boiler through the walls of tubes (heat transfer surfaces), and this process is still used where weight and initial investment are not considerations. The steam drove a piston or turbine. The big step forward that made the automobile and the airplane possible was the invention of the internal-combustion engine, where the heat is produced directly in the working fluid (air in this case, not water).

As I could see from the diagram (always the diagram, isolating the problem) that the chief engineer was sketching for me, a turbojet engine was being proposed in which the air, after flowing through the compressor, was not squirted with kerosene but flowed through a high-temperature nuclear reactor. Oh, so easy to draw: a cylinder lettered "R," with holes through it like a Swiss cheese, the air receiving its heat energy from the hot walls in which uranium was fissioning.

The principle was not at all difficult to understand. After the war the press had made much of the fact that a sizable portion of the Columbia River was diverted through the three plutonium production reactors at Hanford to absorb the heat of the fissioning uranium, and still, with this vast mass of coolant, the temperature of the river was raised a significant amount. From the moment the first nuclear chain reaction was demonstrated, there must have been a growing army of minds speculating about how to apply this new source of heat energy to everything from power plants to Toastmasters.

Thinking of this new source in relation to the airplane, I momentarily visualized wings sprouting from the Hanford reactors. These were originally called "piles" because they are just that: piles of graphite blocks in which lumps of natural uranium are dispersed in a very special lattice, surrounded by a thick layer of lead and cement to shield the lethal radiation. But lead and cement were hardly aircraft materials.

"But the reactor!" I exclaimed as the gist of what was being told me sank in. "How can you make one small enough to fit in an airplane?"

"You'll have to wait for a Q clearance to hear that. Let me say, though, that the stakes are high. It's no secret that the heating value of a pound of uranium consumed in fission is about 2 million times the heating value of gasoline. If you can replace the weight and volume of gasoline with a reactor, you have a plane of unlimited range."

When I left the chief engineer's office, I could sense the monumental problems involved. Everything about a reactor is big and heavy, and a flyable reactor is what the project was all about. "It has to be a small reactor," I thought, "but then how does one get the heat out?" It was not until several years later, when I glanced out the window at the K-25 power plant, whose boilers were several stories high, and then looked down at the drawing of the reactor, 3 feet long and 3 feet in diameter (the size of a large garbage can), and realized for the first time they were of almost identical power output, that I felt the enormity of the problem.

"Well, what do you think?" asked Roger, after we showed our passes to the guard and headed for his car.

"I want to be part of this," I said, "even though you haven't told me much about the nuclear rocket," and it was only then I realized I had made the choice of my first real job. "No wall-to-wall engineers here yet," I thought. "I'll be in on the ground floor!"

"Wait until you see X-10," said Roger. "I don't know whether you'll feel the same way I do, but just looking at it, even off in the distance—it's fenced in too, you know—well. . . ."

We turned off on the side road that I had noticed earlier in the day, and the hillsides covered with pine and cedar steepened, more of the land that "just sorta holds the world together." Then another turn to the left and the narrow valley widened, exposing a complex of buildings on a plateau to the right, the most prominent feature of which was a tall white smokestack (with nothing coming out of it). The smokestack appeared to be attached to a rectangular building, about the size of a large hangar, whose roof was studded with ventilators. There were a number of Quonset huts nearby.

"There it is, the X-10 pile," said Roger, "in the building next to the stack."

I was filled with awe as I stared at the building and tried to conjure up a picture, from all I had read and heard, of what was going on inside. "Just to be here," I thought as we sat by the side of the road, "near the second chain reaction ever started." The first one had been started in the "pile" built on the squash court under the west stands of Stagg Field at the University of Chicago. I even remembered the date the reaction was first sustained, because when I read about it after the war, I tried to recall what I had been doing at the time. I suppose everybody does this, more or less, with important events. It makes you realize that while you are so concerned with the ordinary things that make up your day, there may be men in a room somewhere—or even on a squash court—who are doing something you don't know about at the time but which will eventually affect your destiny.

There is a rich reward in gazing quietly at a nuclear reactor to the point of truly becoming aware of it, of "seeing" it in terms of itself. Then, as with all great creations, something of the universe and something of man is revealed. That day by the roadside, though, I had little to bring, and took little away. I was like a schoolboy standing before Picasso's *Guernica,* trying to grapple with all that was there, grasping for a function, a use. "It looks like . . . Picasso must have been trying to. . . ." But the schoolboy grows up and one day returns to the museum, bringing with him all that he has read, seen, felt—in short, all that he is. Perhaps now the painting speaks to him in its own terms and he experiences the artist's sense of discovery.

What is it that I see now as I hold the picture of X-10 in my mind's eye?

At first I see white, the white of a concrete cube two stories high and the white of the men's laboratory smocks as they move about the catwalks sprouting from its sides.

Then I see black, inky slippery black, as my gaze penetrates the ten-foot-thick walls and comes to rest on the cube of graphite within—a cube made of machine-cut graphite bricks whose razor-sharp edges stack together in tactile joy.

To know what is going on inside that cube is to be swallowed up by the blackness and shrink until one's scale is the scale of the particles that make up all matter; the blackness, as I look out, becomes the blackness of night sky, and all that is substance is concentrated in the bodies that fill the heavens.

The cube is alive with billions of particles called neutrons which are the theme song of the chain reaction. Fast neutrons on the loose, caroming off the nuclei of graphite atoms with which they exchange some of their energy in a subatomic game of billiards, becoming slow neutrons, to be slurped up in a process which next engages my attention. And the incredible thing is that these neutrons travel on the average of one inch between collisions, so filled with "sky" is graphite. Dwelling on this fact, I feel for the first time the essential emptiness of matter. I see with a clarity hitherto denied me the atomic structure of graphite: a small, heavy nucleus, in which nearly the entire mass of the atom is concentrated, surrounded by a largely empty region in which electrons move somewhat like planets about the sun.

Finally, I see gray, as I visualize the slugs of uranium metal, the size of a can of frozen orange juice, heavier than lead, latticed through the black cube, a looking-glass world where the raisins are gray and the bun is black. But then suddenly the gray becomes yellow—in my mind, for I have never seen pure uranium, only one of its compounds which all the world knows as the yellow of a ceramic vase. (The universe must have smiled its special smile of irony as it watched man fashion his own orange-yellow sun at Alamagordo from the same element whose former use was to provide color for his art objects. Who but man, given the power of conscious thought, could rearrange his world thus?)

The yellow that has pulled the eye to the vase now must coax it deep within matter if it is to be understood in its new role. I take the plunge, and as I break the surface, a whole new world appears before my eyes. My first impression of this world of uranium is that it isn't very different from the world of graphite: the same essential emptiness, the same concentration of mass in nuclei orbited by electrons, the same immensity of members, for just as a corner of our universe is filled with billions of stars, so a cubic inch of uranium is filled with countless billions of nuclei (thus making it solid on our scale). But the uranium is up to much more than graphite's game of billiards with errant neutrons. When I take a good look at the nucleus, I see not a single mass but a cluster of particles, 238 tiny marbles, all of about the same mass but with 92 carrying a positive electrical charge (protons), the remainder no charge (neutrons). The 92 negatively charged electrons orbit the nucleus to balance off the positive charges. Had I undressed the nucleus of the graphite atom, I would have seen a far simpler picture: 6 protons, 6 neutrons, orbited by 6 electrons. At first, with the light elements such as graphite, one neutron per proton is enough to keep peace in the family and prevent the positively charged protons from repelling one another. But by the time uranium is reached—the heaviest of the naturally occurring elements—146 neutrons are packed with 92 protons in an uneasy truce.

Until 1932, uranium, constituting about 4 parts per million in the earth's crust (⅓ ounce per average cubic yard), was sought only as a colorant of glass. As the last in a long line of elements—the ragged end of nature's ingenuity at keeping its building blocks together—it coped admirably well with its internal problems, with only a few tired nuclei giving up the fight and decaying into elements with a more stable assemblage of particles.

What then brought about the change? As usual, it was a man in a room somewhere, doing his thing, in this case a Mr. Chadwick in England who discovered the neutron by correctly identifying the nature of a previously puzzling radiation. In the depression year of 1932, three other men in another room somewhere discovered deuterium, a heavy form of hydrogen that is an ingredient of the hydrogen bomb (the bomb stuff is said to be lithium deuteride). Had society known what was cooking while it fretted about the gold standard, a few additional souls would undoubtedly have taken the plunge. (What were you doing in those moments of discovery? I was probably sitting near the newel post in our house on Penrose Avenue, listening to the voices from the kitchen, ". . . and Mr. Mueller says he may have to let me go.")

It took some years, though, for the discovery of the neutron to threaten uranium's peace and quiet to any significant extent. Men (and a few women) around the world bombarded all sorts of elements with this new projectile which was particularly effective in producing nuclear change because, being uncharged, it is not repelled by electrical forces. And in 1934 Enrico Fermi bombarded uranium. "Very interesting, very interesting—but puzzling!"

Finally in late 1938 Hahn and Strassmann in Germany discovered that barium was produced by neutron bombardment of uranium, and Hahn immediately communicated the details in a letter to his former close collaborator, Lise Meitner, who had fled to the safety of Sweden only months before. It is she who, at the age of sixty, took the bold intuitive leap and guessed that the absorption of a neutron by a uranium nucleus sometimes causes that nucleus to split into two approximately equal parts with the release of enormous quantities of energy, a process she called nuclear fission. The key words in the drama had been articulated and the sentence was quickly completed in laboratories around the world.

It is not too difficult to imagine what her moment of creation might have been like: a mind, filled with a lifetime's work in the nuclear field, poring over Hahn's letter, many old hookups coming into play, a few new ones. One fact stands out, and the mind plays with it—barium, its mass a little more than half that of uranium, half . . . half . . . split. . . . What if the uranium atom was split in half? Could it be? Would it square with the facts?

For a moment there must have been breathless surprise, perhaps not unlike that of a boy who makes a running leap across a brook and finds his feet firmly planted on the other bank, not ankle-deep in water. Quickly, her mind must have cast around for a model of fission, an attempt to see what was happening and its consequences. What was the first sketch like? It must have contained elements of size and complexity, the packing of the uranium nucleus with its 238 separate particles, vulnerable to any disturbance, like a large drop of water whose surface tension is hardly able to hold it together. And then the last straw: one more neutron sinks itself into the assemblage, and a split occurs.

Cosmic instinct must prevail as the particles regroup themselves, a choosing of sides as it were, a quest for stability that rivals in intensity man's quest for certainty. The short-range forces of attraction between the two new groups is overwhelmed by the force of repulsion of the large positive charge each carries, and they fly apart with enormous energy. The energy released in the process is calculated from Einstein's famous $E = mc^2$ (energy is equivalent to mass times the square of the velocity of light). A prominent member of one of the new groups (fission fragments) is Hahn's barium. And since proportionately fewer neutrons are needed in the nuclei of lighter elements, several neutrons find themselves on the loose, left over, as if the process had been, for them, a game of musical chairs.

Interesting. It looks as though fission may produce more of the neutrons that produced it in the first place, and then . . . and then . . . the mind boggles. If each neutron produces a fission, which produces several more neutrons, which . . . and the time between generations is a few millionths of a second, in just one second. . . !

All of the uranium in the earth's crust must have given a cosmic shudder as it sensed the lady's thoughts. It was now only a matter of time before it would find itself in increasing amounts in man's matrix of black.

But why not in nature? Why doesn't uranium fission in nature and create a chain reaction in itself, one asks. There are always a few stray neutrons around.

Why not, indeed!

All during 1939, discovery after discovery was reported. The word "breakthrough" has become overused in describing such a scientific event because of the success with which it evokes the feeling of flow, of heightened activity, that follows the original act. Men measured, counted, figured, pondered. They determined that between two and three new neutrons were produced per uranium fission. Earlier in the thirties they had discovered that the nuclei of all elements have a tendency to absorb neutrons in a nonfission process, called parasitic capture, as well as a tendency to scattering them (the bullet disappearing in the water as against ricocheting off the surface); that some, like boron and cadmium, are real neutron eaters, and a neutron in their midst has little chance of escaping; that in others, like graphite, the probability of scattering is vastly greater than the probability of parasitic capture. These probabilities were called "cross sections"—the scattering cross section of graphite, the parasitic capture cross section of boron—and, with the dry humor that often creeps into scientific endeavor, measured in units later called "barns," "that area a poor marksman would have difficulty in hitting."

It must have been clear very early that a chain reaction could not occur in uranium ore. With such a tight budget—2 to 3 new neutrons per fission—and the requirement that at least one survive to produce a new fission (the requirement of a stable population, for example, that each father on the average have at least one son who himself becomes a father), the overwhelming probability was that parasitic capture by impurities in the ore and escape of neutrons from the surface, never to return, would eat up all the neutrons. What about a large chunk of pure uranium, though? The question was answered by a single fact as the avalanche of measurements continued: uranium itself has a parasitic capture cross section that is especially large at certain neutron speeds, almost amounting to a crevasse into which neutrons fall without producing fission. Calculations showed that even a block of pure metal of infinite size would not meet the tight neutron budget.

The end of the road? But natural uranium consists of 99.3 percent of U-238 and 0.7 percent of a lighter isotope U-235, which is identical except for the absence of 3 neutrons. It was found that the U-238 has the affinity for parasitic capture, that U-235 is much more likely to fission—in fact, that it fissions beautifully on a diet of slow neutrons.

It is at this moment, based on this single fact—the great probability of U-235 fission with slow neutrons—that I see a picture forming, a supremely beautiful blending of yellow and black. For I see an artist at work. "Is it possible," he asks himself, "to return enough neutrons to lumps of uranium as slow neutrons by embedding them in a special matrix, call it a moderator, to sustain a chain reaction?" His mind is reaching, trying to round out the edges of his thought. "What would the properties of the moderator be—low parasitic capture, high elastic scattering—to slow the neutrons down? What would be the ideal size and spacing of the lumps to maximize the escape of the neutrons at the speeds when they are most likely to be captured parasitically by the U-238 so that it is highly probable they will wander back in as slow neutrons and cause fission? How large would the whole pile have to be so that the number of neutrons staying in it (a volume effect) is sufficiently large compared to those escaping from it (a surface effect) to sustain a chain reaction?"

Some such line of thought, itself a chain reaction from a fact tossed into a mind with sufficiently low parasitic capture and surface leakage, preceded the conception of the graphite-moderated pile. Enrico Fermi is the man generally credited as the artist.

What could tell man more about the qualities that distinguish him from all else than this picture of yellow and black? A handful of neutrons are tossed into the inky blackness, and as they find their way to the yellow, some cause fission and several more of their kind are ejected, like bright stars from a Fourth of July rocket. In a twinkling they spread throughout the black, colliding with graphite nuclei an average of 200 times before they reach the yellow, just slow enough to be captured by the U-235 in fission.

Every fraction of a second one becomes more than one, and the total number of neutrons increases to the pile's power limit, and the boron control rods move in on the scene, soaking up just enough that now one becomes exactly one and the population goes joyously on its way, reproducing exactly itself each generation. But in it all lies man's mind—not changing anything, for the neutrons, the atoms all do what they are born to do, there's no changing that. Things are just rearranged so that the yellow is lumped in the black at just the right place in the neutrons' short lives. . . .

As Roger and I drove away from X-10, on our way to Y-12 and the sunset on Outer Drive, I recalled with a shock of recognition Professor Templeman's favorite line from Horace: "The inky night has precipitated in the sky, and the sleeping stars have awakened."

7

Oak Ridge

By the end of my first week at Oak Ridge, all the hopes that had been building in me in the long months following my spring visit had been realized. Work was not work but a fenced-in playpen where atomic secrets were the jack-in-the-box. And my project seemed the most exciting of all: to design a nuclear propelled rocket capable of orbiting a 10,000-pound payload (a figure spoken of in hushed tones as the weight of an atomic bomb).

Come Saturday night, and there was a plutonium punch party in the living room of the Stud Farm, a sizable crowd of men and women, mostly under forty, with whom I immediately felt at home in a way I had never experienced before.

Plutonium punch, I should explain, was an eerie green concoction in a large glass vat, gurgling with white puffy bubbles of dry ice to simulate the boiling water reactor on which one of our hosts was working during his more serious hours. On my first visit to the punch bowl, Lilly, our only female physicist, was describing the fruit fly experiments at X-10, in which successive generations of offspring from irradiated parents are watched for mutations in search of an insight into the effects of radiation on future generations of humans. Two heads, no legs, one eye. . . .

Now, as I approached the bowl for a refill, I heard her say with considerable emotion, "Why, it takes the fuzz right off your balls." Had I been the English butler of the movies, I would have spilled my drink down somebody's back. As it was, my free arm moved involuntarily toward my groin at the thought of the terrible invisible rays. "But think of the difference in upkeep over the clay courts," said Roger.

In my absence the subject had changed from fruit flies to the new municipal tennis courts surfaced with asphalt.

This pervasiveness of things atomic, even in cocktail talk, gave a unity to life in Oak Ridge such as is probably felt by people on an Army base or in a space city like Huntsville, Alabama. Seldom for a moment could you forget the purpose of the place. Like the green of the plutonium punch. Or the ditty sung at parties, ending in "getting more miles to the gallium" when this relatively rare metal in liquid form was being considered to carry the heat out of the airplane's reactor ("pile") into its turbojets. And fences, always the fences. And the long, swaying whip antennas. And liquor confiscated at the gates (although it was successfully smuggled in from the liquor store in nearby Clinton and freely available at parties). The origin of the place, too, was suggested by the "Moontinies" and "Moonhattans" served by Jean, who could trace her birthplace to the surrounding hills where a jug of "white lightning" could still be bought.

"This is black rain," explained Al, one of our metallurgists. "It fell where the shot tower had been at Alamagordo."

What could be more historic, I thought, as I rotated the small glassy black bead flecked with faint yellow between my fingers, and I immediately wanted to possess it. I knew that Al had been at Los Alamos and had had a part in fashioning the first atomic bombs. But now, as he showed me his little globules of treasure in his living room after the party, I was incredulous.

"Right from the atomic cloud? These are from the first atomic cloud?"

"Yes, the fireball vaporized the tower and the bomb casing, of course, and a lot of the sand beneath it. When the mixture of vapors reached the stratosphere and cooled down, it coalesced into many thousands of these beads which became spherical as they hardened during their fall to earth. A friend of mine was in the lead-shielded tank that went in soon after the blast to collect samples, and he found the black rain, as it was named, all over the desert floor."

"Aren't they still hot?"

"I had them in a lead box for several years until the hard radiation decayed. They still emit alpha and will for many years, but the glass vial they're in absorbs that."

"I'll trade you one of my arrowheads for one of them," I said impulsively, in a tone even one so young as twenty-one finds embarrassing the moment the words are spoken.

But the words were the right ones. Without consciously remembering Al's interest in my collection of arrowheads, I had gone straight to the one thing that would pry the treasure loose.

"Bring your collection over some day," he suggested.

"The white one there—may I see the white one again," he said a few days later.

I handed him the arrowhead, my best one, white as new snow, chipped out of stone to a perfection that only pleasure in the making could have sought. It was absolutely symmetrical about its long axis and in a class apart from the other dozen or so gray flints whose makers had been satisfied with a point and the semblance of a shank that could be slipped into a notched shaft and bound with gut. My Uncle John had given it to me.

"I'll trade you for the white one," Al said.

"How about any two of the others?"

"No, the white one."

"Well, okay," I agreed reluctantly.

Neither Al nor I was aware then, as we exchanged these pieces of the earth's crust—both perhaps from the very same desert—of the irony of it all. The one artifact so much a product of man's hands, the other so much a product of his mind, although who's to say that the intuitive leap involved was in any way less exciting, or less typical of man's unique intellect, in one instance than in the other.

As the months passed, though, I discovered that the uniqueness of Oak Ridge extended far beyond these ever-present manifestations of the purpose of the city, symbolized forever in man's mind by the white mushroom cloud. It extended to the city's bones, in fact, to its very marrow.

Never before had a modern city, with all its needs and services, been built from scratch in open countryside. (Only now, with the problems of megalopolis pressing upon us, do we hear of plans for similar cities, far from present population centers, cities that are systems engineered for living, like a balanced aquarium.) At the heart of the system was the Roane-Anderson Company, organized to provide community services to the roughly 75,000 people in

Oak Ridge, and its name became as important to the average citizen as the word "mother" is to a child. As well as operating the free bus service (at its peak, the transit operation was the nation's seventh largest), the seventeen cafeterias, and a cold-storage plant, Roane-Anderson ran all the railroad facilities in the city limits, a million-dollar-a-year laundry business, and a maid service employing more than five hundred women. The company was also responsible for maintaining and renting the roughly 35,000 dwellings in the city, operating the hotel, purchasing the hospital's supplies, paying the police and firemen, bringing in operators of department stores, shoe shops, groceries, banks, and dry cleaners, maintaining the three hundred miles of roads in the city and out to the plants, the schools, public buildings, water supply, electric system, and steam and sewage plants, and supervising garbage collection and disposal.

And, as might be imagined, this dependency on a single agency evoked the kinds of feelings a citizen in a socialist country might perhaps harbor toward the central government. Housing, for instance, available at an artificially low monthly rental, was supposedly allocated according to family size but was subject to the jockeying and influence that creeps in when ability to pay is not a criterion. My tentative analogy between socialism and life at Oak Ridge, however, quickly falls apart as I begin to pursue it, simply because I don't believe a socialist ever had it so good. Imagine a new city with a new high school whose size and equipment were determined solely by the per pupil optimums from the latest government survey—and police and fire departments similarly structured. Imagine a city with streets named and laid out in a logical fashion, a city with its stores located in several conveniently located shopping and recreation centers (a new concept in those days). Until the outer fence came down in the spring of 1949, there could be no house-to-house salesmen, no surprise visits by relatives. Nor was there poverty, or begging on the street corner.

This, then, was the city in which I first took my place among men, a city which itself had stepped out into the world but a few years before and was perhaps an indication of the future the technologists are even now projecting. My Oak Ridge experience might well have led me in the direction of technological omniscience—neat, controllable objects that can be made to work as planned, swarms of particles that need only the slightest adjustment of a boron rod to bring their population in exact balance—a milieu in which man can play God and decree with the turn of a knob that equilibrium, not growth, is what is now desired, that henceforth it shall be that births shall exactly equal deaths.

It was not destined to be so with me. From the day I arrived in the fall of 1947 to my departure in the spring of 1951, Oak Ridge, for me, was people and a seeking after self-development and self-knowledge that became compulsive in its intensity, however haphazard in its diversity. This is not to claim precocity and say that I experienced the insight that comes to some men later in life. Not at all. I see too much seeking after glory and advantage in my actions to make this claim, and susceptibility to outside influences. Still, in my little scheme of things I believe these were vintage years because they had that density and quality of "packing" that distinguish certain periods of life; life normally proceeds by fits and starts, seeming now to explode when a critical junction is reached, now to dawdle, or simply to be playing out a bad hand.

One reason for this phenomenon of packing is the generosity of older men toward a young man who seems to have possibilities. The slightest show of honest effort and initiative, and he becomes a lightning rod of all the bits and pieces of "If I had to do it over again" that may seem sentimental but springs from the deep well of man's desire to pass a bit of himself along.

All of which seems a rather pretentious introduction to the fact that I became a shoe salesman in my spare time. Shoes, the symbol of my alienation from the gang at Penrose Avenue, became my bridge to the people of Tennessee.

It all started with an invitation from the girl I

had dated steadily during my last two years at M.I.T. to visit her at the winter home of her uncle, who was president and principal stockholder of the Barron Shoe Company. What a pleasure when I received her letter and realized I would be taking my first long drive in my Ford convertible. Now the long weekend was already drawing to a close, and I stood staring at the schooling mullet in the canal behind the Barron house, trying to distract myself from thoughts of the long nonstop drive from Fort Lauderdale to the ice and snow of Oak Ridge.

"I'm sorry I've been so busy while you've been here," said Mr. Barron, as he walked across the lawn toward the collection of beach chairs on the small dock. "Maybe we can get in a few words while the girls are preparing for lunch" (the "girls" being his wife and niece). The sun blister on his lower lip emphasized its natural overhang, and this, together with his portliness, suggested Charles Laughton striding the deck.

I had always enjoyed my talks with Mr. Barron those last years at M.I.T.—listening to his stories of how he came from the west coast where he bossed a track maintenance gang to how he came to start the shoe company. "All you have to do is make a quality product and sell it properly," he would say. I suppose what I liked in him, though, aside from my awe of him as the first millionaire and company president I had ever known, was his interest in my education. "Now don't let money influence your decision," he had said when graduate study became a possibility. "I'll lend you some if you don't get the staff appointment." He was like many self-made men who, while they play up the "school of hard knocks," have a hankering after education and are intrigued by the possibilities if the two could somehow be combined.

This day he had spent most of his time indoors making what seemed to be a mosaic out of small rectangles of cardboard on the dining room table.

"What were you doing with the cardboard, Mr. Barron?" I asked as we sat down.

"I'm trying to work out a new inventory system for my warehouse."

"Do presidents do that?"

"They may not in General Motors, but they do in my company. The president of a small company has to be involved in all phases of the operation. What I was doing might seem like child's play, but it makes the difference of the few pennies that keep us ahead of our competition. Which reminds me, I've been thinking a little selling might be good experience for a young fellah like you who's all tied up in theory. Ever done any selling?"

"I sold milk shakes and things in a drugstore."

"I mean selling, where you go out and develop your market, meet the people. Magazines, newspapers?"

"No."

"Tell you what. I checked our records this fall and found we have no authorized representative in Oak Ridge and the surrounding towns—nearest is Knoxville. Would you like to be our representative in your spare time?"

"But how will I know how to. . . ."

"Fit shoes? That's easy. I've written a book on the scientific fitting of shoes that will make you an expert. And the selling. . . . All of our shoes, you know, are sold door to door, and they practically sell themselves, what with our values and features: they have special arches and metatarsal pads for that extra comfort. The deposit is your commission; the balance is paid on delivery from the factory."

"How much is the commission?"

"That's good, young fellah. You have an eye for money! It's $1.50 on our $9.00 oil- and grease-resistant shoe, but then they sell like hotcakes at garages. Other lines carry a higher commission: $3.00 on our $12.00 dress shoe."

"Say, if I could sell two dozen pairs a week," I exclaimed in a sudden dream of avarice, "I could make as much as I make working on my nuclear rocket."

"Look my boy, you get in with the safety director at the plants with our special safety toe shoe, and you'll make more money than you ever dreamed of."

I never made it that big; for one thing a salesman with a black suitcase in each hand would not have been welcome at the Oak Ridge plants, even if he could obtain the separate clearances. But I did learn a lot and made some money, too.

At first I was embarrassed to sell to my friends (except Don Kendrick, who heard about the shoes and insisted on buying a pair). Instead I drove to the surrounding towns, cruising country roads, looking for houses the way pilots flew down railroad tracks during the war, seeking targets of opportunity.

One hot, dusty Saturday I drove along Outer Drive, top down, marveling at the beauty of the Cumberland Mountains in the distance, and then turned down the hillside, showed my pass at the perimeter gate, and was on my way to Oliver Springs. After entering the town—a filling station, feedstore, and several other buildings—I turned left up a dirt road. No one answered the first farmhouse door I knocked at, although I heard rustling around inside. I trudged back to the car, irritated, because the big suitcases—one filled with samples of each style of men's shoes, the other ladies'—were heavy and difficult to get in and out of the back seat of my coupe which was now covered with a thin layer of dust. A little farther down the road I came to a beaten-up truck parked next to a path that led into the trees up the hillside. A man and a boy were standing in the open back of the truck, stripped to the waist, pouring a foul-smelling mixture of what looked like liquid garbage from a large barrel into a smaller one.

"Can I talk to you about some new shoes?" I said. "I'm selling shoes."

"Naw," replied the man, as the boy stared ahead blankly, enjoying his respite. "We're fixin' to slop the hawgs, but you can talk to my ole lady up yonder, iffin you want to."

I stumbled up the path, picking my way through clucking chickens who looked as if they had backed into a fire someplace, wishing I had dressed more informally. The house, a one-room, weather-beaten wood cabin with corrugated iron roof, was in a clearing heavy with the smell of chicken shit. There was no doorstep, just a sill and a battered door almost two feet off the ground. Carefully placing the suitcases on either side of me, I knocked. A surprisingly young-looking woman appeared, framed in the doorway, her belly seeming about to explode in my face under the feed-sack dress. Several little faces peered out from behind her dress.

"Ma'am, can I take a little of your time to show you some shoes, I'm a salesman for a wonderful line of ladies' shoes."

"Lawdie no!" she said, breaking into a gale of laughter. "Don't you know it's not shoe-wearin' time, young fellah," and to prove her point, she wiggled the toes of her feet as they hung just over the sill. "You come back in October when it's shoe-wearin' time again, and maybe we can do some business," she added, perhaps in reaction to the look of disappointment on my face.

In the following weeks, after several such encounters, I attempted to define my market more closely and finally settled on filling stations, the nurses' dormitory, and the main bus depot on Friday night. As Mr. Barron had predicted, the oil-resistant feature sold like hot cakes. And (if I can be guilty of flattering myself for a moment) the nurses seemed to like me fooling around their feet. The bus drivers are harder to explain. Even though they sit most of the day, I found they were very precious about their feet and complained of many ailments, once the subject had been raised. Maybe it was just a way to spend a little money on themselves after a hard week's work when, paycheck in hand, they encountered me and my suitcases in the drivers' lounge—something a little personal, a little chitchat before going home, perhaps making up for the absence of the local bar. At any rate, after the first few adventurous souls bought, and found the shoes were delivered quickly and in fact did feel better, I sold as many as a dozen pairs on a good night, with the men clustered around while I took sizes with my scientific measuring rule and filled out order blanks.

Had I not been preoccupied with the smells and other distractions, I might have reflected on man's preoccupation with his feet. People feel very special about their shoes, and when your attention is drawn to a lot of them, you see no two pairs quite alike. Seeing a particular collection of leather at the end of some hairy leg, I wondered about the first near-human who had tied something around his foot (or hind leg?), maybe like a bootie, and smiled with self-satisfaction as he hobbled across the rough floor of his cave.

I might have been more aware, I suppose, of the change in my concept of selling from the anybody-may-buy-anything approach that more than hints at a cult of personality to a strategy of identifying natural buying groups. Even then, though, I believe I was aware of what I enjoyed in selling: the feeling of trust implicit in the relationship, the realization that you are being taken at your word, and the knowledge that you would complete the circle.

Increasingly, as the months passed and the novelty of atomic secrets wore off, I looked forward to my selling hours. Here was something I could get to move on my own, where progress was directly related to my own efforts. In short, I was beginning to feel frustrated with my work at Oak Ridge.

This frustration had a number of aspects, one of which was realized by most of us who had been on the project any length of time: in our hearts we knew that the development of a nuclear airplane should not have been started in the first place. Not that anyone was dismayed at the magnitude of the technical challenge—why else had they come? It was as true then as it is today that, given the time and money, a flyable nuclear airplane could be developed. The fact is, though, that producing such a plane would be something like making love standing up in a canoe; aside from a certain element of virtuosity, the same results can be achieved with far more ease (and safety) in a number of ways. But there was a devilish plausibility about the idea of the nuclear airplane that allowed it to survive for many years.

The concept of a plane of unlimited range was a powerful one, especially in the years immediately following a world war in which range had been critical, and easily captured the imagination of the Air Force. At the beginning of the frequent briefings of visitors from the Pentagon, our general manager would address the gathering in the spirit of management everywhere, catching the purpose of the moment with one deft sweep of the net.

"Gentlemen, our boys here are to show you, step by step, the feasibility of a plane of unlimited range," he would say, "a plane that can take off from a base safely within our country and deliver the bomb to any point on earth, over any route. Imagine the element of surprise!"

"Any point on earth" was a euphemism for "any point in Russia." Those were still the days, difficult to remember now, when the thought of "delivering" the bomb to Russia—"delivery" sounds so innocent, doesn't it, like groceries?—was not expressed in print or conversation, not even on our project.

However, at the end of one particular introduction, the manager was carried away by his enthusiasm. "Gentlemen, what we're really talking about here today is a plane that can go in and kick the Russians in the balls!" he said, ending with a self-conscious half jab of his right hand.

In spite of his enthusiasm, the nuclear airplane was destined for the same evolutionary dead end as nature's experiments that develop a capability the new environment no longer requires. Overseas bases won in the war were retained, and new leases were negotiated. The B-52 was conceived. Midair refueling techniques were perfected.

From this point on, the program was the victim of feelings of hopelessness counterbalanced by that constant contrivance, invention, and justification that bedevil the individual conscience when, in neurotic conflict, it pursues a course of action for which it knows there is no suitable outcome. When it was learned that range in fact would be limited not by the power plant's consumption of fuel but by the crew's tolerance to radiation, even with the best of shielding, the emphasis was focused on other mission capabilities, such as high-speed flight at treetop levels (prohibitively wasteful of fuel in conventional jets) to utilize the factor of stealth that was so envied in the nuclear submarine. Each new mission was just plausible enough.

Not everyone was frustrated though. Some, with the bureaucrats' sense of the indestructible, happily plotted uranium investment versus turbine pressure ratios. Others, with the zest of those who make their profit on the trade, be it good or bad, busily mined the depths of material technology as they experimentally determined the modulus of elasticity of beryllium carbide at 4,000 degrees Fahrenheit, or the heat transfer coefficients of liquid bismuth, with only the pigeons high in the girders of the old S-50 building to disturb their delicate instruments.

But there was a special frustration about working on the nuclear rocket, since it received about as much attention from management as the archery team in a college big on football. And this, despite the fact that unlike the airplane there was indeed promise of a suitable outcome—not for military applications but for interplanetary travel. That was the rub. The military was not interested in interplanetary travel.

Fortunately, there were other things in addition to selling shoes that gave a sense of movement to my days. Here again, someone had an idea of what was good for me, this time my Uncle Nathan (actually, my mother's paternal uncle).

"Never lose touch with pee-pul," he cautioned me, as I sat in his office during my Christmas visit home, telling him about my work at Oak Ridge.

Uncle Nathan had always impressed me as being a happy man. "Play your thrumbone, will you Uncle Nathan?" I would plead as a child, until he would assemble his slide trombone from its black case and delight me with its slinky sounds. There were moments when I had my doubts, though. Whenever the family got together he insisted on scary talk about some burial plot he had someplace with just so many places in it, and it was always a question of who would go where. I suppose this was natural enough for a man who felt he was the backbone of a family, many of whom had acted like wayward sheep. Certainly he was a successful man. Starting with no more education than the rest of the family, he had studied engineering in night school and developed a thriving business on his own. "Your Uncle Nathan has made something of his life," my mother said.

Now, in his office, he continued, "I always try to include something for other pee-pul in my life, like my work for the blind with the Lions."

"Lions?"

"Yes, the Lions Club. Certainly you've heard of it." (All I could think of was Mr. Warren's green-and-white-striped blazer and something about the Cedars of Lebanon that never made sense to me.)

"Do you have any plans for lunch?" he asked. "No? Well, then come with me to the Lions Club luncheon. Maybe you'll decide you want to join the Oak Ridge chapter."

It was at the luncheon, in a setting of apparent high purpose laced with mindless good fellowship, that I first became aware of the pleasure and advantage of mingling with others, that peculiar threading of one's way among strangers with only the occasional inner question, quickly suppressed, of why, what am I doing here with my life? "George was a good mingler," says the bereaved widow. "Everybody thought the world of him." Who's everybody?

When Uncle Nathan stood up and introduced me, I decided I wanted to be a Lion if they would let me in.

"My guest today is my niece's son Junior, who got his master's degree from M.I.T. I gave him his first slide rule, didn't I, Junior?" he said looking down at me next to him at the head table. "He's doing secret atomic work for the government, and we're going to make an Oak Ridge Lion out of him."

As he sat down, he explained to me, aside, "You see that's another advantage of being a Lion. Gives you a chance to do some public speaking. And learning to speak on your feet is important."

I returned to Oak Ridge and joined and mixed

and mingled and sang in the chorus line with burnt cork on my face at the annual benefit for the blind. One of my fellow Lions sold me a life insurance policy; another, Dale Carnegie's Course in Public Speaking.

The course extended over a number of months and was given at the local high school by a scrappy little middle-aged lawyer from Knoxville who had recently entered politics. He would stride to the front of the room and, after pacing back and forth briefly, as if to demonstrate his oft-made point that a good speech was never made without the pounding of the heart the novice takes for impending disaster, would launch into an example of the evening's work, with all the smooth-working ease of a well-tooled engine cycling itself.

"I know men in the ranks, who will stay in the ranks!" he bellowed at the start of one of the first evenings. "Why? I'll tell you why"—his tone was now one of level civility as he prepared for the frenzied conclusion—"simply because they haven't the ability to get things done." The last four words were spat out like slugs that might have pierced steel.

For the next ten minutes he repeated these words (known as the "Dale Carnegie College Yell"), each time in a completely different mood, once in laughter, again with the shrugging "so vat's new" of the delicatessen waiter, always with a complete change of emphasis in words, like the poodle owner's "BAD Dog," or "Bad DOG," or "BAD DOG" (for big business on the white carpet).

Then, one by one, we went to the head of the class and tried to repeat what he had made seem so easy. At first the attempts were halting, but as we limbered up, it became fun, this letting-go before others, which most of us were experiencing for the first time. One middle-aged woman with a shrill voice from whose lips "men" became "min" seemed to take too easily to the violence of the yell, and I had the suspicion that leveraging her vocal skills was as dangerous as handing a loaded gun to a child. In sharp contrast was a sallow-faced young man, with all the enthusiasm of Digger O'Dell, whose entire motor apparatus operated as a massive filter for any emotion that might have stirred in his depths. As for myself, I found the yell a convenient way of expressing anger before people, which I have always found difficult when there is a particular target.

Warming up with the "college yell" became a regular part of the sessions, and then the instructor would cycle himself on the next subject. "I am about to introduce to you a man who . . . a man who . . . a man who . . . ," he said one evening with such sincerity and wealth of detail that the empty chair beside him seemed about to be filled by a man as much alive as a character in a Dickens novel.

Another evening was devoted to the heckling

session where the members of the audience were allowed to beat on their desks with rolled up newspapers (shades of Khrushchev), walk out, anything except touch the speaker. I found the fellow who nonchalantly picked his nose all through my speech the most disconcerting.

There were evenings of extemporaneous speaking, too, when we stood before the class and were required to speak for exactly two minutes on any subject that popped into the instructor's head. The Dale Carnegie acronym, H-PRES, was the scaffolding on which we draped our thoughts, a "Ho-Hum" (H) opener (to dispel that feeling), followed by "point (P); reason (R); example (E); and so what (S)"—a not unlikely structure followed intuitively by most speakers.

Some of the sessions were conducted by a fill-in instructor named George—George somebody—whose public speaking was enormously labored. He seemed mesmerized by technique, and it was from him I learned that if intimidated by a particularly erudite audience, I could regain my composure by visualizing them all sitting there nude, or, if temporarily speechless, could remark that the room was hot and ask that a window in the rear be opened. His well-meant suggestions made the podium sound as lethal as an airplane after the stewardess has had her say.

The first opportunity to use my new skill appeared soon after graduation and then fortunately quickly evaporated. The occasion was to be a repeat of the chief engineer's unclassified paper, "Atomic Power and Aircraft Propulsion," before an engineering society in Baltimore. Normally, such a plum would not have fallen in my lap, but I had become identified as a public speaker (having been urged by Kendrick to give a condensed version of my course at lunchtime), and Baltimore was home. But at the last minute Roger decided he would give the paper himself. The morning after his speech, papers all over the country carried the headline "Nuclear Airplane 99 percent Complete." After the secrecy of the A-Bomb, people, even high in government, were ready to believe that such a plane had been developed without their knowledge. Some in the Pentagon called for details. At the project it was as though the U-235 had hit the fan. And all because Roger had said during the question and answer period that "*analytical* work on the airplane was 99 percent complete." The word "analytical" had somehow got lost in the shuffle.

My first opportunities for public speaking came through HB, Assistant to the Chief Engineer, not in connection with work but rather for the United World Federalists of which HB was the local director. For some time both he and Kendrick had tried to interest me in world government, Kendrick espousing a first step that joined together the Atlantic nations, HB insisting on a single step to total world government including the Russians. Gradually, HB's arguments began to interest me, and sensing this, he invited me to dinner at the Stud Farm with the vice-president of the United World Federalists organization in New York, to be followed by a meeting of the local chapter.

Roger answered the door and showed me to the living room where HB was seated on the couch with a deck of cards perched on his left knee. His guest, straining forward in his chair, was asking, "But how do you make your so-called runs while you're driving?" Before he could answer, HB saw me standing in the doorway and after a brief introduction brought me into the conversation:

"My ESP is really working today," he said. "I managed to get an average of 12 hits in an 8-run series during the drive back from Knoxville this afternoon, and I've been telling our distinguished visitor something about it."

"An average of 12," I said somewhat startled, for I had become interested in the work of Doctor Rhine at Duke University—again through HB—and had read his book on extrasensory perception. I knew HB was talking about his own work with ESP cards, a deck composed of 25 cards, 5 each of the following symbols: star, rectangle, cross, circle, and wavy lines. At odd times I had seen HB stare at the deck, face down, and then turn the cards over one by one, scoring himself for a "hit" each time he correctly guessed in advance the symbol of a card—all in the fashion of Rhine's experiments on precognition, the ESP of future events. From chance alone, an average of 5 hits per run through the deck is expected. In 8 runs, the odds are 150 to 1 against an average of even 6.5 hits. But 12 hits!

"Yes, 12," HB insisted. "In one run I got 6 hits in a row."

"I still don't see how you do it while you're driving. Doesn't it take all your concentration?" his guest persisted.

"Shuffling is the difficult part, and I only do that on the straight stretches. The rest is easy. I balance the deck on my left knee, like this, with my right leg free for the gas and brakes. Then it's all a matter of staring down through the steering wheel and turning the top card over to see if I'm correct in my choice. It makes wonderful use of the time usually wasted in driving."

"Sounds dangerous to me, but the results are very interesting. What has all of this to do with world government, though?" the guest continued.

"It has everything to do with it. As long as man operates at such an abysmally low percentage of his true potential, how can we ever achieve world peace under a system of world government?"

"Now I didn't mean that." HB blurted out, as if speed would help erase what he had said. "It's just that if we were better human beings, it would be so much easier. Maybe I need some food in me. Shall we eat?"

The guest's young son, who had been playing in the yard, joined us at the table. More and more he made a nuisance of himself, banging his glass on the table, "More milk, I want more milk, daddy!" and feeding his French fries to the dog, until his father leaned over and whispered something in his ear. Whereupon he sat bolt upright and finished his meal in silence. HB, always on the prowl for occult knowledge, was visibly impressed by what must have seemed to him the exercise of great wisdom. As we left for the meeting, I overheard him say, "You certainly handled your young man well at the table. May I ask what technique you used?"

"I told him if he didn't stop, I'd knock his God-damn block off."

I saw the look that swept over HB's face, the same look I had seen a number of other times when he was confronted with the human condition. But it was a momentary reaction, and soon, as he stood before the group in the local high school, he once again radiated faith in the future of mankind as he wrote on the blackboard in large letters "V.D." and proclaimed, "This is what the world needs to make it a better place, more V.D." Only toward the end of his talk, and then by inadvertence, did he use the words "verbal discussion" instead of the U.W.F.

code words which HB in his intensity assumed were universally known.

The guest speaker's subject was "Suppose there was no cop on the corner." The argument for a supranational world government with its own standing army—the cop on the corner who prevents the chaos implicit in the question—seemed very compelling to me at the time, so compelling that I subsequently became deeply involved in the U.W.F.

It's pretty heady stuff, these moments of youth, when with one crackling surge of imagination you short-circuit the existing structure and achieve your dream of being old even before you are young. But just as today (as never before, I believe) the young are on to something beyond the subtle personal aggrandizement that is implicit in challenging the old order of things, so was there a component to my feelings (and HB's and others) that bears scrutiny. It was the feeling, perhaps born of our constant association with the heretofore impossible, that a new day had dawned, that man capable of unlocking the secrets of the atom could indeed find ways to live in peace with his fellowman if he but set his mind to it. The bomb both pointed to the need and supplied inspiration for the solution.

Young people today aren't much interested in world government. Quite the contrary. Our major argument would impress them as ludicrous. "What the hell are you talking about, man: 'Suppose there were no cop on the corner.' Why man that's heaven!" But the depth of their floating preoccupation with a better world suggests something more than my courtly minuet with U.W.F. It suggests the anxiety of the man who is finally approaching the truth that he can no longer avert his eyes from himself and in one last spasm cries out for change in all but himself, all the while pleading in his heart of hearts to be shown how to see.

Not long after I became interested in the U.W.F., Kendrick called me into his office. He told me a decision had been made at the highest level of the Air Force to terminate further work on the nuclear rocket and to concentrate all effort on the nuclear airplane. As for my future there was an immediate opening in his heat transfer group, he said, but he felt it only fair to tell me that HB wanted me as his assistant and that I would be faced with the decision of staying in engineering or going into administration.

I heard only his first words; the rest seemed unimportant at the time. "May I talk to the colonel?" I asked impulsively, reaching out, if only in my imagination, for a respite from the finality of Kendrick's words.

"Yes, if he'll see you."

The colonel was head of the Air Force group

stationed at the project and had his office next to the general manager's. He was tall, easygoing, had a neat moustache and the look of a man who might pinch a behind if given half a chance. Surprisingly, he was willing to see me.

"Sir," I began, "are you at liberty to tell me some of the factors that went into the decision to cancel the nuclear rocket project?"

"Well, it's really very simple," he replied. "There is no application for the nuclear rocket that cannot be done better several other ways."

"But Sir," I protested, "we know, on paper at least, that we can build a ten-thousand-pound-payload nuclear rocket that can hit any point on earth."

"Yes, I know, but it's the completion of this preliminary work that has forced our decision. The next stage would involve hardware and the expenditure of big money. And you know as well as I do, even with the best theoretical growth any of you have predicted for the guidance systems, the rocket would miss its target by several miles, and even with the A-bomb that just isn't good enough. The job can be done much better with a plane. And with an atomic propelled plane of unlimited range, much better still."

"But Sir," I persisted, "maybe we'll have more powerful bombs someday; maybe guidance will improve in a way we can't forecast. Anyhow, if we can make such a rocket, we should, because it would allow us to orbit, which would be the first big step to the moon."

"You never say anything about the moon as an objective in your progress reports. Not that I don't know that is what all of you have in mind. You think it is more politic to talk in terms of the military requirement. And I'm not saying that if you talked the moon instead of ballistic missiles, we'd listen to you. It's just that a moon mission didn't enter into the decision. Look, if you really feel as deeply as you seem to, if it is a commitment of the heart and not just a commitment of the head, then do something about it, if not here, then somewhere else. Maybe we're missing a great bet. But getting to the moon is not our business. Delivering a bomb on target is."

I left his office muttering something to myself about "power levers." That's it. I would seek to get closer to the power levers, and someday. . . . Without knowing it, I was about to become a has-been in the space program even before it started.

Now, twenty years later, the epic flight of the Apollo 8 astronauts in orbit of the moon has just been completed.

"Why, you have tears in your eyes," said my wife the morning of lift-off, as we watched television in the privacy of our bedroom.

"Yes, I do. I guess I'm proud."

"It's more than that."

She was right. During the final minutes of countdown, as the rocket stood deceptively still and lonely, my imagination had been captured, as never before, by the density and flow of conscious thought I was witnessing. My eyes swept the giant bird from top to bottom and visualized the structures, valves, bearings, bits and pieces of every conceivable size and shape, all embedded with grains of thought of tens of thousands of men's minds. And then, as if tuned in on some private circuit, I heard, almost felt caught up in, the orgy of data transmission, as the bird electrically felt of itself in thousands of places and in turn was poked and prodded and questioned and soothed by ground controllers. Nor were the astronauts themselves passive. Alert as chipmunks, they scanned and communicated and sent their own signals from electrodes taped to their bodies.

Momentarily, upon ignition, when the orange-white exhaust of the engines sent huge clouds of white smoke up from under the pad, my attention was captured by the sheer beauty and power of the sight. Then as the bird rose slowly through the smoke, painfully slowly at first, I began to delight in the thought of its swiveled engines dancing ever so slightly in their gimbeled mountings, delicately changing the direction of thrust upon command from the bird's brain, almost as a child's finger moves back and forth to balance a vertical lead pencil.

"Yes, there is more to it," I said, as the rocket began to slant from vertical seeking its programmed trajectory. "It's the interaction of all those men's minds out there, the density, the packing of it all. I think it's the most human thing I've ever seen."

Three days later, on Christmas Eve, my wife and I watched the pictures of the moon televised live from Apollo 8 and listened to the voices of the astronauts as they described their impressions of the surface. I was sitting on the edge of the bed, peering intently at the screen, distracted only now and again when a log in the fireplace next to me popped. And then it happened. A spark lit on the rug, and as I walked back from putting it out, through the window I saw the moon hanging in a clear sky directly over our blue spruce on the lawn lighted with Christmas bulbs. "My God," I shouted, "I never thought to look. Look out there, the moon! If you stand here you can see the moon at the same time you see the pictures of its surface and hear the voices. Think of it. Men are actually up there!"

Not until that instant did it really sink in to the point of true awareness that man had left the earth. And only then by accident, by virtue of a shock that momentarily lifted me out of myself and made me strangely aware of my relationship with television screen, moon, Christmas tree lights, burning logs—and of my oneness with all things.

Now that the mission is over, it seems to me that the silent step toward the mountaintop occurred not when men were "up there" for the first time but when the camera was unexpectedly turned back on the photographer—and the earth, all humanity, was reminded of itself for the first time through the eyes of men returning to its warmth, its color, from some other place. It is as though the mission were a drama with the homecoming the recognition scene, and the earth would never be the same again.

The earth had seen itself before—in men's imaginations, drawings, even a picture from an unmanned probe on the moon. But it was the combination of human voices with the pictures of television and the knowledge that everything was occurring in the present, in real time—you are here, they are there, now—that showed humanity to itself. This is not to say that all men were touched. The earth did not become conscious overnight, any more than man became human when life first became aware of itself and stepped silently out of the shadows. But there was a beginning, a turn.

The supreme art that moves men cannot always just happen as it did on this flight. Artists, poets, philosophers, writers, theologians will all one day journey into space to render their experience for their fellowmen. It is even possible that a painter or sculptor, cradled in space in the warmth and safety of a machine that is so obviously the embodiment of men's minds, will come to see the machines as friends and be moved to show man the human content of technology here on earth. Rather than hang a tire atop a twisted mass of axles and I beams in an act of rage and ridicule, he will be moved to show what it is about the common tire and the minds that live in it that allows it to serve man.

As Rheinhold Niebuhr has said, "If the self-centered self is shattered by a genuine awareness of its situation, there is a power of a new life in the experience." Might not the space experience prove to be truly a shattering of the world self, thus enabling mankind to take a quantum jump to a new level of existence and a new set of values?

Or are we to continue profoundly unaware of our situation, relating everything to our narrow self-interest? I wonder—particularly when I recall the attitude of a fellow club member upon the return of Apollo 8.

I was sitting alone in the large room just off the entrance of the club, the room to which television is banished. Just as Borman, Lovell, and Anders were stepping out of the helicopter onto the deck of the *Yorktown,* he rushed into the room and, hat and coat still on, asked, "How far did they land from the carrier?" I looked behind me and saw a large, vigorous man, the type to whom time was obviously precious.

"The announcer says less than three miles," I replied.

"What fantastic accuracy! All that distance, and a miss by less than three miles! Why, that's well within the H-bomb's circle of destruction. You can bet that's what the Russians have their eye on today. Think of how accurate our missiles must be," he concluded sternly, and rushed off without another word, the total significance of Apollo 8 now stored in his personal computer for frequent instant replay.

His comments brought back to mind my meeting with the colonel in Oak Ridge. The decision to cancel the nuclear rocket program was correct (for the Air Force) even if for the wrong reasons. When the development of the H-bomb and accurate guidance systems assured the success of a ballistic missile, it was found that chemical propellants could adequately do the job. Nor was nuclear propulsion necessary to reach the moon, as Apollo 8 dramatically proved. Still, it has a place; at present it is the only feasible final stage propulsion for manned missions into deep space, say, Mars or Venus, and for this reason the program was started again in the late 1950s. On the other hand, work on the nuclear airplane was stopped (after the expenditure of one billion dollars) by President Kennedy shortly after he came to office.

I have a final feeling about my meeting with the colonel—a feeling of wistfulness—heightened somewhat by the fact that what I tell of it in this chapter was completed just minutes before Apollo 8 was approved for translunar injection out of earth orbit (a chance happening that HB would profess to understand).

"I have a new job now," I wrote to my mother after my interview with the colonel. "I'm on the right road. I'm Assistant to the Assistant Chief Engineer. I don't do much actual engineering anymore; it's an executive position. I have to interview people for work, see that everybody is kept happy in the company, help write the monthly report for the project, and see that nobody is doing anything that isn't in line with the project. I have an office and a phone with lots of buttons on it—I'm an administrative engineer."

Careful now. A man must deal gently with those moments in life when he has made his choice, or thinks he has, whereas in truth his choice makes him—those moments that roll off the young man with the ease of water from a feather as he gathered about himself the stuff of the will, confident he can do, if not one way, then another, and quite unaware of the extent to which outside influences continue to motivate him.

8

Alex

". . . follow the fellow, follow the fe-el-low, follow the fellow who follows a dream."

Nancy completed the song with closed eyes and a demure nod of the head as if she were on stage and anticipating the riotous applause of the audience.

"Wonderful, Nancy, hurray for the Mighty Atom," exclaimed her father, moving closer to the piano and putting his arm around her.

"Now come on Alex," said her mother, "it's late, it's time to go. Mackie and Nancy must be exhausted from that long drive up from Oak Ridge. Besides I think you've had a long evening yourself."

"Okay Mary," he said, draining the last few drops from his brandy snifter, "we were just having a little postprandial fun, weren't we Nancy?"

And then, as we all moved toward the front

door of the restaurant, he raised his index finger and said, to no one in particular, "Oh thrice, and more than thrice happy, those whom an indissoluble connection binds together."

It had been pleasant having cocktails high above the blue waters of the bay, with the white sand dunes of Sandwich in the distance still glistening in the evening sun, but I felt a little drowsy as we waited in the heavy August air for the attendant to bring the car. It had been a long drive to Cape Cod—nonstop, as a matter of fact, except for a brief visit with my mother in Baltimore. The kind of cross-country, devil-may-care, distance-eating driving that people do in their youth and never again until later in life—and then by proxy when their children take to the highway.

I had met Nancy in Oak Ridge just a few weeks after the nuclear rocket project was canceled. Hal Shipley, a balding engineer in my car pool who was noted for his inexhaustible supply of jokes and his Walter Huston manner of accompanying himself at the piano, had asked me, "How would you like to date an actress friend of ours at a party we're giving for her Saturday night?"

"Would I!"

"Then why don't you drop over Saturday afternoon to meet her?"

She was seated at the piano playing "Clair de Lune" as Hal showed me into the living room. It was a brief visit but long enough to determine that she had just finished summer stock in Arden, Delaware, would be leaving the Shipleys after a week for a visit with her parents, and was about my age.

Before the week was out, we were engaged.

"He's not an actor, is he?" her father had asked when she telephoned him from Baltimore to say she was bringing somebody very special home with her.

"No, he's an engineer."

Now, as she and I sat alone on the screened porch of her parents' summerhouse overlooking the beach at West Dennis, I asked, "What were you and your father talking about so seriously during dinner?"

"I told him we were planning to be married next June on my birthday. I hadn't intended to tell him so soon—it just seemed so natural after we got talking about you."

"What did he say?"

"I told him you had just started to work and don't have much money, but he said that isn't important. He said what's important is that a man has a goal, a dream, and from talking with you just a short time, he feels you do. He likes you."

The next morning, before breakfast, I found her father on the porch swaying back and forth slowly on the swinging sofa, reading the *Wall Street Journal*. I sat down next to him.

"Sleep well?" he inquired and then went back to his paper.

"Yes. I love the salt air."

Silence.

As we continued to sway back and forth, I grew increasingly apprehensive, for I was perceiving him with that stripe in me, left over from childhood, that interprets another's action, or lack of it, or even tone of voice, in direct relationship to my own inner concerns of the moment.

Finally, I had to know.

"Well, next June isn't far off, is it?"

"It's almost a whole year away," he replied, matter-of-factly, after a momentary quizzical glance at me.

More swaying.

"I mean the time will pass so fast, there's so much to do, what with the arrangements and all of that."

There was a swift change of visage, the kind that is said to sweep over a banker's face at the mention of a loan.

"What arrangements?"

"Well . . . well . . . I mean our wedding and all of that."

"Wedding . . . ? Wedding?" For a long, decidedly uncomfortable moment he stared at me as if desperately trying to recall something that eluded his grasp. Then suddenly he shouted, "Mary, Mary, come here quick. There must be something I don't remember from last night."

I got out of my chair at one end of the deserted waiting room and walked over to the large forbidding swinging doors with the sign No Admittance under each of the small see-through panes of glass. "What's the matter, what's wrong," I thought as I peered into the quiet of the corridor beyond, straining for some indication of movement, some shred of evidence that something was happening in one of the two rooms on opposite sides of the corridor, both marked Delivery.

I slouched back into the chair. Then, "My God," I thought, "I haven't fed the dog all day!" I could dash back to our apartment just across the street from the hospital. But no, it had to happen soon. So I just sat there and worried a little. Not about the dog, Buffer. About money. Money is always good for a quiet worry. Soon Buffer was back in my thoughts, for it was he who had loused up my budget. "Damn his hide!" I thought of the large triplefold piece of calculation paper on which I had broken down expenses and income by the month (with a column for estimated and actual) and by type (including fixed, semifixed, and variable). At the bottom of each monthly column was a figure labeled "Net Increase in Savings" which allowed me to plot "Savings in Dollars" versus "Month" on an accompanying sheet of graph paper. A straight line sloped pleasingly, if gently, upward from $452.62 on December 31, 1949. I had viewed the completed graph with every bit as much satisfaction as I had once reserved for "Gross Rocket Weight" versus "Maximum Reactor Temperature."

But as the year unfolded and my dotted line representing actual savings drooped like a wilted stem as it edged across the months, I was dismayed. "Rent" held steady at the budgeted $35. "Household Operation" wiggled a little around $100. All the other expenses were plus a little, minus a little. "Contingency" was the culprit, for it was here that I had entered the cost of Buffer's almost weekly trips to the veterinarian for shots of the new wonder drug, Aureomycin, intended to cure his periodic attacks of coughing during which he stood in one place and hacked and wheezed and finished by quietly depositing whatever had been in his stomach on the floor in one big "Urp." "American Cockers do tend to be overbred and nervous," someone had warned me.

"Damn his hide, why did I buy him?"

The swinging doors flew open, and a nurse swept by me.

"Miss, Miss, . . ." but she continued on her way, and I was left with my imagination as I once again stood by the door, staring through the glass.

But this time there was something to see down the corridor: the doctor rushing across the hall out of one room into the other, his rubber-gloved hands held upward in front of him. What's wrong! And then, in a minute or so, he strode even more urgently back across the hall. And shortly, back again.

"Miss, Miss, what's he doing?" I pleaded, as the nurse returned. "I mean rushing from one room to another like that. Is it an emergency? Tell me!"

"Well, young fellow, now I guess he's just trying to get from one place to another."

"Sadist!" I mumbled, as she pushed her way through the doors.

Finally the doctor appeared in the corridor, this time walking slowly toward me, without his white smock, a wan look on his face, for it was well after midnight.

"Congratulations! You're the father of a baby girl. I just wish she hadn't chosen the same moment to be born as the other little girl across the hall."

On the table in front of me are several pieces of paper that have been in an envelope in my safe deposit box during most of the last nineteen years. (Do I have a mania for holding on to every scrap of the past? But why?) One is a white file card that I had tied with ribbon around Buffer's neck the day mother and daughter came home from the hospital.

On the front is a pen-and-ink sketch of a plaintive-looking cocker spaniel above which is lettered "Welcome Sarah"; on the back is the message, "Although your presence will definitely lower my prestige with the folks, I look forward to the many years of companionship we shall enjoy." Then there is another file card on which I had lettered "A Chair for Nancy and The Little Lady—From her Daddy—10/17/50" and pinned to the back of a surprise rocking chair for the homecoming.

Finally a note to myself I wrote in the vestry of The Church of The Holy Spirit on Cape Cod as my best man chatted with the minister: "At 4:30, March 10, 1949—I am about to be married. I've never been so happy and am not a bit nervous. In ten minutes my life will really begin. The wedding party has just arrived."

Were it not for these paper footprints, I would have forgotten the fervent stride with which I approached marriage and fatherhood. "Life will really begin." Yes. There is always the excitement of rebirth, of renewal, in marriage. The feeling of a fresh new start that hovers over a meadow in springtime —or a boy wending his way to school on an autumn day, a new notebook under his arm.

"A dollar for the first and a dollar for the biggest," said my father-in-law as he eased himself into the sturdy plastic-and-chrome swivel chair on the aft end of our fishing boat.

"What do you mean?" I asked, bracing myself against the roll of the deck as I prepared to sit next to him.

"You know, a little bet for the first fish and again for the biggest."

"Fish, what fish?" I thought to myself as I looked over the stern at the massive ocean swells that towered as high as a telephone pole when we were in a trough. "This is certainly no day for fishing."

Yet, when we had arrived at Miami the night before, the air was still and filled with the smell of jasmine, in sharp contrast to the biting wind in Knoxville that made Sarah's face as pink as the blanket she was wrapped in during the short walk between terminal and airplane. Even after the drive to Pompano Beach, when we all stood on the dock in front of the house before going to bed, the only movement was the powerful beam of light that flashed in our direction every twenty seconds from the tall lighthouse on Hillsboro Point, just a quarter of a mile or so away across the inlet. The palm fronds on the spit of sand that ran toward the inlet and formed Wahoo Bay directly in front of us were silent. The ocean beyond was still.

The next morning, though, I awoke to an ominous, muted roar, and when I became fully conscious of it, I lunged to the bedroom window and identified the source: a white foaming cascade of waves breaking periodically in the narrow inlet, a thundering wall of water as high as the flying bridge of most fishing boats.

"I've already called Captain Bob," said my father-in-law at breakfast, "and he says he thinks he can make it through the inlet. It won't get any worse because the tropical disturbance is far out to sea. What do you think? Still want to go?"

"Now Alex, you're a fool to go out there today."

"Mary be quiet! It's Mac's vacation. Let him decide."

As our boat milled around in Hillsboro Bay a safe distance from the inlet, I could see Alex was apprehensive. Captain Bob was on the bridge holding the bow into the angry waters flooding into the bay by a skillful manipulation of the rudder and alternate bursts of power on the port and starboard engines. A large cabin cruiser, presumably caught at sea by the storm, was on the ocean side of the curtain of water, itching to get in, and its skipper appeared to be doing the same thing as ours—studying the rhythm of the waves, their frequency, the time interval between the formation of the tumbling Niagaras of water. Several fishing boats were now milling behind us, obviously awaiting the outcome of Captain Bob's dash.

And then, during a moment when the inlet was

relatively calm, the boat at sea started a run for it, full power, like an arrow aimed for the narrow cut between the steel jetty to its left and the pile of rocks off Hillsboro light to its right. Groups of people had gathered on both banks to marvel at the fury of the ocean on an otherwise clear day. The sound now was the sound of raw diesel power.

"Jesus Christ, he timed it wrong!" shouted Captain Bob as a dark mound of water rose behind the boat and began to overtake the stern. The boat floated up, and for a moment it appeared the wave would pass under it. But No! it had started to break, and when it was amidships, it tumbled over. The bow was now pointed down and the boat, stern high, rudder and propellers momentarily out of the water, threatened to broach. And then it did, as its stern was flung to the right, and it rolled over, seemingly flat on its side. Had she capsized? Wait! No, she righted herself and rolled violently to the other side, all the while being propelled forward by the wave like a surfboard. The oscillations grew less and less. She had made it!

Alex's eyes, normally small, became downright beady as Captain Bob maneuvered into position for his run. He looked more portly than ever as he strained to reach the overhead handrail in the open cabin.

"All set!" shouted Captain Bob.

"The Lord is my shepherd," Alex said, with a

brief smile in my direction. I knew him to be a complete agnostic and the touch of humor relaxed me.

The boat shuddered as the throttles were thrown open and both propellers bit into the water against the deadweight. And then we sped forward, all eyes on the water ahead. But it was soon clear that Captain Bob's timing was flawless, and I almost felt cheated as we rode effortlessly up one side of the approaching mountain of water and down the other and watched its top curl over and thunder down astern of us in the inlet.

"What a nice thing to do," I thought, as I saw the look of relief on my host's face and realized how he had put himself out so as not to disappoint me on my first deep-sea fishing trip.

"Give Mr. MacDonald here the ballyhoo and the outrigger," he said to Captain Bob's young assistant Emil, who was now opening the bait box on the stern. "If there's a sailfish out there, I want him to have a good chance of bringing it in."

He explained a few things about deep-sea fishing. The sailfish, it seems, prefers to feed near the surface, and, instead of gulping his prey down in the initial strike, first stuns it with a sharp scissorslike motion of his long bill after a swift dash through the water. Then, turning in a sharp radius with the aid of his sail, he returns to the smaller fish and takes it. Thus it is important that the fisherman understand the nature of the first "rap" on his bait fish and immediately pay out some line behind the moving boat to make the sailfish believe he has achieved his kill. Otherwise, he is immediately suspicious. The beginner usually does nothing or else gives an immediate heave on the line. To prevent this, the line, instead of trailing directly behind from the tip of the rod, is clipped in a clothespin and hoisted like a flag to the end of one of the two outriggers that extend from the boat like the outstretched arms of a priest blessing his congregation. Then, when there is a rap, the line is pulled out of the clothespin, and the slack allows the bait to lie still whatever the novice does.

"Here, Mac, look at your bait a minute before Emil throws it over the side. See how carefully he has inserted the hook in the stomach. And how he left a stub end on this wire after attaching it to the hook, so he could push it up through the bone in the bill and neatly twist it around." (Only a young man with little confidence in his athletic prowess, who sensed in his father-in-law's attentions an implied encouragement and expectation of competence he had never dared entertain, would remember almost twenty years later the trivial details of a bait fish more clearly than many things of just yesterday.)

Yes, I could see it. All I had noticed before was that the bait itself looked like a baby sailfish, only a foot long, all silvery, with a small beak but not much of a sail. Now, I felt a twinge of excitement, the excitement of perceiving craftsmanship. But it was more than that, it was an appreciation of personal style. Things can be done one way, or they can be done another.

It was a little like the day Alex noticed me standing in the line of vision of a friend who was about to putt, and later, as we were walking to the next tee, explained that while talking was the unpardonable sin, there are many other fine points to behavior on the green that are more a matter of courtesy. Or like the time we were opening clams together, when he saw that I was cutting into the body of the clam as I moved the knife straight in between the halves of the shell, determined only to sever the muscle that was holding them tightly closed. "Try moving the tip of the knife down and around like this," he suggested, "so that you don't cut the belly. They make a much more appetizing presentation that way." "Presentation." It was important to "present" clams in a certain way. Or like the day on Cape Cod when he paused on top of a hill on the golf course and used the word "prospect" to describe the view of the Bass River in the distance. "What a lovely prospect," he said, and although I had never heard the word used in that context, it seemed so right, so fitted to the emotion of the moment. I started making lists of words that appealed to me in a similar way in my reading and looked them up in the dictionary.

My bait was now 50 feet or so behind the boat,

and I watched intently its silvery glint as it worked its way through the water just beneath the surface, fully expecting a strike from second to second. After a half hour of this red alert I thought of my earlier prognosis—"This is certainly no day for fishing"—and settled back in my chair.

Alex had taken off his shirt and seemed to be enjoying exposing his deeply tanned chest to the hot sun with no threat of his wife eyeing his bulging girth and remarking, "Alex, it's disgusting. You're getting fat!" Life had become a series of "encounters" for Alex. "How do you expect me not to gain weight, Mary, during a noble encounter like this," he said, while visiting us in Oak Ridge on the way down to Florida. "Same old story," she replied, and reminded him of all the other encounters he faced—with his friends in Florida, and again in the summer with a different group on Cape Cod, and all the stops along the way.

The sun went behind a cloud, and he removed his peaked fisherman's cap, exposing his bald head to the cooling breeze.

"What made you decide to retire when you did?" I asked, "you were only fifty, weren't you?"

"I wanted to get out while the getting was good. I was on top once before, during the twenties, and then in the thirties I lost most of what I had. I promised myself if ever again I was on top, I would get out. And I did, just before the end of the war. We liquidated our inventory of wool in complete secrecy and went out of business. You know the saying, 'Fool me once, shame on you. Fool me twice, shame on me.' And just in time, too. At the end of the war the wool market went to hell, and it's been down ever since. I would have been locked in for good."

I knew how much money meant to Alex. He never got over the sting of being poor as a child. Poverty and an early bout with tuberculosis denied him of all but a few years of formal education. From then on it must have been hustle, hustle, first as a butcher and then in the woolen mills around his native town of Lawrence, Massachusetts, where his father had settled after arriving from England. Before he was thirty he had made himself indispensable to the owner of a mill. When asked to train an assistant, he quit and went into business on his own with his father and younger brother, on Summer Street in Boston, as a wool topmaker. To hear Alex tell it, it was a tough competitive business where you bought with the attitude, "Cut your asking price in half and I'll make you an offer," and sold with at most the hope of "preference at a price."

A man might well want to quit when a business like that had served its purpose. But to a young man starting out, retirement seems so final, so connected with the end of all things.

"Have you ever been sorry you retired?" I asked.

"Not for a minute. Oh, I've had periods of depression, but then I had them before I retired too. I guess you've never seen your father-in-law during one of his spells. It's the damndest thing, Mac. When it's over, I can't imagine myself acting the way I have. For weeks on end I pace the floor, fiddling with my watch chain and thinking, always thinking. And then at night I have trouble sleeping. It must be terrible for Mary because I don't want to talk to anybody or even see anybody. This last time, just before you met Nancy, I couldn't decide whether to make an offer on the house we now own in Harwichport. But that was only part of it. I had to invest my money, and it looked as though we were headed for a depression. On the other hand, like the politicians, I knew you can't beat Santa Claus, and one way or another we were in for inflation. Everybody said, 'Buy the house, Alex, even if you pay too much. Make a decision!' Finally, I made an offer way below the asking price, and Jesus, the old lady accepted it. Then I knew for sure I overpaid, and felt worse than ever. But the indecision was over, and gradually I became my old self."

"It's hard to imagine you that way."

"I hope for everybody's sake I never have to go through it again."

"Have you always read as much as you do now?"

"Yes. Maybe that's why I never found it difficult to contemplate retirement. I've had a love affair with reading all my life. First, as a young boy, the poets, Shelley, Keats, Shakespeare. Oh, how I loved Shakespeare. 'If the truth were known, who among us would escape a thrashing!' My God, Mac, how can you beat that for expressing yourself. Then, as I grew older, and began to see what makes the clock tick, it was easy for me to educate myself in any field that seemed necessary at the moment. Why, I even remember plowing through Blackstone's *Commentaries* when I decided I should know something about the law."

What makes the clock tick? The first time I heard the phrase was just after our honeymoon trip to Cuba, when Nancy and I stopped off in Florida on our way back to Oak Ridge. Alex and I and a friend of his, Fritz, had driven to the yacht basin at Bahia Mar to look at the boats. Fritz was a tall man, considerably older than Alex, with a homely face and a charming German accent. He had emigrated to this country after serving as a sailor in the Kaiser's Navy and settled in Erie, Pennsylvania, where he worked for years as a waiter before he started an amusement park named Waldemeer. ("Ah, woods by the sea," were his first words, in German, upon being shown the tract of land on which he was to build the park, according to Fritz, who had a story for everything.) Had the two men known one another previous to their chance meeting on the beach several years before, I don't believe the friendship would have flourished, for they were entirely different by nature. As it was though, Alex was ready to be amused, and Fritz, with all his devilish ways, filled the bill.

Except, perhaps, for that day at the yacht basin. As we were leaving the main dock, he stopped and, looking back at the collection of boats, said slyly, "I'll bet der aren't many engineers represented in der, eh Alex?"

"What do you mean?" I asked hesitatingly.

"Shall ve tell him vat makes der clock tick, Alex?" he replied, in mock wonderment at my question.

"Come on, cut it out, Fritz," Alex said sharply, wanting, I realized afterward, to spare my feelings. For although I had already made the first halting steps away from engineering, I still identified myself with the profession and might be sensitive. Alex needn't have worried, although it is true that for a moment, when the implication of what Fritz had said sank in, I felt hurt. But the next instant I knew it had nothing to do with me. I had become an administrative engineer.

"Say, Fritz, I'll bet you're right. I'll bet there's not a single one of those boats owned by an engineer," I said, as if I had been cut in on some great wisdom.

What makes the clock tick? Over the next several years I learned that it was a favorite expression of Alex's, and whenever he used it, my heart skipped a beat. I would like to say it stirred the same feelings in me as the word "overview" so popular on campus today. But it's not the same thing at all. Overview implies to me a grand, lofty look at hitherto disconnected elements that have been viewed separately, a perception of the whole. This was beyond me in Oak Ridge. The shadowy world beyond my experience that gave rise to my anxiety, the world that I increasingly felt was there impinging on my ideas, dreams, ambitions, I could not see at all, much less overview. It took the magic words, first of Fritz, then of Alex, to bring it into focus.

"Speaking of what makes the clock tick," said Alex, as we continued to drag our baits over miles of ocean, "how are you coming with the Forbes Stock Market Course I sent you?"

"I'm on the next-to-last installment. Nobody on the project knows as much as I do now about the stock market.

Practically from the first day I met him and learned something of his background, I had grilled Alex at every opportunity on the subject of business and finance. At one point he suggested sending me his *Wall Street Journals* after he finished them. Then, when he found I actually read them, he gave me a subscription of my own for Christmas. This just led to more questions. "What's the futures market? Is a bond the same thing as a debenture? An irrevocable letter of credit . . . ?" Soon he was sending me *Barron's* after he was finished with it and his old copies of the *Value Line Market Survey*. Finally, after cautioning me he didn't mean to be throwing his weight around (an expression he used whenever he wanted me to know he was aware of my desire to provide for myself and thought there was something I should have I could not afford at the moment), he said he wanted to stake me to the Forbes Course.

"The advertisement for the course says it teaches you to read a balance sheet and profit-and-loss statement," Alex said. "Would you like me to send you the annual reports of a few companies I own shares in after I'm finished with them?"

"I'd like to practice beyond the tests in the course," I said. Actually, I had hated the obligatory course in economics at M.I.T., probably because business seemed like work, and I never thought of engineering as work. I thought my roommate was being a smart aleck when he would open the paper and tell me what his favorite stock, General Motors, was doing. Now suddenly it was fun to look at a balance sheet and think of all it told me about a big sprawling corporation, all there on one piece of paper and, with it, the profit-and-loss statement to show what flowed through the corporation during the year.

"It's like a thermodynamic system," I tried to explain to Alex, "almost like a heat transfer equation. I guess that's what I like about it."

"Have you run across the small tool account yet?"

"No." I thought he was serious, for I had read something about a special category of fixed asset with a useful life of under one year.

Alex laughed. "During the war, when all of us on Summer Street were subject to the excess profits tax, one of our vigorous competitors was noted for wining and dining the customers, including ladies for the night. The story was he buried this extra expense in the small tool account. But seriously, I'm tickled you are learning something about this side of life. One day soon I suppose you'll want to try your hand at picking a stock."

I didn't know what to say. Just before coming to Florida, I had sold the one hundred dollars' worth of stock in the Scudder, Stevens, and Clark Fund he had given Nancy and me as our first Christmas present and bought twenty-five shares of Packard Motor Car Company instead. For months I had plotted the price of the stock day by day on engineering graph paper, watching it get cheaper and cheaper, until it seemed to bottom out—4, $3\frac{7}{8}$, $4\frac{1}{8}$, 4—almost half of book value. All those assets! What a steal! I put in my order at 4, not a "buy at the market order," because Alex had told me, "You can usually save an eighth or more that way." The day after my order was executed, the stock jumped up half a point. Up $\frac{1}{2}$! Peanuts, on a stock priced as high as IBM. But on my five-dollar investment, an increase of over 10 percent on my money! A veritable discontinuity, I thought, as I plotted the new price on my graph and connected it to the old one, with a near vertical straight line. And then it kept moving, 5, $5\frac{1}{4}$, $5\frac{1}{2}$. My uncanny ability frightened me a little.

I decided I did not have to tell him I sold the Scudder stock. "I've already taken the plunge, I bought Packard just before it went up!"

"Well, I can see you have a predilection for the dogs," he said, smiling, but I didn't think it was funny.

"They were selling way below book and near their net quick assets value," I countered.

"The only hooker is, the automotive industry is a fast track and you can eat up a lot of net quick in a hurry. Come to think of it, I believe I read it was rumored they are going to receive a large tank contract from the government."

"When it gets to 6, I'll have made 50 percent on my money and I'm going to sell. Remember your saying 'trees never grow to the sky'?"

"My, you intend to be a real in-and-outer,

don't you? But you're learning. Remember though, even a stopped clock is right twice a day."

I had to ponder his last remark a moment.

"How are things at work? Have you decided what you are going to do?"

"They're as crazy as ever. We've been told the nuclear airplane is going to be pursued with 'renewed emphasis'! But with GE running the project, not Fairchild. As a matter of fact, a GE man has already interviewed me and said they definitely want me as part of the new team. I'm going to make the break, though. After this vacation I'm scheduled to go to Long Island for a meeting with the president of another Fairchild division. . . ."

"Which division?"

"The Stratos Division. They make aircraft pressurization and cooling equipment. It's a new field and they've made me a definite offer as a sales engineer. It's not exactly what I want, but I think I'll take it."

I was musing about the Stratos job when I heard Captain Bob's shout, "Look sharply at those baits! We may find some dolphin near that debris over there."

I could see what appeared to be a palm tree, fronds and all, floating in the water a hundred feet or so abeam of us. Alex was explaining that fish often school around flotsam, when it happened—just a slight tug on the tip of my rod, but enough for me to look up and see that my line had been pulled out of the clothespin.

Zing! The slack was gone, and the reel was now spinning out line as if propelled by some high-speed electric motor.

Zing! Almost at the same moment another zing next to me.

"Uh, uh!" remarked Alex.

"We've got two on," shouted Emil to his skipper.

I thought I would be pulled right out of my chair but decided that at all cost I had to hang on to the rod. Then, fearing that my spool of line would be exhausted any second, I started to tighten up in the friction drum in the reel.

"For God's sake, don't touch that," screamed Captain Bob from the flying bridge, "you'll break your line! Just keep the pressure on him. Don't stop winding in."

It was obvious we hadn't hooked sailfish. "A dolphin, maybe, or Spanish mackerel, or even barracuda," observed Captain Bob, "but whatever they are, they're big!"

After the fish's first run, I made a little headway as I feverishly wound the reel, leaning forward with the rod, and then pulling back—getting my back into it, as instructed by Emil.

But soon again—Zing! Whatever it was, made off with all the line I had reeled in, and more.

"How are we doing, Uncle Mac?" asked Alex, as he too wound in line with all his might.

"Okay, but my fish seems to have crossed over your line. See how they come together out there."

"That's all right," observed Emil, "just keep them coming in."

Finally, as I worked my fish toward the side of the boat, Alex's now seemed to have crossed under mine, for his line was near the stern of the boat.

"Damn!" he exclaimed, as Emil gaffed my fish, "I guess the propeller cut my line. It's slack."

But then as my fish was lifted over the side—a huge cow dolphin that later weighed in at 42 pounds—we saw two leaders running from its mouth. Evidently she had gulped down my bait and, not yet feeling the hook because of my slack, had crossed over to Alex's bait, making a meal of it, too.

"Dominus vobiscum," Alex said, "we've both caught the same fish!"

Curious how people sometimes come into one another's lives at just the right time. Take Alex and me, for example. A few years earlier I wouldn't have had the slightest interest in business. As for having him as a father, I can't think growing up with him would have been much fun; he would have been too uptight.

"Sell down to the sleeping point" was one of the maxims he quoted me in referring to people who felt themselves overcommitted in the market. In a sense this is what Alex did when he retired. He blossomed out, and his new leisure allowed him to enjoy a son-in-law as he never could have enjoyed a son. I suppose I am particularly sensitive to the element of time because now I see in my relations with my own children how much time, freedom of fear and pressure, it takes to be right there with the helpful nudge instead of thumbscrew authority.

I don't mean to imply that Alex made me a sort of retirement project. Not at all. In any complete description of him you would have to include the word "selfish." It's just that there were so many things he didn't have to do. He didn't have to make money, and I didn't have to be a success; after all, I wasn't his child, something of him wouldn't be lost if I failed.

"Hold close with open arms." We had fun together but seldom for more than several days at a time. "After two days both fish and guests stink," he would say. Being caught up in his gusto at our dinner table on family occasions was a joy I had never experienced before. Toward the end of the meal, after polishing off a thick slab of roast beef, he would sit back in his chair, his right hand wrapped firmly around his wineglass, and blink his eyes a bit (I think there were tears in them). He seemed so aware of the moment, as if he knew now was the best, and better might never come. Then, likely as not, he would be swept away into verse, and quote one of his favorites:

The Moving Finger writes; and, having writ,
Moves on: nor all your Piety nor Wit
Shall call it back to cancel half a Line, . . .

Or he would offer a toast to "Uncle Mac," or to the wine. "I can't remember her name, and I can't recall the place, but Oh! My God! The wine! It was Chambertin!"

Once, shortly after we had moved from Oak Ridge to Long Island, he came North alone—his first plane trip—to visit the bank in Boston. He stopped off in New York, and the three of us went to the old Chambord restaurant. "They're going to sock it to me, I know," he added, after explaining it was reputed to be one of the finest restaurants in the world, "but nothing is too good for Uncle Mac and the Mighty Atom." As callow as I was in such matters, I sensed our waiter was exceedingly proud of the quality of the meal he was about to serve us, and I thought I detected a pained expression on his face, as though he had been jabbed in the stomach, when Alex ordered his second martini before our filet of sole bonne femme was presented. He seemed pleased, however, at Alex's choice of wine after a discussion with the sommelier. But his spirit darkened when Alex ordered Green Chartreuse as an afterdinner drink. And he actually fled the table when presented with a request for a bottle of Tuborg as a nightcap.

Had Alex been in the least socially pretentious, I might have felt in all his help an attempt to dress me up for his friends. I can imagine my reaction to a different type of father-in-law. Both may have had the notion that anybody who's anybody at all plays a good game of golf, serves well-opened clams, makes money so that he can retire from the working life of which any true gentleman is contemptuous. But Alex operated from a different base. "Here's a young man," he seemed to be saying, "I can help to self-confidence in a milieu his intelligence is seeking."

Some years later when I got the bit in my teeth, I talked to him about my plans for coming-out parties for my daughters and my wish that they become interested in the Junior League. "Well, I don't know what to advise you, Mac," he said after patiently listening to me. "I never did it for the girls, but then you know how I feel about that sort of thing." Yes, I did know. He had a special phrase for anything that suggested snobbery—a name, a club, perhaps a resort—"than which there is no whicher."

All in all, I see something beautiful in the man, a beautiful, wonderful sensitivity. Lest I do him the injustice of suggesting perfection, though, I must add that I see now there was a lot of Babbitt in him. Strange, of the things that used to bug me, one in particular comes to mind. I can't remember a single time he ordered a meal at a restaurant without a scene. The minute the plate of roast beef was set in front of him, tension would spread around the table. Was it cooked properly? Most of all, was it big enough? Alex would quietly simmer, a martyr to chefdom. And then Mary would say, "Alex, now speak up if you don't like it. Don't be an old fool. It's ridiculous to sit there and take it from them like that!" Whereupon he would call over the waiter and complain, without a shred of humor, "Young man, is this piece of beef meant to be the appetizer, or the meal?"

There was another possible blemish on our relationship which, if true, was not nearly so trivial. With what I know now about the unfinished business of childhood I brought to my marriage, it is entirely possible that I competed with him for his daughter's love. Were it not for my having left engineering before I even knew him, I might be completely convinced that every ounce of my life's work for the past twenty years was an attempt to outshine Alex at his own game. It can happen.

I haven't seen Alex for the last eight years. Nor

have we been in touch with one another. But he had to speak out here, and I am left with the overwhelming feeling that people become part of other people.

9

Entrepreneur

Things were never the same for me at Oak Ridge after HB's sudden departure. The story I heard later was that he had begun complaining to his roommates that the Russians were trying to pry atomic secrets out of him. Then he drove to Knoxville, got on a plane for New York, and was next found walking around inside Saint Patrick's Cathedral in a daze. HB was replaced by an older man from California, and another new addition, the chief project engineer, talked me into going back into engineering to work on a new concept for an aircraft reactor. But after the freedom and excitement of administration I found the work a bore and began a letter campaign to find a new job.

The first possibility turned up while I was on vacation, some nine months before I accepted the job with the Stratos Division of Fairchild, and I would have preferred it by far. I had heard of an opening at S. T. Winston & Company of New York City, which impressed me as an ideal bridge between engineering and the world of business.

"What do you plan to do about it?" asked Alex when I told him about the opportunity, upon returning to Cape Cod from Cambridge.

"One of the partners is an M.I.T. graduate. I think I'll write him when I get back to Oak Ridge."

"I wouldn't do that," Alex advised, "not if you are really interested. Call him on the telephone now. You're flying back Monday. Rearrange your plans to stop off in New York. Tell him you're interested in the position and can meet him in his office Monday at an hour of his choosing. Be direct and say as little as possible. He'll respect you for it."

I arrived at Rockefeller Plaza an hour in advance of my appointment and went to the arcade, which I remembered from my wartime visits, for a haircut and a shine.

"Make it a trim," I told the barber, "I'm going to an important business meeting." I was twenty-four and looked younger. The barber looked more amused than impressed.

And then, with time still to spare, I went into a shop and bought a small plaster reproduction of the bust of Queen Nefertiti that looked just like the picture of the original I had admired so much in high school.

When the interview was over, I stepped off the elevator and looked for a phone booth. "I think I have a chance," I told Alex excitedly. "They're going to decide at a firm meeting next week. I can't imagine a better job in the whole world!"

Yet I had only a vague idea of what the firm did. The first partner had explained they were a risk capital investment company, started by Stan Winston after World War II with some 10 millions of capital. The idea was not only to make money but also to offer a source of capital to deserving young enterprises, particularly those based on technology or innovation. All that money! And the chance to have some part in investing it.

It was exciting to think of myself working in these plush offices with such men as the three who interviewed me. It was as though my eyes had suddenly become the lens of a Bachrach camera. Who has ever seen a Bachrach picture that speaks of incompetence (though I was to find there are many incompetents in business). I compared the men I was talking to with my new boss in Oak Ridge who would take a pair of scissors from his drawer and trim his frayed shirt cuffs during our early morning conference, all the while talking in a desultory manner about what he thought we ought to be doing. I was on the way to becoming a business snob.

"Ever had any business or financial experience?" the managing partner asked me moments before I left.

"Not actually, but I have studied the Forbes Stock Market Course and a book on accounting and one on corporate law."

"That's very interesting. Keep it up," he said. "Whether you come with us or not, it will be very useful to you. I was a practicing lawyer at one time, you know, and I'm a great believer in a man's being able to broaden himself from any sound base, whatever it is."

When he accompanied me to the receptionist's office and helped me on with my raincoat, my spirit soared. I left feeling confident except for one thing—my moustache. I had mixed feelings about growing it in the first place. Most people I knew disliked moustaches; I didn't like them myself, but then I had to look older some way.

The day after I returned home, the headline in the *Oak Ridger* read, "SOUTH KOREA INVADED." Several days later I received word that "in the light of the international situation," S. T. Winston & Company had abandoned plans for enlarging the staff.

The year at the Stratos Division of Fairchild seems to me now to have passed so quickly it was hardly more than an interlude. I was given the job of conducting a market survey on the requirements of a family of new, small turbines for various auxiliary power applications for aircraft, including a gas turbine manufactured by Turbomecca in France for which Stratos had just negotiated the American rights. Then just as the results of my work and extensive trips all over the country were about to bear fruit, a letter arrived at our rented house in Babylon, Long Island, forwarded from our Oak Ridge address. I ran my finger over the engraved lettering of the firm name in the corner of the envelope and wondered about the 230 Park Avenue address, and especially the "Esq." after my name.

The letter was written by one of the partners of the firm. In it, he explained that my name had been given to him in confidence by a friend of his, the managing partner of S. T. Winston & Company. Would I care to submit details of my background and arrange for an interview, he wanted to know.

"Look at this, just look at this," I shouted to Nancy, waving the single discreet sheet of paper enclosed with the letter, on which were listed in quiet elegance the names of dozens of major corporations, with the note, in parentheses, "transactions totaling upward of $250,000,000."

I hadn't the slightest idea what the "transactions" were all about. But "two hundred and fifty million dollars!"

I was greatly impressed with JT (as I would

come to know him) at our first meeting in what I assumed was the boardroom, with its long, rich brown table, ashtrays and pads and pencils neatly arranged at each of the ten places, brown leather chairs and sofa, and etchings of Wall Street. The Phi Beta Kappa key dangling from his watch chain indicated a scholarly attainment beyond my reach. Later when I learned that after graduating from the University of Virginia he had become a Goodwin Memorial Fellow in International Law at Harvard and then gone to Oxford as a Rhodes Scholar, I understood his close questioning of my education.

JT explained that the firm was engaged in three types of brokerage: real estate, private placement of corporate financing, and purchase, sale, or merger negotiations. He was primarily interested in mergers and would want me to work with him in this area. The best background for sale or merger work is law or engineering, he said, mentioning his own legal background and work at Sullivan and Cromwell. Another partner (called Commander by everyone, I was to learn, because of his naval rank and love of sailing) had started as a real estate broker and had brought JT into the firm in the mid-thirties, with the intention of developing a position in the new business of private placements made attractive by the recent securities acts. After World War II, JT, seeing what he thought to be a real opportunity for the company to become professional merger intermediaries, had hired an engineer to specialize in the work and later, another lawyer who worked on mergers too, although a good deal of his time was spent on real estate and financing.

I had no understanding of what I was hearing for I could relate it to nothing in my experience. Small wonder JT concluded our discussion with the comment that he had wanted someone with more experience. Still, he said, he liked my background and wanted to think about it.

I waited a full week and, not hearing from him, called to ask if he needed any additional information about me, references perhaps. Persistence in itself is an admirable quality, he allowed, and asked me in for another interview during which I met the other members of the firm. And then tea at his house in Scarsdale the following Saturday afternoon. As Nancy and I were leaving, he walked us around his property, stopping at a small chicken house (the thought of being slightly self-sufficient seemed to please him immensely) where he found two fresh eggs. When we were in our car and saying our goodbyes, he handed us the eggs. "Here, you have them as a small token," he said.

"All I can say," remarked Nancy on the way home, "is I'll sure look good if you don't get the job now."

The next morning we each had a fried egg for good luck.

As we sat around the table in the large dining hall in the Harvard Club, no one said very much, at least I didn't, heeding the advice given to me when I left Stratos: "Keep your mouth shut and wear Brooks Brothers clothes." Actually I had purchased the dark blue suit I was wearing in Oak Ridge, but I hoped it might pass for Brooks Brothers with the senior partners. At least it was not shiny, for I had only worn the suit on special occasions.

Naturally I was elated to have been invited to lunch so soon after joining the firm. And relieved to feel part of the organization as a whole, for I had begun to feel I was looked upon as JT's boy. Early on, one of the two junior partners had cautioned me, "Never forget it was JT who brought you into the firm, and never for a minute forget that he is boss no matter what the situation appears to be." I thought it was generous of him to say that. After all I was a potential rival, and he could have been hoping for my failure.

The Commander was our host at the club. At seventy he was close to twenty years older than JT and nearly three times my age. But there was a twinkle in his eye, even on the most serious occasions, and I could never look at him without remembering the piece of oakum he carried in his pocket and sniffed now and then for its smell of tar and reminder of sea. In truth, I was awed by his very presence. I had heard any number of times that he was one of the best-connected people in the country. Apparently many people had connections, but few were well connected.

The talk at the table turned to whether General Eisenhower could hasten the end of the war in Korea and then to the election itself.

"What do you think, Mac, who do you think will win the election?" JT asked to my surprise.

"General Eisenhower," I said without hesitation. At first I was proud of my answer, but then I began to worry if I had gone too far out on a limb and might be proved wrong. This was not the first time, nor the last, when I spoke spontaneously from conviction and then worried about what I'd said.

My worry then, however, was interrupted by the waiter. As the Commander was being served his glass of buttermilk, it slipped from the waiter's hand and splashed down the front of my vest and into my lap.

"Oh, it's nothing, nothing at all," I lied (not much, only my best suit), as I dabbed around with the extra napkin supplied by the waiter, all the while sitting erect and trying to seem oh-so-unperturbed.

At a Stratos luncheon my reaction would have been anger rather than shame. But then the drink would probably have been my boss's whiskey sour instead of buttermilk, and the hilarity of the event would have increased the normal flow of salesmen's jokes and badinage, which always made me feel ill at ease.

How I bent myself to my surroundings in those days! (Have I stopped even now?) I was not ready to see that quality is not a matter of unfrayed cuffs and buttermilk for lunch. I felt I had entered the best of all worlds and was totally preoccupied with establishing myself in every nook and cranny. "You're on the merry-go-round," was Alex's way of putting it. "Now all you have to do is hold on tight."

It never occurred to me I might not make the grade in the business world. After all, there were books, and I bought the most recent ones on accounting, corporate law, and corporate finance. Impressed by JT's emphasis on short, well-written letters and memos, I made a special project of grammar and punctuation, again by studying. But most of all it was listening to and observing the partners, particularly JT, whose words and manners I aped.

On his part JT seemed as willing to teach as I was to learn. It was truly a golden opportunity for a young engineer who had set his cap for a business career.

Not that there was a large and complicated body of knowledge to be transmitted. It was more a matter of learning to handle oneself, bits of advice I copied down in my notebook after each discussion, like "Don't say, write, or send anything until you have thought ahead and can see a positive good," or "Natural to feel you want to fill the vacuum, that something should be done, and then act when you shouldn't."

"Serious, disarming, no fuss, just goes on sawing his wood," was JT's admiring comment on Robert Anderson, then Secretary of the Treasury.

It was not until years later that I came genuinely to perceive the essence of a businessman. I was trying to describe to a client the shortcomings I felt in a mutual acquaintance who had an important executive position. "He never seems to click," I said. "He either pushes too hard, or too little, either gathers too many facts, or too few." On and on I went, bound up in words. "You mean he's not a businessman," said my client, with a simplicity that took me aback. Like a caricaturist, he had completed the picture with one deft stroke.

Later in the year, after the presidential elections, Nancy and I were invited for a weekend at the Bucks County, Pennsylvania, farm of a well-known playwright. His wife and Nancy had grown up together and continued to be close friends.

The last evening of our visit our host and I went downstairs to the playroom for a game of darts before dinner. The room was actually at ground level and opened out onto a terrace and artificial pond beyond. Despite the sprawl of the place—numerous wings had been added onto the original stone farmhouse—the interior was cozy, and this room the coziest for me with its rich wood paneling and polished copper fireplace hood that reached to the beamed ceiling.

The two of us had never hit it off very well; I always felt he liked to pick on me, usually after too many drinks. Maybe he resented my youth—I was twenty years his junior. Or perhaps I reminded him of something in himself he did not like. At the time I never thought about the reasons; I just felt his sting.

Tonight was no exception. Our host became more and more combative after each of his frequent visits to the elaborate bar which lacked only a bartender behind it. Finally he looked at me sorrowfully over his glass and said, "Why did you do it, Mac?"

"Do what?"

"You left it."

"Left what?"

"It was beautiful and you left it, that's what you did. Oh, Mac, why did you do it?" I half expected him to wring his hands.

"I haven't done anything," I said defensively.

"Not everybody has a dream, Mac. I mean it was a glorious dream, and you went and left it. Your rockets and space travel and all that. How could you do it, Mac? How could you leave it all for Wall Street?"

"I'm not on Wall Street."

"You might as well be. Trying to be a tycoon, Mac?"

And then in a hushed, almost conspiratorial tone, rubbing his thumb and forefinger together, he said, "Did you leave your dream for money?"

I felt like telling him *he* should talk, he the gentleman farmer with 250 acres, who had written one big hit and not much since. That's what I wanted to say, but I didn't. I just felt uncomfortable. Could it be there was a grain of truth in his accusation? Even though he was plainly in his cups, maybe there was something to what he was saying.

"I haven't left engineering," I said. "It's useful in my business."

And suddenly I remembered my going-away party at Oak Ridge, and one of the gifts my fellow engineers had given me. It was a mock book, and its title was *How to Become a Millionaire.*

"Mac's lost his dream," he mumbled, clutching the bannister for support as we went upstairs to dinner. "Mac's lost his dream." And I wanted to kick him in the slats for making me doubt myself.

My first visit to a client's plant made me realize the importance of engineering to my new career.

The visit had been arranged following a meeting in our office with the head of a medium-sized machine tool company. The industry, whose business was apt to be cyclical, had experienced a drastic decline in new orders following World War II. Now, with the end of the Korean War in sight, he wanted to purchase a smaller company as a diversification, one however that was "in character with our basic business," as he put it. He had come to us to help him find such a company.

"You sound like you have a technical background," he said, after I had described a packaging machinery company whose owner had expressed some interest in selling.

"He's an M.I.T. engineer," JT said. "You're a renegade engineer, aren't you, Mac?" he added, putting me a little more at ease. While I had sat in on conferences almost from the beginning, this was the first time I had ever initiated a negotiation.

"Sounds like a good fit with our business. And the geography and size are right too. You said about one million of net book value? When can I visit the plant?"

I could see JT was pleased with the way I had handled things. As for me, I was excited by the prospect, however distant, of contributing a $50,000 commission to the firm after my long period of apprenticeship.

"Call me Charlie," our guest said, as I showed him to the elevator.

"Okay, Charlie," I replied, feeling rather important to be on a first-name basis so soon, "I'll call you the minute I have confirmed the date."

Several weeks later I met his company plane at the small airport in Keene, New Hampshire, and drove him to the country inn where reservations had been made for us.

"I hope the plant is in better shape than this place," he remarked, as we felt the old pine planks in the entrance hall sink beneath our feet.

I was prepared for him to grill me about the company we were to visit in the morning, but when we sat down to dinner he seemed tired and distant. Groping for contact, I spoke of the difficulty I had machining a piece of stainless steel into a rocket motor at M.I.T.

"Were you using a carbide tool? Maybe your speed was too high," he said, and soon he was talking with surprising openness about his products and his competitor's, the machine tool industry and his position in it. "Those last three companies I mentioned should be merged together; their lines complement one another perfectly," he commented at one point. "If I were your age instead of mine, I might try my hand at it. Trouble is, they'd all want to be boss."

"Ever think that a machine tool is the only nonliving thing that can reproduce itself?" he asked, as he mellowed a bit.

"I don't mean that literally, but think of it, not

a single piece of machinery could be made without machine tools. And what makes machine tools? Other machine tools! I told this to a professor friend of mine, and he said I was anthropomorphizing. Never looked it up. Do you know what it means?"

"Beats me."

"Say, you look like a quiet fellow," he continued, now with a distinctly confidential tone in his voice, "a man whose business gets him around in some pretty interesting quarters. I'd appreciate it if you'd keep your eyes open for a number two man for me."

"Number two man?"

"Yeah, somebody who can take over from me some day. You must run into some top caliber fellows who are restless."

"Don't you have anyone in your own organization?"

"That's just why this whole thing has to be so quiet. First time I've ever mentioned it to anyone. Sure, I've been bringing three fellows along. Each one of 'em thinks he is going to get it. But they're all turning out to be Boy Scouts. Oh, they're good where they are. Best in the business, as a matter of fact. But for my job, I need somebody who can be a sonovabitch when the situation calls for it. Do you know what I mean?"

The feeling that he is taken seriously can give a young man quite a lift. I had already learned that one of the swiftest decisions a businessman makes is whether to take someone seriously or lightly. I had not had the feeling of being accepted as an equal at Oak Ridge. Engineers, like wine, it seemed, require a natural process of aging, even on a project involving as much new technology as ours. It would be years before I could ask myself the question, "Who and what do *I* take seriously?"

The plant was located in a tiny New Hampshire town not far from the inn. It was the only plant in the vicinity, I gathered from the reaction of a filling station attendant when we asked for directions. "Oh, you mean 'the shop.' Looking for the shop, eh? On the other side of town, past the creek. Can't miss it, them red buildings."

The receptionist looked a little like Granny, I thought, as I signed the visitors' log on her desk in the sparsely furnished lobby. "It's not just that it's cold outside," she observed, as Charlie and I thumbed through the tattered trade magazines on the table. "It's such a *penetrating* cold."

The president's office was at the end of the hallway that led from the lobby, and he was standing in the doorway as we approached. "Nice to see you. My name's Kettle, Bill Kettle," he said. I had expected him to take off his rumpled fedora before he sat down. Why did he have it on in the first place? And that black rubber bow tie!

My God, I thought, is he trying to ruin the deal

before it's even started? Ever since the chairman had visited our office to discuss selling his stock in the company, I had wondered how his number two man would react. Besides, it was the first time I had ever "brought the parties together," an important and delicate moment, and I was anxious to get the meeting off to a good start.

The hat and the tie may have embarrassed me, but they didn't seem to bother Charlie, I noticed. Apparently he felt inclined to chew the fat with his counterpart sitting across from him in a swivel chair, his back to his rolltop desk against the wall. "Like to fish?" he asked, pointing to the framed photograph over the desk. A dozen or so men were standing side by side dressed in Mackinaws and boots, each proudly displaying a single large fish for the cameraman.

" 'Bout the only selling I do," Kettle replied, turning to look up at the picture. "Once a year I take a group of our customers to my island down Maine."

"And that sailfish over there. Must have been a record."

"Caught that last year in Florida visiting our chairman. He's retired there, you know. Never shows his face around here anymore."

"That's probably the only reason he'd consider a move of some sort with the right party," I interjected, seeing my opening. "Move of some sort," a euphemism for the word "sale." Months ago I had learned a fact tinged with Oriental mysticism: no seller is for sale. There is a tribal dance, a ritual that must be followed.

"Yes," added Charlie, taking up my cue, "Mr. MacDonald emphasized the company isn't in any sense for sale. Our companies would seem to be a fit, though, wouldn't they? Aside from the selling channels, that is."

"Well, they both manufacture machinery, if that's what you mean."

"I mean our industries are contracyclical, don't you think?" Charlie said. "Packaging machinery should be up when machine tools are down."

"Look, I'll be straight with ya. I don't have any interest in any merger except for one thing, and that's to see this business grow and to see my eggs hatch."

"Eggs?"

"Here," he said, pushing back the top of his desk and exposing the stack of rolled-up blueprints within. "Been working on 'em for years. There's my latest one," he added, pointing to the drafting board in the corner.

"Say, that's a neat-looking design," enthused Charlie as we gathered around the board.

"Been trying to get the stockholders to give me the money to build this new line. Completely obsoletes our old machines, but all they think of is dividends. Had enough trouble getting the money for the new boring mill out in the plant. Speaking of that, would ya like to take a walk through?"

In the plant I felt uneasy whenever my eyes met those of a workman, perhaps the way a real estate broker feels when he's showing a house amid the anxious stares of the children still living there. Uneasy, and a little sneaky, too. For, unlike the children, the employees usually are not told about an impending sale (although somehow they always seem to know).

I felt completely at home with the machinery as we walked down the aisles stopping at each of the important tools. The patient "zing zing" of the surface grinder as it removes ten thousandths of an inch from the steel slab beneath its abrasive wheel, drenched in a flood of coolant looking like gray milk. The more aggressive bite of the planer as its tool moves back and forth over the surface of an iron casting, removing metal with the apparent ease of a carpenter's hand tool. And the high-pitched squeal of a lathe reducing the girth of a spinning shaft. Specialists, all, in metal removal, who go about their sculpting with a rhythmic determination, the accuracy of each reflecting the accuracy of its progenitors.

"Say, what wonderful housekeeping, everything so orderly," Charlie commented as we watched the new horizontal boring mill boring out a hole in the side frame of a packaging machine. Such astute observations were not yet part of my vocabulary, and I listened with admiration. Nor was I less pleased with his praise of Kettle's rapport with his men, evidenced by a casual encounter with an elderly drill press operator. "How is the little lady," Kettle asked, "recuperating well?"

Now, perhaps warming to Charlie's flattery, Kettle, making sure we were not within earshot of any of the men, spoke of an attempt to unionize the plant. "This here feller came up from East Boston to try to organize us. Little, scrappy runt of a guy, a real rabble-rouser if I ever saw one. Hung around here for days, talking to the men. Finally, I buttonholed him at the gate one morning. 'I'll make you a proposition,' I told him. Could see he was suspicious but not suspicious enough. 'I'll make it easy for ya and call a meeting of all my employees. They won't listen to a little runt like you.' Got him sore as hell, I sure did, and at the meeting he spent the whole time telling my boys what a terrible man I was to work for. Got downright personal, yes he did. End of the meeting I walked up beside him, my hat on and all, and asked my boys, 'Do I deserve this? Maybe we don't always have everything the way we would like it, but are we going to let some guy we don't even know stand up here and say these things? Are we going to let some little foreigner from out of state run our business, from East Boston, mind ya?' My boys just shook their heads no, and that little runt disappeared back to East Boston where he belongs.

"But say now, I'm probably telling ya more about pandas than you want to hear. There's the only place that really counts," he added, pointing to the loading dock where several completed machines were being crated for shipment.

Back in the office Charlie made his one mistake of the visit. He asked the price.

"Price, what price?" replied Kettle. "The business ain't really for sale, you know. You'll have to talk with our chairman about that. I'm just the hired hand."

"Whatever we finally do," Charlie countered, "to be a good deal, it has to be good for both sides." On this note of profound reasonableness (it sounded so original at the time) we left for the airport.

As it turned out, there would be no deal, either good or bad. Charlie made an offer—"Sure, it's below their book net worth," he explained, "but my own stock is selling way below book"—and the owner rejected it. My budding negotiation had gone the way of most: it collapsed. Presently, I read in the *Wall Street Journal* that the company had been acquired by another firm in a related part of the packaging machinery field. Truth is, they had a more logical reason for owning the business (and, for those days, a high-flying stock) and could afford to pay more.

As with Mr. Kettle's loading dock, the only thing that counts in the merger business is a consummated negotiation, and I was learning that they are few and far between. What would the percentage be? I have been at it now for 18 years and have participated in some 75 mergers, an average of around 4 per year. And plant visits? Perhaps 500. Negotiations, well over 1,000. At any rate, a very small percentage of negotiations are ever consummated.

But isn't this true about any endeavor? Most work consists of the in-between time, when nothing seems to be happening, the time when we seek movement—oh, if something would only move forward! And yet, life *is* this in-between time, and triumphs are few. Even Mr. Kettle, whose machines leave the dock with regularity, is looking for something more: the hatching of his eggs.

I wish that over the years I had enjoyed the in-between time more. On one level I obviously did, for I remember vividly the hundreds of little towns, and some not so little, where I observed the things of this nation being made. Little details like town squares and churches and trees. I have special trees all over America! And the getting there. High above the clouds. Through cornfields; red clay banks by the roadside. And each town a place where something is made. Not the big obvious things like automobiles or airplanes—in fact, I have little to do with such companies—but the myriad of things around us that we often take for granted. Like Formica. And toothpaste tubes. And plastic-coated wire.

I remember, too, the men who ran these companies and their peculiarities. The otherwise stuffy chairman of the board who offered me horehound drops from a paper bag and a Cuban cigar at the beginning of each private conference. The man from Dayton who delighted in the robin's nest on the top of the hanging lamp in his porte cochere.

Only two sale or merger transactions were completed during my first year with the firm, one on the last day of December just before the new tax law went into effect.

The year 1953, though, was a banner year with five transactions, three of them over five million dollars apiece. While I had not originated any of them, still I had worked on all but one and felt a growing participation in the success of the firm. Two days before Christmas, JT called me into his office.

"We're all very pleased with your work, Mac, and we would like you to have this token of our appreciation," he said, handing me a check that had been tucked face down in the corner of his blotter. "Perhaps it will help with your new young lady," he added, referring to my daughter, born in September.

"Will it!" I enthused. "Why it's two months'

salary," I said, looking at the $1,500 amount. "Thank you very much."

The check had a greater significance for me than its face amount. That night, I sneaked up behind Nancy as she was peeling carrots before the sink in the kitchen and slipped the check around in front of her face.

"Look at this, just look at this," I could hardly contain myself. "I've made over $10,000 this year."

"A man's reach should exceed his grasp, or what's a heaven for," said Browning. For a young man who once thought of $10,000 as a lifetime goal, this moment was truly heaven.

Something strange was in the air. I could feel it. Ben, the junior partner with whom I shared an office, had seemed unusually glum when he came in a few minutes before nine in the morning and tossed off a perfunctory "good morning, Mac." I knew he had been having a lot of trouble with an infected wisdom tooth, but this was something different. He stood motionless before our window for a few minutes, seemingly preoccupied with the baggage and mail-handling activities next to Grand Central Station some fourteen stories below. Then he sat mum behind his desk, hunched on his elbows, chin resting on clasped hands, one leg crossed over the other and swinging nervously. I thought he fidgeted a bit when the Commander passed our door at his usual 9:10 on the way to the corner office, but the glimpse I got of the Commander revealed nothing one way or the other. He looked the same as he had every morning for the past two years; tall, spare, the turned-up brim of his old brown hat detracting somewhat from the look of determination emphasized by his protruding lower lip as he strode through the main office space, dispensing his patrician "good morning" to the secretaries, while staring straight ahead.

When JT ambled by at 9:20, Ben shot a sideways glance at the doorway and began sucking on the hole left by his wisdom tooth as he resumed staring at the wall.

Without having had more time than to take off his hat and coat, and perhaps receive a message over the squawk box that connected all our offices, JT again passed our door, presumably headed for the conference room just off the entrance lobby. A few seconds later the Commander stuck his head in the doorway.

"Are you ready, Ben?" he asked, looking right past me, without the customary smile and glance in my direction to acknowledge my presence.

"Yes," Ben said, grimly I thought, and as they turned toward the conference room, they were followed by the other junior partner.

They were obviously having a firm meeting. But why the first thing in the morning? Could it have anything to do with me? My senses told me something important was about to happen. Normally, the surge of fear that accompanied the thought of my involvement would have persisted. But suddenly I felt elated. It was April 1, 1954, just six days short of my two years' anniversary with the firm. Almost, but not quite, I had allowed two words to creep into my consciousness as the date approached, the words I remembered most from my first interview with JT: partnership caliber, the firm was looking for someone with partnership caliber. Was it going to happen?

My musings were suddenly interrupted by the sight of JT passing my door at a rather brisk pace (for him), his head somewhat lowered. After a brief but significant interval, the Commander and two junior partners passed. Moments later the Commander's voice spoke to me out of the squawk box: "Will you come into my office a minute?"

JT's door was closed, but when I saw the Commander's door was closed as well, my original feeling of fear returned.

"Uh, uh," I thought, as I opened the door and saw the Commander seated behind his desk, one of his cut-in-half cigars in the paper cigar holder in the corner of his mouth.

"Do you want to be happy and have lots of fun, or make lots of money?" he asked abruptly before I had a chance to sit down.

I searched the junior partners' faces for some clue in the interval it took me to frame an answer.

"Well, I guess I would like to do both," I replied, satisfied with my straddle. "Why? Do I have to make a choice?"

"Yes, you do. I have just given JT formal notice that I am dissolving the firm effective July 1. The three of us are setting up a new firm, and we would be happy to have you join us."

Businesses come and go, the statistics show, partnerships do break up, but at that moment I felt sorry for JT. And then scared, scared of how he would react; perplexed by what this would mean to my career. I knew JT had crossed the Commander on a number of occasions. But dissolve the firm? And after one of its best years?

"Do I have to make up my mind now?"

"No, you have a reasonable time to decide."

When I returned to my office, I called my broker and canceled the buy orders I had put in well below the market on several favorite stocks, hoping to invest my year-end bonus at bargain prices. Then I steeled myself against my natural inclination to initiate a discussion with JT to cut the painful suspense.

JT spoke to no one the remainder of Thursday

and all Friday. Now I had the weekend for uninterrupted thought—in the main, stretched out on the bed, staring at the ceiling, thinking about the business itself. I had decided almost immediately after leaving the Commander's office that as a matter of self-respect I had only two choices—staying with JT if he wanted me (on the proper basis) or doing something totally different. Did I really want to be a merger broker? After all, I was twenty-eight and had a second daughter less than a year old.

Finally, Sunday evening I called Alex in Florida, telling him of my decision to continue in the business with JT if at all possible.

"Actions based on loyalty are always a safe bet," he remarked. "But remember, keep your sight high, don't sell yourself short!"

Monday morning passed without any word from JT. How I ached to fill the vacuum. Finally, after lunch, he asked me to come to his office.

"I intend to form a new firm," he said, "and would like you to join me as a partner."

Strange, there was only one thought on my mind when I heard his words. The junior partners had told me that whereas they were called partners of the old firm, they were subject to dismissal by either of the senior partners. Somehow, in my mind "general" partner or "full" partner would cover this point.

"Will I be a general partner?" was my only question.

"Yes," he said.

The first anniversary of our new firm passed without our having closed a deal. In one memorable week, four negotiations JT and I had been patiently developing collapsed.

One, a division of a large company, had seemed like a sure thing. But coincident with receipt of a satisfactory offer, the president, who wanted to sell the division, stepped up to chairman. One of the first acts of his successor, now chief executive officer, was to withdraw the division from the market. Like Churchill, he was not about to preside over the dissolution of the Empire.

In another, the controlling stockholder, who had made a handshake deal with the purchaser, got cold feet when the stock he was to receive dropped a point or so and disappeared to his home in the Carribean while the papers were being prepared.

As the fall approached, I became nervous. My guaranteed minimum income, my old salary, was about to terminate. Under our partnership agreement I would be sharing not only in the firm's profits but also its losses. And I now had a third daughter, born in the spring.

And then lightning struck.

I was having lunch at my club with a man about my age who had just become the executive vice-president of a privately held company. "Get to know him," a mutual friend had advised me, "he has lots of ideas and is going places." Before we had finished our drinks, he had told me his firm's main objective was to acquire a "vehicle" on the New York Stock Exchange, a controlling interest in a company into which they could subsequently merge their own business. It couldn't be too large; they wanted to end up with control.

As he spoke, I compared his requirements with a company JT and I were working on. Thirty percent of the stock was closely held. The rest was scattered among many shareholders. A perfect fit, I thought, and so did my guest as I described it to him.

"I'll go over the figures in Moody's when I get back to the office, and call you," he said.

He called at 2:00 P.M., saying his boss was prepared to pay $21 per share for the block, a premium of $4 per share over the market price. JT immediately called the chairman of the big board company at his office in Pennsylvania but was told he was lunching with a number of the directors at the Bankers' Club in New York. What luck! I enthused. A call there brought him to the phone.

"Yes, our group might consider something close to $21 a share," he said, with just the right mixture of positive and negative in his tone. "I'll be in your office at three o'clock."

My luncheon companion was astounded when I told him we would produce the seller in our conference room in half an hour. "My boss and I will be right over."

After the usual pleasantries the negotiation was fairly brief.

"We have to have $23!"

"No, $21 is all we'll pay!"

Many times I had observed sellers start above the line, buyers below. Now I just sat there hoping to God there was a line. Finally, after much irrelevant talk,

"All right, $22, nothing less."

"No."

"What will you pay?"

"$21.50."

"It's a deal!"

Could there be a slip this time? JT and I thought not. The chairman had telephoned the bank in Pennsylvania while we were all standing there in the conference room and advised them to send the stock certificates to the Irving Trust Company by messenger for a closing the following day.

But when we met downtown at noon, everybody was there but the buyer, and it was clear that his number two man was conducting a delaying action for his boss.

"He'll be right here," he kept assuring us.

Finally, in the late afternoon, when even he began to wonder, his boss showed up, an enigmatic smile on his face. "Now we can start," he said, and he began signing the carefully prepared documents that snowed steadily down on the walnut table before him. By six o'clock, the paper work completed, a check for $3,000,000 passed hands and, with it, control of the company.

"The deal went so fast, I had to scurry around to get the cash funds into the bank," the buyer complained.

Soon we were all off in our separate directions; it was Friday night, and there is little ceremony in such matters. Nancy and I were expected for the weekend on Cape Cod, and when we finally arrived at 1:00 A.M., Alex met us at the door, a glass of sparkling burgundy in his hand.

"Here's to Uncle Mac and his first deal."

The next morning I dropped by the newsstand in town, hoping to read about our coup on the financial page. The headline read, "IKE HAS HEART ATTACK."

The market plunged on Monday, and had we not closed on Friday, it is fairly certain we never would have.

As often happens in the merger business, two

negotiations that collapsed in 1955 came to life the following year and were consummated. With the favoring winds of the business climate—the stock market was at an all-time high—we closed five more during the year. The largest transaction, the sale of a machine tool company for some $12,000,000 of marketable stock, had its roots in my first plant visit.

That Christmas I got little sympathy from Alex when I complained (somewhat proudly, I admit) of being in the ninety-percent tax bracket.

"Bring Uncle Mac the crying towel," he said.

10

Getting to Know Myself

"The mass of men," wrote Thoreau, "lead lives of quiet desperation." I was one of those men. Outwardly, as the world wags, and indeed by my own standards, I had arrived, I was a success. But inwardly I was increasingly aware of my discontent.

Here I was with enough money (but not really enough), the owner of a big white house with black shutters on two acres in Westport, a house with a gracious winding staircase which would be suitable I knew, even as I bought the place, for the eventual weddings and toss of the bouquet to the eager hands below when years later my daughters would be married. Yes, I was a success, but nobody paid me any more attention than they did the kid on the corner of Penrose Alley in his fifteen-dollar shoes. That griped me. It seems absurd, and it was, but how many lives are wrecked on the reef of such absurdities?

It was not only my own discontent I was aware of. Nancy was in the same boat. It was plain to both of us that our marriage was not a happy one; we weren't getting along, nor had we for some years. Naturally I blamed her for this, consumed by the infuriating thought that my wife was the one element in my life I could not control. It's so easy, and so human, to place the fault in the other. But deep down, there lurked the question: Was I part of the solution, or part of the problem?

That Nancy and I were both part of the problem never occurred to me. Still farther from my grasp was the recognition that our contributions to the problem were similar, at least on one level: we both had a need for unhappiness. Marriage is an especially fertile field for satisfying one's quota of unhappiness; a choice of mate guarantees a lifetime harvest.

In 1958, Nancy started seeing a psychiatrist at the suggestion of her doctor who expressed concern for her health. She was desperately tired all the time, and drinking was becoming a serious problem for her. Plainly she needed help that I was unable to give her.

As the Soaring Sixties got under way, JT and I

closed deal after deal, many of them holdovers from the recession years of 1958 and 1959. "We are pleased to announce," read our placement sheet at the end of 1961 "that merger transactions of $100,000,000 in approximate amount have been negotiated by this firm in the past two years, including major placements of five to thirty millions as follows." Twelve in all, but more important than the number was the quality. We attributed nothing to "financial legerdemain," nor was there a "quickie deal" among them, to use another of JT's favorite expressions. All were corporate "fits" and would be described in today's jargon as "synergistic."

It is curious to recall that whereas many men at this point would have increased their profile, I lowered mine. Convinced that I was in pursuit of a simpler, more trouble-free way of life, I sold our large Ford station wagon and replaced it with a black Volkswagen, insisting there was more than ample room for Nancy and the three girls. My 1950 Chevrolet was good enough for driving to the station.

Yes, "There is a tide in the affairs of men," I reminded myself, "which, taken at the flood. . . ." And each time I thought of this my whole body tensed with apprehension. One misstep—worst of all, letting success go to my head—and my ship would founder in the shallows. Fear was at the tiller of my life.

One day in the fall of 1961 when Nancy and I

were returning from a weekend with friends at their cottage on a lake in New Hampshire, the tension surfaced.

"You're annoyed with me again," Nancy said, as we turned off the narrow country road onto the highway.

Maybe a little fresh air would help, I thought, and reached up to slide back the sun roof of our Volkswagen.

"I can tell when you are annoyed with me," she persisted.

I slammed back the roof and gripped the steering wheel tightly in both hands, staring grimly ahead.

"Say something, anything. You never say anything."

Those trees over there, I thought to myself, noticing the forest of dead trees by the roadside. Wonder what killed them, the water they're standing in? Maybe a beaver dam's in there.

"You don't approve of me, do you?"

Silence.

"I hate you, my God how I hate you," Nancy shrieked and suddenly turned on me. In the ensuing tussle the car almost left the road at high speed. My hands were trembling on the wheel as I fought to control the feeling of despair that was sweeping over me. Was this really happening to us?

The rest of the trip I was alone with my

thoughts, more alone than if I had been by myself. By the time we reached home, I knew it was necessary that we each go our own way.

For months, though, I agonized over my decision. First the problem was Christmas; can't leave before Christmas. Then JT; what will JT say? Best to wait until he leaves on his cruise in April. And Nancy, how would she take it? All along she had insisted I wouldn't have the nerve to leave the children.

Like a sailboat in irons, I had lost all steerageway and could turn neither to the left nor right. Finally, I made an appointment to meet her psychiatrist.

"Well, now, I see you aren't eight feet tall," he said as we looked at one another for the first time. I was perplexed. Had she told him I was tall or something?

Ostensibly I was there to find out how Nancy might react to my leaving. "The human spirit has a way of meeting a challenge rather better than we might imagine," is all he had to offer.

What I really wanted to hear was that she was getting better. If I would only wait. If I would do this or that. . . .

"There *is* deep anger," he observed.

And her father, how might he react? I asked.

"Now that's his problem, isn't it, Mr. MacDonald?"

When I sat down on the edge of Sarah's four-poster bed, it creaked and threatened to collapse as it had each evening for years. Tonight, though, I welcomed the distraction, for the moment had come to speak to my daughter. Her younger sisters hadn't really understood, but she would, I knew.

For a moment there was only the sound of air bubbling up from the aerator in the aquarium near the window. And then Sarah burst into a flood of tears. For a while I just sat there, trying to look through my own tears at the piece of coral in the aquarium (where at least a shark or maybe an octopus could hide). Out of the corner of my eye I could see Sarah's horseshow ribbons, red, blue, and pink, strung out down one of the posts, topped irreverently by the silly hat and furry monkey she had won at a carnival. It was too much for me; I fled the room.

Later, just before I left the house, the world really fell out from under me when I heard Sarah consoling her younger sister: "It's all right, Devon, Mommy says it's like a broken leg, it will heal."

"My, what ambivalence," the analyst said, shaking her head.

"You mean Nancy?"

"No, I mean you."

That's what I was afraid she meant. Toward the end of the hour I had the uneasy feeling she was directing her attention to me, not my description of Nancy's problems. True, I was talking urgently, but there was so much to tell if she were to give me a sound opinion on whether Nancy would be helped by a different psychiatrist.

"Ambivalence?" I said. "Isn't that when you are attracted equally to men and women? I'm not that way."

"No. It means opposite and conflicting feelings about somebody. Love and at the same time hate."

"Then you think it is all my fault. Is that what you're saying?"

"No. But it's obvious this separation has put you terribly off balance, and I think you could benefit from psychotherapy."

Well, at least it will help me understand Nancy's problems, I thought. Still, and always, it was the other who was at fault.

"Can you take me?"

"Let's schedule another session and see how it goes."

At first it was more of the same, my sitting there each session, watching her face intently for clues as I unloaded my grievances against my wife. No reaction, though, except for unsettling comments here and there. "My, what a terrible thing to have happen to you! Why were you smiling as you told me?" "Smiling, me smiling?" I asked, averting my eyes.

One day she cocked her glasses up on her forehead and gave me a particularly knowing look. "Oh, come off it, Angus," she said. "You knew she drank the first day you met her."

"No I didn't."

"Didn't you tell me last week. . . ."

"But I didn't think. . . ."

"But nothing! You're an intelligent man. You saw a red light, and you chose to go through it. Seems to me you want to be a martyr to a woman."

My head was pounding with anger at having been trapped. All those weeks I had thought I was making my point, and now she springs it on me like this. A lawyer, that's what she is, a damned lawyer, I said to myself. Nevertheless, something did get through to me.

"Why would I want to be a martyr to a woman?" I asked.

"Let's talk about you for a change and maybe we'll find out."

"Can you give me a clue?"

"I think you'll find it has a lot to do with psychological dependency and guilt over success."

"Psychological. . . ."

"Time's up. Bring me some dreams next session."

Get a load of her, I thought, as I left the office. Bring me some dreams, she says, just like that.

I had been aware of my dreams over the years —a few now and then, like anyone else, I suppose—

but now I remembered several each morning, some in vivid detail. And the very fact that I did, on command so to speak, involved me more deeply in therapy, for I was beginning to see that there are forces other than those I had neatly analyzed on paper at M.I.T.

"What do you think it means?" I asked, after reporting one of the early dreams in which I had crashed upon takeoff in a supersonic airplane.

"What do *you* think?"

"Well, you know about these things better than. . . ."

"It's your dream, Angus, what do *you* think?"

"I've been dreaming a lot about airplanes crashing, haven't I? And always on takeoff. And this one, a supersonic transport. I was looking at the delta wing when we stalled. It's as though I'm trying to go on a trip. . . ."

"Journey?"

"Yes, a journey, it must be a new journey because the SST hasn't been designed yet. A dangerous journey, too, because I crash."

"Yes, but didn't you say you were walking around the wreckage later and told somebody you must have hit a severe downdraft?"

"Yes."

"In other words, you survived the crash."

In the following sessions it seemed easier for me to talk about my childhood. Before, I had avoided the subject, preferring to talk about my immediate problems. Sure, it might be interesting to go into "all that," I told myself, but what for?

For the first time I began to perceive my close identification with my mother. Yes, I walked in a hurry every place, just as she did, and talked with my hands. True, I felt she had inspired me in my schoolwork. Still, what of it?

And then. . . .

"I had a dream last night," I said, through pursed lips. "You remember my telling you about giving my classmates at City the impression my father was a lawyer?"

"Yes."

"And about one of them catching me in the lie when my father and his compared notes about their sons?"

"Yes, your father called on him regularly to sell him cookies."

"Well, I'm standing in the same grocery store, with a black leather display case, trying to sell the owner its contents. When he seems doubtful, I say it's not just a matter of charity, I'm really selling Sunshine Cookies, and I open the case to show him four packs inside. Then my mother appears in the background. I become embarrassed and ask if somebody else was already selling him cookies because I didn't want to cut in on another salesman's territory."

"Interesting choice of words: 'didn't want to cut in on his territory.' "

"Do you think it has something to do with trying to be better than my father?"

"Competing might be a better word."

The next session I graduated to the couch. "Take off your coat and lie down," she said as I entered.

"Me, lie down?" I said, frightened at the sudden change in rules.

"I think we'll make better progress this way from now on. I want some free associations. Tell me what's on your mind."

For the first few sessions I lay there feeling uncomfortable, staring at the ceiling, my words about as spontaneous as a State of the Union message. It's not being able to see her that worries me. What's she doing? I wonder. Taking notes? And the unstructured time. I can stare at the ceiling all session for all she cares. But with the knowledge that every session was costing me $30 I felt betwixt and between. Like shooting skeet, when aiming at a fast-moving target. "You have all the time in the world," a friend had said, "and you need every second of it."

"You're doing fine," she reassured me at the beginning of one session. "Some people can no more allow their thoughts to roam freely than they could run down a flight of stairs with their eyes closed.

This mental leap in the dark doesn't come easy to anyone."

"But I don't seem to want to say anything today."

"Why don't you consult your feelings?"

Silence.

"I feel bored, that's it, I'm bored and feeling sleepy."

"You speak of boredom frequently. Could it be you are using boredom in some way?"

"You get bored, you don't use boredom," I said testily. But something in her comment produced an echo.

"How could anyone be bored unless he wanted to be?" she said gently.

"Last weekend I watched a squirrel eating at our bird feeder. He was constantly on the alert as he ate. Is this man's problem, that we no longer have as much dangerous input to our senses from the surroundings and . . . ?"

"Angus, you're intellectualizing again. Why do you want to be bored?"

"Boredom . . . yes, I do get sleepy when I read a book . . . not business . . . something I really want to get around to like Aristotle . . . Mr. Warren, he used to sleep on the couch all the time . . . I like to sleep on the rug in front of a fire . . . Maybe I *am* using boredom . . . I don't have to be bored

. . . I want to be able to read, so many things to read . . . Maybe I am using boredom as a block. Why? Do I want myself to go so far and not any further? Active-passive conflict maybe? Why not let myself go all the way? Dick Fleming, I wonder if he's home. I should call him to wish him Happy New Year. Say, that was Dick's theme song at parties when he had a few drinks: 'All the Way.' "

"What was the rest of the song?"

" 'When somebody loves you, it's no good unless she loves you all the way.' My God, do you think I felt so close to my mother I was afraid we might go 'all the way?' "

"Cutting in on your father's territory, so to speak?"

"Does this have anything to do with guilt over success?"

"Maybe. It's interesting you should think of it."

"I don't mean just from the sexual standpoint."

"Now you're cooking."

"I keep thinking of that dream about my mother and the final exams. The one I had after I showed you the letter I wrote to my mother when I was at Harvard. You know, the letter she saved."

"I remember the letter well. You were telling her what a dirty trick it was for your sister Jeannine to go live with your father. What were your words? 'Don't feel too bad about it, Mom. I love you very much, and I'll never forget you or leave you no matter what happens, honest. Some day you'll be real proud of me. My marks are still good.' "

"Gosh, how can you remember?" I asked. All along I had suspected her of taking notes.

"I'm paid to remember."

"In the dream, my mother actually took the exam. I could see her sitting there behind the desk at City. But I was the one who went to the head of the class to receive the report card and the perfect grade."

"She was the power behind the throne."

"Yes, but it didn't make sense when we first discussed it. I was trying to interpret the dream in terms of my mother wanting to dominate me, and she's not that way at all. She encouraged me, sure, but to this day she never asks anything for herself."

"She lets you know how unhappy her life has been."

"Unhappy, yes. There's something I'm reaching for. . . ."

"Keep it up."

"I know *I* got the marks, *I* did the work. But what if some part of me deep down felt I was only doing it to please her, that if she withdrew her support I would be nothing? In a sense my success would be unjust enrichment. Here I am on top of the world, and there she sits in Baltimore with nothing. What I'm seeing is that things don't have to be literally true to exert a tremendous influence on my life. Am I being too intellectual?"

"Your intellect is all we have to work with, and you're finally allowing it to interact with your feelings. Time's up."

I couldn't tell from the matter-of-fact way she spoke whether she approved of the progress I had made or not.

"I'm going to make a schematic drawing," I said as I was leaving. "I want to show how things like anger and dependency and guilt connect up."

"You'll find a lot of lines going around in circles," she said.

The next session I arrived half an hour early, and while I sat in the anteroom, I inspected for the hundredth time the wall-to-wall carpeting, the double doors leading to the consultation room, and the painted-over wiring that ran along the baseboard to the lamp on the table next to me. What was the rest of her apartment like? I wondered. And her husband? Were there children?

Presently the doors opened, and the same hollow-eyed girl I had seen before slipped past me and out the entrance door.

"I heard you arrive half an hour ago," the analyst said as I entered.

"Oh, my cab didn't run into any traffic," I lied.

"Have you always worn those glasses?" she asked casually.

"Since I was seven, mainly for reading; my eyes strain easily," I said, as I stretched out on the couch.

"You're so quiet," she observed, "and yet you seemed so anxious to get here."

"I *was* anxious."

"You aren't happy to be here?"

Silence.

"Why don't you consult . . . ?"

"My feelings, I know, consult my goddamned feelings. So I feel like shit running through a goose, does that satisfy you?"

"You feel resentment."

"I don't resent anything. What have I got to resent. It's just that my right arm aches again and I feel uncomfortable."

"You speak a lot of your arm aching. What does it actually feel like?"

"Tense, like I am holding it tight."

"Holding it back, maybe? Do you want to take a swing at somebody?"

Silence.

Something she was saying made sense. The ache subsided a bit.

"When did it start?"

"After you asked about my glasses, I believe. What's the matter, don't you like the way they look?"

"They look fine."

"Do you think I ought to have different frames?"

"No, I was just asking a simple question."

"But you implied. . . ."

"I didn't imply a thing. You perceived my question with your infantile megalomania."

"What's that?" I said.

"It's the thing we see in young children, the reason we have to be so careful not to hurt their feelings. You forget a child's birthday, and he is absolutely crushed. He isn't loved. He feels he's done something wrong. It never crosses his mind that you might have plain forgotten, or are sick, or in general that it had nothing to do with him. It's a holdover from infancy when the child experiences no separateness from the mother and in a very real sense is dependent on her. Then, if mother is neglectful or angry, it can in reality be a life-or-death matter."

"Then you're saying I'm immature."

"Not in the sense that you mean it. Let's say there is a stripe of it that runs through your personality."

"Why me?"

"I think there was a time in your teens when you bound your emotions with hoops of steel and with that mind of yours rose like a phoenix from the ashes. Tell me, how did you feel when you left here last session?"

"Frankly, I felt sort of disappointed."

"And yet you obviously made great progress."

"I got the feeling toward the end that you didn't think so."

"But what did *you* think, Angus."

"I thought it was quite exciting to begin to see how dependent I was on my mother for approval. I had read about such things, but last time I could feel how it might be working in me."

"And yet you felt disappointed."

"Yes, I see what you mean. At the very moment I was making my discovery, I was looking to you for approval without realizing it. It's almost funny, like a leaking dike, I plug it up one place and it spurts out in another."

"You were transferring your dependency needs onto me. Let's talk about why you arrived so early today."

"Well, I *was* sort of anxious to get here."

"To find out if I thought any better of you, if I finally realized how brilliant you were last session?"

"Maybe. I guess so."

"Think of the resentment, Angus, when we tie ourselves to people, and they don't meet our grandiose expectations. Think of the hostility that builds up over the years. And not only from the imagined slights. A part of you came in here today—your immortal soul, some would call it—eager to get on with your journey of self-discovery, and you were completely sidetracked by a casual question about your glasses. All of us sense a certain promise in our youth, and none of us takes lightly what we ourselves make of it."

"Strange," I said, "how all this comes on the heels of one of my most successful sessions. It's as though I were looking for ways to pull myself down."

"The lines do go around in circles, don't they?"

Not every session was productive. At times I would stick on dead center for weeks on end, not willing (or was it not ready?) to see. But even these periods had their value. A skillful listener always learns more from what isn't said.

Gradually, I became aware of signs of change in myself. Little things that many people take for granted, like reading. Hardly a week now went by without my finishing a new book, and soon I had read more than in all the years since leaving college.

In little ways I was becoming free of the incessant need for approval. On one occasion the evidence was dramatic. Shortly after President Kennedy's assassination, I had taken my daughters to a resort hotel in the Poconos for a long weekend. Now, standing on the edge of the indoor pool, I prepared to dive. Gone was any feeling that all eyes were on me, that I would stand or fall depending on the way

I handled the dive and the strokes across the pool. I was simply there for a swim. In I went and for the first time I swam instead of propelled myself across the pool. After several smooth, effortless strokes—at the moment my antennae told me I would be half-way across as measured by my years of contrived swimming—I bumped full tilt into the far end of the pool and split my head open. (How do you explain that to your children? "Well, Daddy's more relaxed now. He used to be too uptight.")

Too uptight! The way I was, for instance, at skeet shooting until I got a new view of myself one Sunday morning. Who would think that those clay "birds," "flying" black and yellow against the sky, could have something to say to a man if he would only listen.

You have twenty-five targets and twenty-five shells and to be any good at all you have to hit all twenty-five, time and time again. In fact, if you go to a contest and miss one in a hundred, you might as well have stayed home. There's no way to fudge, no partner to blame, no opponent to return your shot, making an even poorer performance than you, no possibility of a brilliant recovery after the first poor shot, as in golf. One slip, one stray thought, and the target is missed—forever.

To stand up to the station in a major shoot and know you have a hundred targets coming out and can't miss one can be pretty trying on the nerves, if that's where you're shooting from. Yet in one way, it's very easy. A twelve-gauge shotgun has a three-foot pattern of pellets at the target so there's no excuse for missing except inattention, or getting your ego involved, which may be the same thing.

That's what I used to do. I'd be doing great, hitting twenty of the first twenty-five—unselfconscious, enjoying myself—and then I'd start shooting at every target as though I *had* to hit it. People were looking, people were judging; my "reputation" was at stake. It was as if I would be less of a man if I didn't hit that next target. Was I holding my gun right? Were my pants baggy? Was I swinging loosely enough? Zing! That target was out and missed, and then another, and another. The game was over for me.

To hell with it, I thought, that Sunday morning I speak of. It was a lovely spring day, and I was going to the gun club simply to enjoy a few hours of fun. Nor did the fact that it was the day of the Annual Club Shoot concern me, for somehow I had the feeling I didn't give a damn if I missed a hundred targets in a row. I left clutching the huge silver President's Cup, the first time I had won a prize of any significance.

"Hold close with open arms," I remembered, and then Horace in his epistle to Numicius: "If you want to make yourself happy and stay that way, Numicius, perhaps the only successful rule to follow is, marvel at nothing, never be spellbound. . . ." Marvel at nothing, admire nothing, covet nothing; there are various translations, but they all suggest nonattachment, nonidentification, as the way to freedom. I had heard the words from Professor Templeman and been exposed to his fine example, but now I felt the wisdom might begin to act in my life.

"My arm hurts worse than ever," I said, as I took off my coat and stretched out on the couch.

"How do you feel otherwise?"

"Well, I feel sort of numb all over, sort of brittle, like I just want to lie still here and not disturb anything."

Silence.

"I had a dream last night," I said, "one of the most vivid I have ever had."

Silence.

"I was a young man standing on a big dock—it was a Navy pier—and my father was in the water doing a sidestroke with one arm and pulling on a hawser attached to the bow of a ship with the other. The ship was large and gray—a destroyer, I think, that's it, a destroyer—and my father was struggling to get it alongside the dock. But every time he had made a little headway the wind, which was blowing hard off the dock, would push the bow out—just like it does sometimes with my sailboat when I'm coming in for a landing—and he would struggle against the waves, which were now quite choppy, to get it back again. I became more and more anxious, as it seemed to be getting out of control."

Silence.

Silence.

"How do you feel now?"

"More tense than ever."

"What do you see in the dream?"

"Uh, nothing, except it's strange I have my father pulling the boat when he can only do the dog-paddle. I don't understand it."

Considerable silence during which I felt mentally constipated.

"How do you refer to a boat?"

"You mean by name?"

"No. I mean how would you describe a pretty boat to me?"

"I'd say she's . . . she's. . . ."

Bells didn't ring. Lightning didn't flash. I simply felt light, like a feather. And free, suddenly free, for the first time as long as I could remember, of any tension.

"What was that, what happened to me?" I exclaimed, when I finally realized something had happened.

"How do you feel now?"

"My arm feels like it's floating. I've never felt like this before. I feel so peaceful. It's the way I wanted to feel but didn't when I studied those exercises for release from nervous tension in Oak Ridge. Something important has happened, hasn't it?"

"Yes, it has, but you've been approaching it for some time. It's called catharsis, but catharsis by the doctor since I had to nudge you a little into the association of the boat with your mother. When you see it all yourself, it will be called catharsis by the patient."

I left her office only a fraction of a percentage point or so higher up the scale of potential self-understanding, but that was a huge increase over what was already there. I had been totally unaware of my anger at my father for not being able to control my mother, for being unable to bring her into the wind, so to speak.

During the ride back to my office, I couldn't help reflecting upon the nudge the doctor had given me—the way it was handled, the whole spirit of a helpful nudge in a relationship—and suddenly I saw all the opportunities I had missed to help others over the years, how I had so often clumsily rubbed something under the nose of some friend and frightened him off just as he was about to see. But instead of "woe is me," what I felt now was a sense of confidence and decency. It was not simply a resolve to do better, it was part of me.

In the ensuing weeks I came to see the many

ramifications of my original insight, among which was the fear I must have unknowingly brought to marriage that the same thing would happen to me and guilt over my subconscious resolve to prevent it by being better than my father. It is a continuous process, though, and only now, as I once again stare at the scraps of paper that for so long lay in my safe deposit box—the notes that accompanied the presents when Sarah was born, the note to myself in the church on Cape Cod—do I realize that my "fervent" approach to marriage was, beneath it all, a grim determination. Life became a sequential matter, rather than swirls and eddies, a 1, 2, 3, 4, 5 sort of thing where a right start was all important and everything, no matter how trivial, had to be done just right.

In my heart I had feared being a father, and in my head I had to see myself as a perfect father. It's as though a part of me, anticipating an eventual day of reckoning, wanted enduring proof, something I could one day hold in my hand and sentimentalize: "It's not your fault. You tried. Just look at that picture of Buffer. Remember how cute he looked with this card hanging around his neck. And writing down your thoughts like that just before you were married. And giving Nancy the rocker she said she always wanted. How many men arrange everything perfectly like that, I mean try to make everything perfect the way it should be. You were not content with being a good father, you had to be a perfect father!"

It is not the least of life's ironies that as you pursue strategies to protect yourself against realizing your deepest fears, you neglect the real needs and problems and thus help bring about the very fate you dread. Even this has an answer, though. Better the dread fate—once—than the worry about it always.

Of Men and Machines

Watch out there, old boy, I thought as the cock pheasant darted across the runway and into the brush. A little closer and you could have been sucked into one of our jet engines.

We were next in line for takeoff, and as we turned into position, I glanced back at the string of jets behind us and the busy terminals beyond. Always at moments like this, as I savor the glint of sun on burnished metal outside and the feel of cleanliness and comfort within, I get a lift thinking of the beauty and freshness of an industry still young enough to be committed to futures. At such moments I would like to see the quarrelsome passenger across the aisle who snarls at the smiling hostess, "Guess we're finally getting the hell outa here," condemned to do time in foul-smelling train toilets whose fixtures open onto clacking rails below or sit in seedy waiting rooms where peeling wooden benches and dank odors bespeak an industry geared to the past.

As I waited for the takeoff, I recalled the beach coat that had been sucked into the compressor in the Gas Turbine Lab at M.I.T. Who'd a thunk it, indeed, I mused, that almost twenty years later I would be sitting here ready to fly to Rome at over 500 miles per hour.

Now the pilot was announcing that we were cleared for takeoff, and we turned onto the runway. The plane sat there, as it does in those few seconds of ultimate alertness before takeoff roll begins, aware of its parts like a diver about to jump who caresses the end of the board with his toes, flexes his fingers, his arms held at attention at his sides. And then the lurch forward as the jet engines feed on the juice of fossils that millions of years ago were living organisms, kerosene coursing through arteries, the push and pull of hydraulic fluid on tendons that flex the control surfaces, electrical impulses that flow through the bird's nervous system at the speed of light, monitoring temperatures, pressures, flows, speeds—a great bird given life by an alien brain in the cockpit, a brain to which it is connected not by some delicate surgery but rather by a pair of eyes, a pair of hands, a pair of feet.

Now we are racing down the runway as the turbines keep calling for more heat like a child in a swing, "Higher Daddy, push me higher." And then suddenly, "Oh! that's enough, Daddy, that's enough!" as maximum turbine inlet temperature is reached and the full raw power of the four jet engines is used to accelerate the plane and overcome the clutching drag of the assortment of wing-leading edge slats and trailing edge flaps that extend and droop down to coax enough lift out of the air at the relatively low speed of takeoff.

The plane feels light and for a second floats up and down on its extended gear, then leaps skyward with an authority that turns it back on the choking, coughing, lumbering climb of the piston engine plane.

Thump, whomp, slam, bang!—the noise of a steamer trunk falling down the stairs as the main gears are retracted and the plane composes itself for high-speed flight. The "slam, bang" brings to mind my senior year design problem, "linkage that will retract wheel completely," and I am mesmerized by the retraction of the slats and flaps as they slide smoothly upward and inward against the force of several hurricanes, forming finally the perfect, smooth airfoil.

"Is there anything wrong with the plane?" asked the passenger in the seat next to mine. "I mean the way you have been looking out the window so intently."

"No, nothing at all," I said, "I'm just looking at our plane, trying to take it all in I guess."

"Taking it all in? What is there to see?"

When he had first stopped in the aisle next to me and politely asked if the seat were empty, if he might join me, I was somewhat put off by his appearance. Actually, it was flawless—was that what I found unsettling?—from the black bowler he carefully stowed in the overhead rack, to the rich, well-tailored worsted so in contrast to the shiny fabrics worn by the Latins on the plane. At least he wouldn't snore, I thought, or grouse about the service like the jerk across the aisle.

Now, as he spoke, I sensed a certain awareness and purpose about him, and I felt myself warming to him. Besides, immediately after sitting down and fastening his belt, he had opened his black leather portfolio and begun adding a word or sentence here and there to the broad pointed writing on the yellow pad within. No salesman's memo this, nor a letter. And those newspaper clippings and pages of magazines stuffing the pockets of the portfolio. My curiosity was aroused.

"Oh, there's plenty to see," I replied evasively to his question. One learns, particularly in business, to be on guard against enthusiasm. Spontaneity is so often taken for immaturity, and we do have to be big boys, don't we?

"Look at that off to the left, that's Cuttyhunk

Island down there," I said, "and the tip of Cape Cod in the distance after less than fifteen minutes in the air. It takes me days of sailing to get there.

"Do you fly a lot?" I added, removing the subject one step further from his question.

"I did, before I sold my business. I used to be in packaging machinery, and my customers were all over the country."

Later, in the course of our conversation, he told me he had given up his United States citizenship.

"Given up your citizenship!" My face must have shown my surprise, even shock.

"That seems to be everybody's reaction," he said calmly. "I could have done anything, run off with my best friend's wife, anything. But give up your citizenship! My father was English, and I've always had strong ties abroad. When he died, I decided I had had enough of commuting every day from Darien to the plant in Brooklyn. I sold the business and became a citizen of Liechtenstein . . . for obvious reasons. I have no regrets. I served my term. I even had a bar with one whole wall papered with over twenty-five years of the New Haven's commuter cards. Tells you something about me that I would save them, doesn't it? Now it's over though, and I'm joining my wife and children in our apartment in Rome and am about to do what I have wanted to do for some time."

"What's that?"

"Write plays—or at least the one play I've wanted to work on," he added diffidently. "Surprised you again, eh? Well, I even surprised myself, but I was determined not to repeat my father's life. Once I got the tax moves in motion, I couldn't wait for last week to come, to be specific, October 3. Everything had to be done by then."

I was perplexed. While not a lawyer, my work on mergers had deeply involved me in tax law, and I could recall nothing in the code that would suggest October 3 as a limiting date.

"Were you on a fiscal basis or something?"

"No," he said, obviously pleased that I asked. "October 3 was my birthday, my fiftieth birthday, and I had told myself, 'Life begins at fifty!' "

My first feelings of uneasiness about him returned as "Society" in me whispered its warnings. It's one thing to break the ten commandments—or some of them; who hasn't? But giving up your citizenship, avoiding taxes, was something else again. Any way you slice it, I thought, a businessman-turned-playwright at fifty was bound to be suspect.

It astonishes me now, as I reflect on my reaction, or rather, prejudice. How quick we are to judge others, as if they were of another flesh.

"Have you always wanted to write plays?" I asked, curious in spite of my suspicion.

"No, not at all." He stroked his moustache

thoughtfully. "I think it was fear of becoming like my father that got me started. I came to see how empty a so-called successful life could be. I began to visualize certain aspects of our relationship as scenes on a stage. But then, I had always thought a lot about human motivation—probably why I was good at my business even though I wasn't an engineer; liberal arts major, you know. I began reading more widely and found myself writing short stories, and then one-act plays, usually about some aspect of the father-son relationship."

For a long moment there was silence between us, and then abruptly, with surprising intimacy, for he was obviously by nature a reticent man, he turned to me and said, "You know something! We like to fool ourselves. I thought all along it was my father I was trying to understand, and then one day I woke up to the fact that it was myself I wanted to see more clearly. And you know something else? It was only at that moment of realization I began to love the man for himself instead of regarding him merely as my father."

I felt that he had overstepped the boundary of reticence and would now retreat into himself. Sure enough, the next moment he said, with a charming smile that masked his embarrassment, "Look, I don't want to bore you with my life story. By the way," he offered his hand, "my name's Bert Allen."

The stewardess was smiling down at us with trained affability. "Would you like a cocktail before dinner?" she said.

Later, as we were sipping our drinks, my companion said, "I'd still like to know what you were observing so intently as we were taking off."

"Well," I said, "you know, I started life as an aeronautical engineer, and whenever the plane takes off, I seem to trace the airflow, particularly through the engine—this sounds silly as I put it into words—in my mind's eye."

"No, not silly at all!" he said.

"I suppose it's the beautiful simplicity of those two nacelles out there that intrigues me. You can almost see their entrances being molded on a potter's wheel, so graceful and friendly are their curves to the air. Nothing seems to move, nothing vibrates, no glint of sun on a whirling propeller disk that suggests action. And yet there is an incredible complexity and richness beneath the surface."

"Richness?"

"Take the turbine disk out there in the nacelle," I explained, "rotating at thousands of revolutions per minute. Whenever I fly to the West Coast, I look out at one of the engines and then at the mining country below. I visualize the iron, nickel, chromium, molybdenum, tungsten lying quietly, happily beneath the surface in their earth forms. Think of the improbability of their one day finding themselves—after being dug out, separated, and purified by men's minds and backs—joined together in the stainless steel of a three-foot turbine disk, high above their birthplace, holding, as a hand does its fingers, the turbine blades that extend from its periphery."

"I see what you mean," my companion said.

"Yes, richness in the sense of the hundreds, perhaps thousands, of men's minds that live inside that nacelle, hovering over the main turbine bearings, assuring them a supply of oil at the right temperature. Those minds are dynamically alive in the turbine blades, too, as they become cherry red and stretch outward under the effect of temperature and centrifugal force—only to within critical clearance of the casing, that is, and never beyond their yield point."

"How interesting. You seem to think of metal as alive."

"It is, the minute it's used for a purpose. Even if it is used for a doorstop, a certain amount of engineering is involved: a choice of shape and weight. A door pushes and a conniving mind says, 'Heh, heh, heh, there, no you don't!' But think of a turbine or compressor blade. Some men spend their whole lives working on these blades. What is alive and what isn't? I sometimes wonder whether iron might not be the wood of some distant universe."

He smiled, though he was obviously intrigued. "Maybe," he said. "Anyway, you've aroused my curiosity about just what happens in that nacelle. With all the machinery I've been exposed to, I haven't the slightest idea of what happens out there except that air comes in one end and out the other."

"That's essentially what happens. A man is born, he dies. But, oh! the in-between. Seriously though, I will try to tell you the way I think about it now, because after all I've been away from it for over fifteen years."

"Yes, I meant to ask, what do you do now?"

"Let's not change the subject," I said, rather annoyed I suspect. "Visualize a little bit of air, ten miles ahead of us there. Define its boundaries; it's a particle of air, a slug of air perhaps, maybe you would say the size of a pea or a raindrop, a very particular piece of air. There it sits, a bit cold—say fifty below zero—but pure, still, unsuspecting, and as yet unaware that it will be part of that sausage of air between here and Rome that will pass through our right inboard jet engine. In one minute we'll be there, and since we're traveling at close to the speed of sound, our friend will have very little warning of our approach. If we were traveling at a supersonic speed, it would have no warning at all, for our plane would be moving through the air faster than the pressure wave, or sound, it is creating.

"As it is, our particle feels our approach seconds before we arrive, and then in the twinkling of an eye it has entered the inlet, been slowed down to a fraction of its original speed, which increases its pressure. It twists and turns through perhaps a dozen stages of whirling compressor blades, receiving a further boost in pressure from each one, enters a combustion chamber where it is squirted with kerosene, burns to a temperature exceeding two thousand degrees, squeezes through a nozzle increasing in velocity, passes through the turbine blades to which it imparts some of its energy, and then finally expands further, dropping in pressure and temperature and increasing further in velocity, through the tail pipe.

"With the help of the heat energy from the kerosene, it has been able to spin the turbine. And the turbine, being on the same shaft, spins the compressor that has induced its flow in the first place—a classical bootstrap operation—and still it has enough vigor to leave the engine faster than when it came in, thus providing the thrust forward. Newton's law, you know, 'for every action there is an equal and opposite reaction.' Something is thrown back, something wants to go forward. The garden hose for example . . . Oh hell! Here I am with a piece of seaweed; the more I pull, the more of it comes. I see a little line flowing through that engine, twisting and turning, slowing and speeding, hot and cold, lean and dense, on a journey whose proper description would more than fill a book."

"Come now," my companion was saying, "you told me to choose a particle of air, and having started this love affair, you want to leave me dangling. The least you can do is tell me a little more. For instance, you said as it enters the engine it's slowed down to a fraction of its original speed. What do you mean, 'slowed down?' It wasn't even moving?"

"I was looking at it from the engine's point of view. Think of an elf in the inlet who can see neither ground nor clouds to judge that the engine is moving through the air. To him, the engine is still, and the air is coming at it at a speed three times that of the wildest hurricane. He sees the air abruptly slowed down before it enters the compressor cascade."

"Cascade?"

"Yes, the air literally cascades through a series of blades shaped like miniature airfoils. The first set is rotating and turns the air onto the adjoining stationary set with the precision of a figure skater closing a figure eight. Then the air is picked up by another moving blade and directed properly at the next stationary set and so on."

"Now you speak about air flowing. What about our particle?"

"We're still looking at it. It's as though we are looking at a single bubble being carried along by the stream. You look at one particle, passing over one compressor blade, through one nozzle, one turbine blade. If you don't, you never get started, everything is a big smear, like the average person trying to describe an experience. Then you make your design and later try to take into account two-dimensional, and finally three-dimensional effects."

Our conversation was interrupted by the hostess's announcement of dinner.

"Steak and lobster, that's all this airline ever has," remarked our neighbor across the aisle. "Or chicky, chicky, chicky. Damn it, can't you girls pass on the passengers' complaints and see that something is done about this. I would think they could show a little originality!"

Having spoken his piece, he buried his nose in his glass of wine, and I hoped for a sudden gust of clear air turbulence.

I love meals on a plane. It's the same sort of snugness I enjoy on a sailboat at anchor, the feeling of being enveloped by the peace and quiet of the cabin, a small space where every inch counts, and everything must be designed with an eye to violent motion. The smells aren't the same, the kerosene of the lamp and the slightly musty taint that most women hate and all sailors love; still, the plane has a smell of its own, like a new car. You settle back in the boat's cabin and spear smoked oysters from the open tin and artichoke hearts dripping with olive oil from the jar between sips of a gusty Portuguese wine from a paper cup. And then cold ham with English mustard and crisp green salad.

There's something about going topside after dinner and standing on the bow of the boat alone, whether there is a flat calm and the anchor line coils limply into the water, or is pulled bow tight, groaning in its chock. Looking up at the stars, I want it all to stay, I want to feel it, see it, hear it deeper and deeper. And then I lose it all in the grasping. But even having lost it, I stay, and look, and wonder.

In a curious way I had some of the same feeling now as I settled back in my seat after dinner, aware of the hurricane outside between me and the stars, and at the same time of an inner peace and contentment. One by one the overhead lights were flicked off . . . it was time for drowsing. . . . But I wanted to stay with that feeling of an elusive something hovering there behind my closed eyes. A kind of happiness. My analysis had come to an end and I could see, I could sense how it had pried me open not only to myself but to the world. My companion, for instance. The ease and frankness of our approach to one another. In other years, had he spoken of business I would have been all over him for information without ever touching the man himself. My suspicions and prejudices would have erected a barrier between us and we would have spoken as stranger to stranger. Oh, to keep this feeling of openness always . . . for myself . . . for all men and all things. . . .

I woke with a start to the sound of "thump, whomp" right under my feet, as if all the baggage in the compartment below had suddenly shifted.

"The sound you hear is the normal sound of the landing gear being lowered and locked into position," intoned the stewardess over the loudspeaker. "We are preparing to land, so will you please extinguish all cigarettes and fasten seat belts."

My companion was leaning across me, pointing excitedly out the window. "There's my apartment down there, that penthouse on the top of that new apartment building. See it? By the way, I hope you'll visit me sometime. Will you be here long?"

"Just long enough to change planes for Milan. I'm on my way to the International Machine Tool Show. But I'll look you up next time."

We were now in our final approach pattern, and the laboring noise of the hydraulic system heralded the lowering of the wing flaps. It was as if our proud lady, at the end of her journey, were preparing for rest and knew that it didn't matter now if a little stuck out here and there.

12

Shearwater

"Life is fired at us point blank," says Ortega y Gasset. Indeed it is, I thought, as I observed my daughter Sarah, already sixteen, talking to an unknown young man as we stood on the dock in Bermuda waiting for the boat *Shearwater* that was to take us scuba diving. So much happens so fast. I was suddenly seeing my daughter in a new light, no longer mine but a young woman with her own life to live.

But then I seemed to be seeing so many things in a new light these days, which is perhaps only another way of saying I had begun to question, to ponder my life instead of taking it for granted. There was, for instance, the question of inevitability. And what did "inevitable" mean? Was everything that "happened" to me inevitable in that it was stamped in the original pattern, so to speak, and so foreordained. Did we, by our very nature, cause to happen that which seemed to be happening to us? In this sense, was it inevitable that the unlikely opportunity of going to Harvard and M.I.T. should come my way, or that my passion for rocketry should be diverted to a business career, or . . . and here my thoughts faltered . . . that my marriage should prove to have been a failure?

But perhaps inevitability is merely a fine name we give to chance—after the fact—in our endeavor to impose order on chaos? Then was it chance alone, I asked myself now, that the boy of twelve who sat on the bed with his mother and heard her say what he already knew in his heart, that she was leaving his father—was it chance that he should find himself, a quarter of a century later, sitting on his daughter's bed the same month of the year and she the same age as he was at the time, explaining why he was leaving her mother? The same cry of unhappiness from Sarah and later from her sister Devon. And the stricken look on Heather's face, who was only six at the time. I was as numb that Sunday evening as a hangman standing on his own trapdoor, about to push the button on himself.

Yes, it all had to be, I thought, as I watched the *Shearwater* approaching. Much that happens between two people is irreversible, as perhaps everything is in this life. As I stood in the glare of the hot Bermuda sun, I could only try to reassure myself that never again would I allow a relationship to deteriorate beyond repair. Never again! How we like to delude ourselves with finalities. At any rate the indecision about the necessity of divorce was over, the on-again, off-again attempts at reconciliation had come to an end.

I suppose it takes a shock to make a man look deeply within himself. I wonder sometimes what if my marriage, too, had been an apparent success, as my business was? Would I have ever come in touch with the reality that is my life, or would I have continued to expand, trying to convince myself that all was as it should be, until my volume could no longer support the bloated surface? Well, all that was behind me now. Only the residue of sorrow remained, and as I watched *Shearwater* approach the dock, I tried to comfort myself with the thought that at least the sorrow I felt was scrubbed clean of self-pity and guilt.

"It's so big, Daddy, it's so big," Sarah exclaimed as the boat docked. "And white like our first sailboat."

Shearwater's most noticeable characteristic for me was her considerable shear over her fifty feet from bow to stern, which I assumed at the time accounted for her name (the dictionary says "any of various long-winged seabirds, appearing, when flying low, to cleave the water with their wings").

Her shelter cabin opened out into a spacious rear deck in the middle of which were racks of air bottles, while scattered about in various places were the implements of scuba diving—masks, flippers, air regulators, lead weights, and harnesses—together with bits and pieces of pottery, rusting metal, and several cannon balls, all heavily encrusted with barnacles.

The main event of our scuba diving vacation was about to begin. Sarah and I had spent the first week learning the basic dives to various depths in the sheltered bay of Breck's Scuba Diving School, finishing with the final deep one that qualified us for open-water diving on the reefs a number of miles out. Getting offshore with the proper equipment and supervision was not easy, though, and it was only after considerable poking around that I was directed to HC, the owner of *Shearwater,* who took out occasional scuba diving parties.

As we stepped aboard, box lunches in hand, HC was there to greet us. "Welcome aboard, MacDonalds," he said, his tone as casual as his dress: blue sneakers that had seen better days, washed-out blue shorts, and no shirt to cover the profuse reddish hair on his square chest.

Soon after we were under way, he introduced me to one of the guests, a man of about my own age, whom he characterized as an expert scuba diver. His name was Hugh Sinclair, and he was to dive with

Sarah and me—the usual precaution of doubling up. In the light of our relative inexperience, I felt a surge of relief.

I had been aware of Hugh even before we were introduced. His movements had the sure, sparse look of a man in step with the cadence of the sea. And his attire—bathing suit, sneakers, brown straw hat with a red bandanna band—were in sharp contrast to the Abercrombie & Fitch adornments of others, particularly those of one young man who sat quietly during the trip out, sagging under the weight of his black rubber wet suit, with wrist-mounted depth gauge and stainless steel sheath knife strapped to his leg.

As we headed for the open sea, Hugh and I edged our way around the outside of the cabin and onto the large foredeck where my daughter was already sunning herself. There was none of the gentle undulation of a bow cutting through ocean swells; the sea was a flat oily calm. Nor was there breeze or cloud to suggest a change. All was still and sun except for the vibration of the engine which gradually receded into the background.

It became clear as we discussed what lay in store for us that Hugh's mind was as uncluttered as his bearing, yet it was with some surprise when we traded backgrounds that I learned he was a professor of English at a private school in Massachusetts.

I was even more surprised that when I mentioned that I was reading Norbert Wiener's *Cybernet-*

ics and Society, Hugh not only expressed a thorough knowledge of the book but went on to review the thinking of Teilhard de Chardin as an opposing point of view. I had never heard of de Chardin, or of his major work, *The Phenomenon of Man,* to which Hugh referred. I look back on our discussion, as stimulating as it was unexpected under the circumstances, with a mixture of amusement and quiet respect for what must always be impinging on me if only I were aware of it.

As we approached the barrier reef, with Bermuda's shoreline barely visible in the distance, I went to the cabin where HC appeared to be involved in an interesting bit of navigation. With binoculars in one hand and a child's type of copybook in the other, he maneuvered the boat on an uncertain course as he peered at distant points on shore. He did not consider my questions a distraction but rather seemed to delight in explaining what he was doing. There were over four hundred known wrecks on the reef, he said, some dating back to the 1400s. The wreck on which we would dive was a French frigate which had gone down in 1810. To locate it, he had turned to the smudged page of his copybook on which he had originally penciled its triangular relationship with several prominent features on shore: a spire, a chimney, and an oil tank.

I found it amusing that he would try to find a speck on this expanse of water with such a crude method. Even with a pelorus it would be difficult enough. But in a few minutes he pointed to dark splotches beneath the water which he said were cannons. They appeared no different to me from the dark coral heads we had seen as we approached the reef. Hugh, standing on the bow, confirmed the location of the wreck and lowered the anchor over the side.

As the others prepared to dive, I continued my conversation with HC about his copybook. He flipped through page after page of similar crude diagrams, each with a few notes about a particular wreck, mainly concerning country of origin and date based on artifacts that had been brought to the surface. Some of the older wrecks were accidental, he explained, but many were caused by island plunderers who years ago used false signal lights to lure ships on the reefs as they passed the island they used as a checkpoint of latitude before turning on their eastward trip to Europe. HC was driven on year after year by the hope of a major new find such as the jewels and gold, now in the Bermuda museum, discovered the year before by another boat on which HC had kept a watchful eye as she trolled back and forth in the distance.

Neither Sarah nor I had ever entered the water from a boat outfitted in the cumbersome scuba gear.

The safest way, Hugh explained, was to sit on the gunwale, back to the water, and, dipping the head back and letting go, do a sort of back flip into the water. Seeing my sixteen-year-old daughter do this and then disappear beneath the surface in a boil of bubbles was more than I had bargained for. I am inclined to be timid unless I have a feeling of control after carefully considering the variables. Then I will do almost anything. Sharks, for instance. I had read, listened, questioned endlessly, and could find no instance of shark attack in memory except two in front of the beach club where we swam, and those under circumstances where the sharks could exert themselves as cowards. My "control" is probably illusory, but it worked for me and allows me to stretch as I otherwise wouldn't.

After a moment's hesitation—I could still ask Hugh to bring my daughter back in—over I went, all arms and legs.

My first impression when I had stabilized myself a few feet beneath the surface was one of scale, the immensity of what spread before me and my smallness in it. There was also a surge of freedom and a twinge of fear, for all of my skin diving before had been in relatively shallow water where the cradling sides of an inlet or the tilted bottom offshore provided a sense of containment. Here there was just a huge expanse of water, and the oily calm of the sea and the granular whiteness of the sand produced a sparkling clarity that allowed me to see at least a hundred feet on all sides and to the bottom that spread endlessly fifty feet below. Water as clear as gin, HC had said, a metaphor that amused me since it coupled together two of the focal points of the island's existence.

There below me, lying in the sand, were twelve cannons, six on each side, still pointed outward toward the enemy with the unmistakable outline of a capstan sticking out of the sand in the center and toward one end. I had to imagine the outline of the ship, for there was no trace of the wooden hull nor any other of its fittings. Nor was there much sea growth in the vicinity of the cannons, which is why they stood out so dramatically against the white sand bottom even with their heavy encrustation of barnacles.

As I followed Hugh and Sarah deeper and deeper toward the wreck, my feeling was one of awareness of all of the inputs of my senses—perhaps like a healthy animal on the prowl. The chill I had felt on my skin at first was leaving me as my nervousness decreased; now the water began to have a soft, friendly feel. My lead belt exactly balanced my natural buoyancy, and the only exertion my muscles felt was in changing position; otherwise I hung suspended, a unique feeling in itself. I had never quite believed that the pressure at fifty feet would not overwhelm my ears, so as I descended, five feet at a time, I was relieved to find that pinching my nose and blowing did in fact equalize the pressure on the eardrums at each level, completely eliminating any sense of pain. I was aware too of the slightly oily taste of the air, although it was compressed with a so-called oil-less compressor, and the hissing sound of my breathing; I was gulping the air as though I did not really believe it would continue to be freely available.

As an overlay to all of this, giving it the necessary dimension of depth, there was the visual input of movements, colors, and forms: yellow brain coral, lavender coral fans, fish singly and in schools of every describable color and shape. And all with no dimming murkiness but set forth as clearly as desk mementos embedded in lucite.

When we arrived at the bottom, the three of us caucused in a tight little circle, checking on one another's equipment and state of mind, for we were all momentarily aware that fifty feet of water separated us from the surface and that, as with all matters involving the sea, lilting ease and pleasure can quickly change to difficulty and fear.

As I touched the bottom, my own immediate enthusiasm was for the sand that enveloped my feet with the consistency of granulated cork. It was a desert of sand in which I felt I could frolic, hampered only here and there by the wreckage of the ship and occasional coral formations and vegetation. There was none of the sinister ooze and vegetation here, just the shifting white sand. It was obvious that this particular area was scoured by currents and storms for, as open water goes, it was not deep, and the silt and fines of the crushed coral had been leached out long ago.

Hugh went off, rooting in the sand, for he had told us on the surface that every storm shifts the sand and can bring to the surface artifacts that have long been buried. Close at hand the cannons looked strikingly different than when viewed from above. Each cannon was several times as long as I was and so wide around it could not be encircled by my arms at the breech end. Together they formed a valley, and in this valley of the cannons Sarah and I toe danced on our flippers down what must have been the center of the deck of the frigate.

Soon we too were lured away by the thought of treasure, and as I groped about in the sand and washed out holes as a fish does with his fins, I was amazed at the profusion of artifacts exposed—not worth a nickel as treasure but a fortune for me. I found the broken-off top of an earthen jar, then the tops of several wine bottles, obviously old to judge by the irregularity of shape. A small conical object of brass defied identification until I got it to the surface. The best guess is that it was once the top of a candlesnuffer. Handsome, hand-hewn, square copper nails, about four inches long and with hobnail tops were everywhere under the sand, the only remains of the hull except for occasional pieces of metal strapping. Rough-hewn stone bricks were also scattered about, obviously the rock ballast of the ship.

Before long I had worked my way off to one side of the wreck where small coral heads, some six feet tall, were growing out of the bottom. Their surface of various types of coral and vegetation was an attraction for smaller fish of every kind. Pulling myself along the sand as I searched, I came face to face with a large fish. Both of us looked at one another with sudden surprise and for a fleeting moment the fish and I had something in common—curiosity. As I looked at the fish's face, I wondered about Nietzsche's "We feel so tranquil and at ease in pure nature because nature entertains no opinion about us." For just a click in the world's scheme of things I thought I saw a wide-eyed awareness, and the fish subsequently reacted to me in a way I can only describe as playfully friendly. His dominant colors were yellow and black, as I remember them, and his size was such that he would have fitted neatly in a medium-sized suitcase. While I had experienced the curiosity of fish before—the small sergeant major has come right up to my face mask on many occasions—I was totally unprepared for the company of such a large fellow who quickly became devoted to swimming by my side. After a while I tired of the affair, but he persisted even to the extent of allowing me to poke his side with my finger, although this plainly unnerved him.

Before he, too, became bored, Sarah appeared, and as she played with the fish, including the finger-poking ceremony, she turned to me and through her mask I saw in her eyes a look of spontaneous child-like joy the years will not tear from me. Here was sheer delight in the new, the unexpected, the unselfconscious jumbling up of the world's components. Gone was every trace of sulking boredom.

As our friend left us, there was just enough urgency in his departure to be inconsistent with his past behavior, and I looked around, and then up and to the side. The sight I saw would have been accompanied in a movie by a few measures of Beethoven's Fifth: a school of barracuda, at least a dozen in all, half the size of railroad ties, hanging motionless in the water like so many logs, their heads slanted toward the surface at a thirty-degree angle.

Although I have been in the water many times with small barracuda, some just a few feet away, and have never heard of a single attack by this fish on a human anywhere, still it was with less than confidence in my data that I viewed my problem. For one thing their size was more nearly that of those I had caught fishing in open seas, and their lower jaws were even more protruding than the smaller ones in relation to their size, giving them a greater measure of that characteristic aggressive leer that everyone finds so discomforting.

Hugh's appearance on the scene was a great relief, especially since he approached with the thumb-touching-forefinger signal of everything is okay. He was obviously an alert and sensitive man—qualities I value even in less frightening circumstances—and he swam in our vicinity, as we continued to search the bottom, until the barracuda ghosted off as quietly as they had arrived.

When we left the frigate, after lunch, Hugh and another diver went overboard with only flippers, face masks, and snorkel tubes and allowed themselves to be towed at the end of two long ropes at a speed of several miles per hour for an hour or more. In this way, with their snorkels several inches above the surface, they were able to look down upon the reef as we motored along it and look for telltale signs of undiscovered wrecks. When at last they saw what appeared to be a rust spot in the sand, we anchored to investigate. Since our air bottles were empty and the compressor on board didn't work, Hugh and several of the more experienced divers surface-dived to the suspicious area on their breath alone.

While the others were investigating, Sarah and I snorkeled around a coral head which approached to within fifteen feet of the surface. We made repeated dives to this moderate depth, for the head was covered with a particularly beautiful assortment of growths, so different from those close to shore which are always completely picked over. As we were about to surface after examining a large yellow brain coral, we looked ahead and there, almost still in the water, on the far edge, was a five-foot shark. In answer to my daughter's questioning glance, I pointed away, and she headed for the surface and the boat. I slowly surfaced, keeping my eye on him. Someone had told me that swimming slowly toward a shark will cause him to move away, and now, looking down from the surface, I paddled in his direction. But instead of retreating he angled slowly up toward me with that well-documented sinuous motion. That was enough! Sitting in the water, I paddled backward, using my arms as oars, until I lost sight of him, and then I swam for the boat at full tilt.

There was a certain quality to the *Shearwater* experience that engaged my attention all during the taxi ride from the dock back to our cottage at the Coral Beach Club, but it did not surface until later that night when all was quiet except for the sound of the tree frogs who filled the night air with their "peep-peeps." The sea, or more particularly, water, has always held a deep fascination for me. Was water a side of my life, I wondered, as I recalled how building a small waterfall in the grove of hemlocks that arched about our terrace had become so important for me when I was desperately searching for a solution to my disintegrating marriage. Had I instinctively felt that the sound of water tumbling down the carefully chosen ledgerock and the sight of the damp moss and ferns that surrounded the pond and hid the circulating pump might give me the peace of mind I so urgently craved?

Be that as it may, the *Shearwater* experience had left me feeling enormously alive and exhilarated—I felt no need of sleep or rest. It was as if somehow the sluicegates of my mind had been opened and I was being carried along on the flood, not so much thinking as being thought.

What, then, I concluded, was the particular quality of *Shearwater* I was groping toward? Was it that through a totally new experience not involving habit I had been able to lower the threshold of what I saw, felt, and perceived? All incoming data was important; I was not so much looking as seeing as I plunged backward beneath the surface of the sea and then slowly worked my way deeper and deeper into the mysterious new world.

"Ripeness is all," I whispered as if the entire day were summed up in this moment of rapture. I saw how so much of my life had been habit, opinion, minute-to-minute influences, which through a gradual accretion finally blocked off new thoughts. Most action, most decisions result from data that have been subconsciously screened to fit a sought-after objective. Contrast this with the quiet, will-less mind, that sees and then acts in the overflowing fullness of the pattern that forms from undistorted facts, not an act that is brought off but an act that happens. Not a happening though, as a bottle is washed up on shore, but rather the unfettered use of mind brought in active contact with the experience of my particular world. An alert mind brought in free contact with all that it passes through—can there be a more exciting thought?

Some weeks after my return from Bermuda, I was walking to work from my Manhattan apartment on a quiet summer morning. My feet moved over the pavement, but my body was once again immersed in the clear water off Bermuda and my thoughts had a particularly tranquil quality. My mind's eye roamed over the rock ballast of the old frigate embedded in the sand and the barnacle-encrusted cannons. A feeling of depth, stillness, rock-bottom stability. A phrase leaped into my consciousness: "Peace of mind has become the rock ballast of my ship."

I played with the thought all the way to the office, as a child rolls his hoop with a stick. For months I felt I had tapped something deep within myself. But one day, when I was thinking about renewal, change, movement in life—everything moves, everything changes, goes on its way—I realized the leaden weight of my observation which, through its half truth, was seductively attractive enough to act as a rallying point for the part of me that wanted to see no more. A sort of comfortable wayside inn.

Peace of mind, hell! What a static goal, as barnacle-laden as the cannons. What a cover-up for not getting on with the true job of movement, change, growth. Movement is all, I thought. Or in the words of de Chardin, "A passionate longing to grow, to be, is what we need."

I was still seeking final solutions, though, substituting one absolute for another. At one moment, ripeness is all. In the next, movement is all.

Maturity is all, I might have enthused in Bermuda, settling for a phrase, but instead I chose Shakespeare's line to express my feelings of the moment, the feelings that maturity is the ultimate goal, that my single desire was to become part of the aristocracy of maturity, the small but growing group of people in the world who seek primarily to satisfy their own inner values which are constantly updated by a free flow between head and heart. The word "ripeness" was not substituted by chance, I saw now, for maturity carries with it the connotation of having arrived, of finality.

How easy it is, on first glimpse of the immaturity of one's life, to set up maturity as an absolute and then identify with it, as if the work was completed. I smoked myself out during that morning walk to work. Peace of mind has become the rock ballast of my ship. Peace of mind, indeed, not the excitement and pain of discovery, is what I had sought all along. And the moment I detected this sleight of hand on my part, I resourcefully set up another absolute—movement, change, growth. Movement is all. Once again I had averted my eyes from the true task of seeing myself as I am, accepting myself as I am.

13

Cuttyhunk

Wooooom . . . Wooooom . . . Wooooom. . . .

The large black whistle buoy at the entrance to Buzzards Bay seemed almost alive as it floated up and down in the passing waves, trapping air on each rise and exhaling it through its low-pitched, mournful whistle as its ballast tank slowly sank back into the water. As I sailed past, the buoy bobbed in a particularly large wave and emitted a plaintive "eee-hoomp" which started off like a donkey's bray but ended on a forlorn note, as if it realized Labor Day had passed and it now faced the angry winter seas.

I had sailed very close—too close, it suddenly occurred to me, remembering the fifty-foot length of line I trail astern whenever I am sailing alone—but glancing back I saw the line slither safely past the buoy without fouling it. Ahead lay Cuttyhunk Island, the last of the bony fingers of five islands that begins with Nonamesset across from Woods Hole and separates Buzzards Bay from Vineyard Sound.

I had chartered the thirty-foot sloop in Sakonnet Harbor, and when I left the mouth of the Sakonnet River across from Newport early that morning, rain had threatened. Now with Cuttyhunk rising on the horizon against the clear blue sky like some Pacific Isle and nothing but the Atlantic to starboard, as the boat hobbyhorsed through the waves on a beat to windward, I felt—well, "as close as a Unitarian will ever get to heaven," as the Commander would have put it.

"Easterly winds from 10 to 15 knots, with gusts up to 20," the Coast Guard had announced. Not bound to any particular timetable, I eased the bow of the boat off the wind to pick up speed when I saw a large wave coming. At the last moment, I could steer the boat hard on the wind again so that she knifed into the wave with maximum force, sending hard water from stem to stern as if thrown from a bucket, while I sat in the cockpit, dry in my wet weather gear and snug as the proverbial bug.

Snug—and at the same time, even as I felt my hand on the tiller tingling with the vibration of the rudder cutting swiftly through the depths, conscious of the absurdity of my feeling of security because the day seemed kindly disposed toward me and the elements for the moment were lenient. I could not help smiling at the thought of that length of rope trailing behind me, my little prop of security in case I fell or was washed overboard and could manage to reach some part of it before the boat sailed beyond me. My lifeline!

And yet I felt aware of my existence to a degree I have rarely experienced, a sensation of the wholeness of my life instead of my usual fragmented self. A moment outside of time? I was still the boy of ten, and it was still that evening on the cliffs near Penrose Avenue after my father had taken me on my first flight in Chamberlin's airplane. I am standing on the edge of the cliff, staring up at the stars, after leaving the gang huddled around the embers of the burning Christmas trees, and suddenly I am intensely aware that I am here and the stars are out there, that I exist and they exist. I am conscious at the same moment of myself as the observer and the stars I am observing.

Many years have passed since then and innumerable things forgotten, but the special and extraordinary feeling I had on that occasion never leaves my memory.

Now I recalled the time I was on a bus pulling away from the Cincinnati airport, bound for a downtown hotel. Riddled with tension, I was straining with all my might to develop some notion I had, as if it were a life-or-death matter. Or was I straining to push the bus faster? Finally, exhausted, I gave up in despair. And at that moment, when my deepest wish was for a vacation from myself, the image of Karl Compton's face flashed across my mind, and with that vision my whole attention became engaged. The look on his face and in his almost impossibly blue eyes, which I had taken during my years at M.I.T. for serenity, became instead the symbol of a tremendous range of thought and feeling which could be mobilized and modulated as circumstances demanded.

While my attention was thus focused on the image of Compton, I also saw myself. I saw myself rushing to the airport in a taxi, straining at every light and delay, although there was more than ample time to spare. I saw myself fidgeting to take off and eager to land, totally unaware of the food and drink I had consumed in between. Hurry to be the first for baggage and then wait for the bus! Tackle that minor problem as if it were a go-or-no-go decision on takeoff! Itch to get downtown so you can then wonder what to do with yourself. This all at once and more, too, as the circle spread to include my whole life.

"Where is my range, where is my range of response?" I thought, and I saw that much of my life was like one shrill note of a pipe, that I was a man living on the edge of myself. And even as I saw this, all tension seemed to drain out of me, and I sat quietly and peacefully without thought until stirred by the bus driver's shout at the entrance to my hotel.

When did this moment outside of time, this moment of self-awareness, dissolve? When did I come back to myself? One never knows, any more than one can fix precisely the moment of falling asleep or awaking from sleep. The next thing I knew I was rounding the red bell buoy in Buzzards Bay and slackening off the main and jib sheets in preparation for a new heading of east-southeast. This would take me on a broad reach to the black can buoy at Middle Ground between small barren Penikese Island, now little more than a mile away, and Cuttyhunk. With the wind now abeam, the boat picked up speed on the final leg of my journey to Cuttyhunk harbor.

As I was approaching Middle Ground, a jet fighter swooped down from the sky and made a high-speed pass over tiny Gull Island. Suddenly my thoughts were enmeshed in a net of associations. (We say "suddenly" when what we mean is we have just seen the tail end of the train that has gone by.) In rapid succession I thought of the jet that had swooped down over the Charles River in salute to General Patton at the end of the war, the first jet any of us had seen, of Patton's shiny helmet as he rode triumphantly down Massachusetts Avenue, of tanks. . . .

Tanks! But had I not dreamt of something connected with tanks the night before in Sakonnet Harbor, only to awake with no awareness of the dream, not even that vague uneasy feeling of something buried that often remains afterward?

Only, unlike most dreams, there was no movement, no sequence of events, but a sort of sketch or drawing in the style of Giacometti's *Annette* with its swirl of lines defining the eyes, the chin, and jaw. (I had been reading a book on the art of Giacometti the previous evening before extinguishing the kerosene lamp and closing my eyes in sleep). But in the dream there was no face, only a human jawbone in all its angularity viewed from the side, with its molars intact, and matched by an upper set held in place by the merest suggestion of the rest of the skull. The teeth were not well defined—swirls of lines, circular—but teeth nonetheless. And sketched lightly around the teeth was a parallel trapezoid of lines giving the dominant impression of a tank tread endlessly encompassing its wheels.

At first I was startled by the abrupt reappearance of the image, and then for a while I simply marveled at its stillness and clarity. But though I groped for the feeling that had accompanied the original, it was gone and, with it, the meaning that had seemed so clear in the dream itself. What would I call the picture, I asked myself, as I desperately sought the road back to the knowledge that had so effortlessly been revealed to me during the night? Death? Certainly there was the look of death about it. But those tank treads. War? Hostility? Aggression? Death of . . . aggression! Yes, that had to be it. The death of aggression. Yet I had simply exchanged one question for another. The picture had a name, but I was as mystified as ever.

Gradually I became aware of the contribution of Giacometti's art to the content of my dream. I had been deeply touched by his central feeling, and the thought had come to me that if you never look inside you could not possibly know the reality of the outside; indeed, the two were inseparable. I could see it expressed in all his work, particularly his *Bust of Diego* with its gaunt, eroded features, man reduced to his insides perhaps.

Inside. Outside. My thoughts, which had been floating somewhere among the gulls circling off in the distance, became more pointed. Hadn't something in Giacometti's work reminded me of my growing feeling of separateness? And hadn't I felt something stir in me last night when I recognized the paradox I had begun to see during analysis? Yes, it was true: the greater my sense of separateness, the closer I felt to people.

There was no mistaking the feeling of warmth,

of light, bordering on ecstasy that was enveloping me. And in that moment I saw the death of aggression as the dream of all men of all times who have taken the first step toward enlightenment.

Approaching Cuttyhunk, I thought of Herman Melville's Ishmael, ". . . not so much bound to any haven ahead as rushing from all havens astern." If I, like other men, was uncertain of the port ahead—except for that ultimate haven we call death—still I no longer felt I was fleeing from all ports astern.

Our society puts great store in "doing." All around us we see people working at it even when they no longer have to "do," as if in dread of a quiet moment that might bring them face to face with themselves. This way it is possible for a man's life to be lost to him, for him to feel at the last moment that his existence had been no more than a bullet fired point blank at the earth.

A man needs solitude, needs time for himself to grow. I like to think my choice of a career wasn't so much happenstance after all, since it has given me time for myself. But in truth, was it actually my choice? Certainly I was not conscious of it at the time. Probably I am only flattering myself by imagining that my successful "doing" in the financial marketplace, that most pragmatic of institutions, was an attempt to serve my sentence as quickly as possible so as to get my "doing" behind me. But even then, when I was in the clutches of the need to be successful, the need to be approved of by others, to do in all things what I supposed was expected of me as son, student, husband, father, partner, citizen, there remained a secret part of me that knew that only in solitude could I find what I was looking for but had no words to define.

In solitude I begin to perceive the ocean of forces in which I live. When I walk among the swarms of particles that hang together, like a galaxy in the sky, in the space I call my body, I see the immense improbability of myself, a power of arrangement that makes man's most ambitious attempts look like a single grain in an ocean of sand.

Everyone must have had the experience, at some time in his life, after an act of seeming urgency, of seeing how little difference most things one considers important really make. I have come to treasure the thought of human impermanence, of the extreme narrowness of each man's couch, how a life can be snuffed out in a single moment of errant chemistry. I stand under the shower, and I look at the new faucet that still leaks and once again remember that the young plumber dropped dead last Sunday. Someone answers "First rate!" when I ask how he feels, and I am startled to realize that old Ned French of Springfield, Vermont, whom I visited for so many years at Jones and Lamson Machine

Tool Company, is no more. Yet strangely enough the thought of the impermanence of men and things is not confining. Such moments of realization have the taste of eternity.

As I entered Cuttyhunk Pond through the narrow channel that leads from the outer harbor, I was struck by the absence of the tall masts that in season rise from the almost completely landlocked pond. Gone, too, were the power boats behind the dunes. The only sign of life was a lobsterman tinkering with his boat at the distant dock and a flotilla of Canada geese and a single swan heading at flank speed in my direction.

"So now you're my friends," I said, remembering the summer months when they wouldn't give me the time of day. While I circled and anchored, they kept a discreet distance, then crowded in, fighting among themselves to get at the scraps of bread I was throwing on the water. The swan—no beggar he—imperiously stuck his head over the gunwale and demanded to be fed.

Unencumbered by the minutiae of summer, the bare features of Cuttyhunk lay exposed to my view: the Pond surrounded by sandy beaches except for Copicut Neck, an eroded bluff that rose a few dozen feet above the water and was connected to the main island by a narrow spit of sand and gravel behind which I had often watched the sun set. And then the sharply rising hillside that dominates all else, dotted with a few houses, and the yellow church spire pointing to another dimension. The whole place had a comforting charm about it mindful of a European scene, except for the Coast Guard lookout tower on the hump of the hill.

Eager to get ashore and poke around, I packed a duffel bag with the bottle of wine, smoked oysters, and tinned sardines I had brought for lunch and rowed in the dinghy to the abandoned Coast Guard boathouse. From there I walked along the macadam road, its blackness hot under the bright September sun, then upward toward the Boswith House, the familiar tangle of wild rose bushes still on my left and on my right the same rusty remains of a Model T covered with honeysuckle vines I had seen on previous visits, upward along the steep road to the country store with a ding-a-ling door, and off to the right on the path that leads to the highest point.

I sat on the scrub grass near the tower, where across Vineyard Sound I could see the eroded cliffs of Gay Head. I looked for the patch of wild heather I had come across years before when it was in bloom but had never been able to find again in the tangle of bayberry and thorn which covered most of the island stretched out below me.

By some association my thoughts turned to the dinner with my daughters at Gino's in New York the previous June, on that day some advertising genius has successfully promoted as Father's Day. Perhaps it was the wine I was sipping that made me remember, for they had given me a book on French wines.

The girls had questions about Vietnam, about the riots, the student demonstrations, and other things of concern to them. "All right, Daddio," Sarah concluded, "do you have any wisdom for us?"

Did I indeed have any wisdom to impart? Certainly I gave little enough evidence of it that evening, for as usual in my eagerness to disgorge everything all at once I ended up stumbling over myself.

"What would I have liked to say to my daughters?" I mused as I watched a lonely white sail that seemed to be putting out from Menemsha Bight. Maybe something like this:

"I can try to give you answers, but wisdom is something else again. What I see when I think about wisdom is a summer garden, green and beautiful. Some of the nourishment and growth comes from the violent thunderstorm, with all its crash and fury. But most of all, it comes from the soft summer rain, dripping lightly from petal to blade to ground, the soaking earth made more receptive by each preceding drop, over days, not minutes. The personal crisis, the strenuous challenge, play a part in our growth, but more than anything, it is the quiet times, the whispering thoughts that count.

"The burning issues of the day are always with us. But unless we can change in ourselves, nothing very much is going to change with the way of the world."

After I had eaten, I decided to hike down to Gosnold Pond, which lay off in the distance at the far end of the island—a tidal pond, abounding with all sorts of creatures, separated from the ocean by a stretch of the finest sand. The going was rough. I knew it would be, having done it once before, and would have been impossible were it not for the deer paths through the thorn thickets.

As I broke out of a particularly dense tangle into a small clearing, I noticed some deer droppings and all at once recalled Sarah's one and only visit to Cuttyhunk, when she was about fourteen. After lunch she had taken the dinghy and rowed to the inviting sandspit near Copicut Neck. An hour or more passed, and I became concerned, but presently she returned, full of enthusiasm. She told of her walk and discovery of Gosnold Pond—the same easy route I would be taking back to the boat this afternoon—and how she had poked around at some of the fish in the tidal flats and then chased a rabbit into the thickets toward the hillside.

"Daddy, you wouldn't believe it!" she exclaimed. "I went into this forest of little trees you could hardly get through and all of a sudden there was a great crashing noise right next to me."

"What was it?"

"I couldn't see anything, but with all the jungle around me I knew it must be a gorilla just like on television, and I began to cry."

The very thought of a gorilla on Cuttyhunk made me roar with laughter.

"Come on now, don't hold me in suspense, what was it?"

"But then I wasn't afraid any more, I knew it wasn't a gorilla, it must be Daddy. Remember how when I was little you would hide in the bushes and make noises like a bear or a lion. I thought you had come across the other side of the island to surprise me. Just as I was thinking this, I saw a white tail flipping up, and a big deer disappeared into the bushes!"

Some weeks later I related this story to my analyst, as something that would amuse her, I thought. "That's interesting," she said quietly, "your daughter associating you with a gorilla." I quickly changed the subject.

Now, as I stood in the clearing, it was as if some final membrane had broken, and in a sudden flash I saw, in fullness and completeness, what I had previously been only vaguely aware of.

Families are people! Dimensional, round, separate people!

Only now, as I stood in my mind's eye between my children and my parents, did I see how I had secretly judged those closest to me with the harshness born of the fear and resentment that inhabit the emotional thickets of childhood. Not even my grandmother, to whom I had always felt especially close, had escaped my judgment. Wasn't she the one who nagged at my mother and father until I could hardly go anyplace outside of Penrose Alley on my own? Wasn't it her fault that when it was snowing I had to watch the gang build igloos in the field from my bedroom window, for fear I might catch cold?

None of this resentment was ever allowed to surface. After all it was Granny who gave me the pennies and cake when I was little and later, in the Navy, sent me cartons of Spuds, when cigarettes were all-but-impossible to buy. She always managed to let me know that no matter how long the interval between visits, every moment since the previous one was devoted to anticipation of the next. Still, she was not at all grasping, was indeed overgenerous. Once, when her husband asked reprovingly, "Boy, why don't you visit your poor old grandmother more often?" she replied, "You leave him alone. Don't you realize he has built a wonderful new life for himself!" How could I possibly feel the resentment I kept hidden from myself?

This feeling of separateness had been growing in me for some time, I soon realized, for I recalled a visit to my grandmother in her tiny apartment in Baltimore the previous year. As we sat among the clutter of Kewpie dolls and knickknacks, the talk for the first time was about Granny herself.

"You mean to say Grandmother Keenan was your mother!" I said. Apparently it had never occurred to me before that she also had a mother. "Why, she died only a few years ago. Who was your father?"

"You knew him. You remember Granpa Keenan. He was the man with one eye. Lost the other from a firecracker. I will never forget how you split your head trying the tightrope across your father's car bumper in front of his house."

"He was your father! But he was married to someone else, he didn't live with Granny Keenan."

"They were divorced. My father drank a lot."

For the first time, as she talked, I saw her as an individual, a person in the round, with her own mysterious life, and without my realizing it all my childhood resentment faded away. When I got up to go, we stood in the center of the room, looking at one another, just for a second, but in that second I really saw my grandmother as she was and her life of competing for affection. And I saw in her eyes that she knew I knew, and nothing mattered. As we embraced, and she repeated the familiar, "He's my boy, he's my boy," for the first time I actually held her toward me, instead of holding her off with a sense of uneasiness as I had through all the years and felt her frail withered body beneath all the layers of padding. That was the last time I saw her.

I was about to leave the clearing, when the thought of my sister Jeannine welled up in me. "Why, why!" I asked in anguish, but even as I asked I knew. Why did I pick on her at home yet defend her whenever the neighborhood kids did the same thing? Everybody seemed to pick on Jeannine, the way animals do when they sense a weakness. I remembered her face the first Christmas I was out of the Navy, when I opened Granny's box with a dozen shirts and socks, and she tore open her packet and tried to look pleased with the single kerchief with the 97-cent price tag still affixed.

I remembered, too, discussing my sister while in analysis and the dream that followed. A little boy was marching down the street, the sidewalks lined with people, to the cadence of rum, dum, dum, a dum, dum. Behind him was a column of two, and then four, until the parade was the width of the street and trailed off in the distance as far as the eye could see. All of the faces were the same, just increasingly older as they marched by. I awakened with a start and wrote down the words of the dream while they were still fresh in my mind.

Rum, dum, dum, a dum, dum,
Little boy, little paper drum.

Cocked hat, wooden sword,
Marching by, marching by.

Smile on the face, center stage,
Happy, happy, pleasing everyone.

Little short pants, suspender hung,
Scuffed-up shoes, playing his drum.

Wooden sticks, lightly held,
Rum a dum, dum, isn't this fun?

A sister now, isn't she fun?
But look at me, look at me.

But most of all, I remembered my harsh judgment of her life as I grew older, the way I turned my back on her, all but closing her out of my life. If only she were here with me now, I thought, I would see her without this ambivalent mixture of love and hate; I would see her as a person in the round. If only! She died two summers ago.

With tears in my eyes I pushed my way into the brambles. It was too late to undo what was done. Too late—isn't that the story of our lives? "Forgive me," I whispered as I continued down the hillside. "I'm sorry."

When I reached the pond, I had no stomach for poking around in its depths as I had on the previous visit. I felt weary and sat down on a large piece of bleached driftwood. As I sat there, my attention was captured by a tiny moving speck of black against the wood's whiteness. Fascinated with my unexpected company, I edged closer and saw it was an ant. Disturbed by my movement, it hastened along a zigzag path as fast as it could under its huge burden, but when I made no further move, continued peacefully on its way. At first, I thought it must be carrying a crumb or morsel of food of some sort. No. When I looked closely, I saw it was a grain of sand. Did the ant know what it was doing, where it was going with that grain of sand?

Did I with mine?

I walked down to the water's edge and then along it, toward Copicut Neck, the water racing up the sand almost to my feet and falling back again, bubbling into the sea. Why is it that a man is so quiet and thoughtful by the water's edge? Can it be that an ancient side of him is touched, the side that recognizes the interface between the earth and the ocean—man's past and present; the side deep within him that remembers the painful journey of the first fishes that were caught on the tidal flats and then edged and flipped and flopped their way to the next comforting pool, giving their progeny lungs and legs; the side that accepts the pain of the present journey of man thrust upon another mud flat, now psychic, where it is a matter of the subtle interplay of tiny electric currents and chemical reactions rather than the growth of new functions or appendages that determine his future; the side that resists the temptation to take the passive road, to lie still and slowly expire, or to nuzzle into the moist sand in a brief quest for certainty rather than make the overland search? Maybe, just maybe, the tide will come in in time.

Halfway to the boat, I noticed a flash of lavender tumbling in the boil of sand and water and picking it up found it to be a lovely piece of sea glass, perhaps part of an old perfume bottle, worn smooth by sand and water. Unaccountably, as I paused to examine it more closely, my head was filled with the sound of marching bands—Rum, dum, rum a dum dum—and it was as though I were back there again, back on the sidewalk on Fifth Avenue, standing in the bright sunlight last March, watching the endless flow of people in the St. Patrick's Day Parade. Little girls, big girls, little boys, big boys. That old lady, look how proudly she walks, dressed in her finest lavender, with her chalk white face and orange hair, making it down the street for one more year. And there's the woman with the Irish setter being pulled out of the parade by the fellow with the official looking button. "No animals, Madam" . . . The three Negro girls standing next to me, clapping with glee every time a Negro boy or girl came by, giggling, "Isn't he cute, isn't she cute." The old man standing peacefully in front of me, his neck bulged on one side the size of an orange, maybe a goiter, maybe cancer; the white stubble on the back of his neck was his hair, his very own. As the crowd flowed inexorably by in my memory, I experienced once again, standing there on the beach, the same overpowering feeling of oneness with them all I had felt that day.

"A heart filled with love," I wanted to cry out. What hollow words, dulled by custom, when heard as preachment. Yet how new and moving when felt for child, wife, friend, or enemy in a moment of understanding, of realizing how we all share life's abrasions, of seeing oneself as a citizen of the world, even the universe, a man among men, living amidst the indestructible life of the universe, infinitesimal in power, yet infinite in strength, sorry to the depth of all being, yet not self-destructive.

When I reached the boat, the sun had already set, and there was a gentle breeze topside. And as I stood on the deck, looking off in the distance yet anchored in myself, a feeling of unusual intensity came upon me, so intense that I went below, lighted the kerosene lamp, and wrote this note to myself:

"I have spent half a lifetime getting rid of or exhausting my clutter of anxieties, juvenile wants, and yes, satisfying the actual needs of myself and my family. There was a time when no one could have convinced me that it was anything but footling for a man not to be working at a lifetime pursuit, not to have made his "mark," whatever that is. Only now have I begun to listen for my resonant frequency. How frustrating to realize there is a limit to what my inner substance will allow me to extract of itself at this time. Pry it, force it, grab at it, and it will flutter away in the morning haze. Maybe this is what is meant by humility. Waiting, waiting, listening for the whispering thought that will point the way to my grain of sand. It will come, I know it will, if I can remember day by day to move closer to myself, to be aware of my false prides, born of equally false self-contempt, that keep me from my core; if I can remember that my work exists because of my being, not I because of my work, that my structure cell by cell is but a momentary trustee of all the hopes of the past. And particularly if I remember how little wear my knees have received."

The next morning I set sail for the mainland amid the screeching gulls that had earlier shared my breakfast. One, bolder than the rest, had taken scraps of bread from my hand, and now he was following close behind. The wind was still from the east, though its weight was noticeably diminished and there were none of the gusts of the previous day.

Ahead was Middle Ground. As I rounded the buoy and set my course for home, I let out the mainsail and lowered the jib which was flapping ineffectually now that the boat was running free before the wind. Soon I was approaching the black whistle buoy at the entrance to Buzzards Bay.

Beyond I came upon a school of porpoises surfacing. For a while they escorted the boat, their black shining bodies arching gracefully in and out of the water, their whispering sighs clearly audible above the sound of the cresting waves. Then, as if drawn by curiosity, they headed for my lifeline. No longer stretched taut astern, it swung sinuously from side to side as the boat surged forward, and I watched my kindly companions roll under it one by one. Then they were gone.

That lifeline! Suddenly I saw it as somehow symbolic of my life, of my need always to be reassured that I could find my way back. All those scraps of the past I was still hanging on to, the toy bank my father had given me, my safe deposit box, the notes to myself tucked away in my wallet.

This attachment to the past, this final dependency. Can a life be truly lived that needs constant proof of its very existence? Now I saw, for the first time it seemed to me I truly saw, that the present moment was all I had. Far from impoverishing, the realization was infinitely rich with the taste of freedom.

The time had come for letting go.